Reforming Teacher Education

Education

Something Old, Something New

Sheila Nataraj Kirby, Jennifer Sloan McCombs,
Heather Barney, Scott Naftel

Supported by the Rockefeller, Ford, and Nellie Mae Education Foundations

RAND EDUCATION

The research described in this report was conducted within RAND Education and supported by the Rockefeller, Ford, and Nellie Mae Education Foundations.

Library of Congress Cataloging-in-Publication Data

Reforming teacher education : something old, something new / Sheila Nataraj Kirby ... [et al.].
    p. cm.
    "MG-506"—P. [4] of cover.
    ISBN-13: 978-0-8330-3982-8 (pbk. : alk. paper)
    1. Teachers—Training of—United States. 2. Educational change—United States.
I. Kirby, Sheila Nataraj, 1946– II. Title.

LB1715.R363 2006
370.71'1—dc22
                                                                    2006018196

The RAND Corporation is a nonprofit research organization providing objective analysis and effective solutions that address the challenges facing the public and private sectors around the world. RAND's publications do not necessarily reflect the opinions of its research clients and sponsors.

RAND® is a registered trademark.

Cover design by Stephen Bloodsworth

Published 2006 by the RAND Corporation
1776 Main Street, P.O. Box 2138, Santa Monica, CA 90407-2138
1200 South Hayes Street, Arlington, VA 22202-5050
4570 Fifth Avenue, Suite 600, Pittsburgh, PA 15213
RAND URL: http://www.rand.org/
To order RAND documents or to obtain additional information, contact
Distribution Services: Telephone: (310) 451-7002;
Fax: (310) 451-6915; Email: order@rand.org

3/20/08

Preface

Over the past several decades, teacher education has been subjected to both scathing criticism and innumerable efforts designed to reform it or to save it from being dismantled. One of the latest efforts aimed at teacher education reform—and one of the most well funded—was launched by Carnegie Corporation of New York in summer 2001 and boldly titled Teachers for a New Era (TNE). Eleven institutions—ranging from large research universities to a private, stand-alone graduate school of education—were selected to participate in TNE. The aim of the TNE initiative is to stimulate development of excellent teacher education programs that are guided by a respect for evidence-based decisionmaking, that are based on close collaboration between education and arts and sciences faculty, and that fully integrate student teaching experiences into the teacher education curriculum. To assist in this endeavor, TNE is providing each grantee with $5 million in funding over five years and substantial technical assistance to enable the grantees to align their teacher education programs with TNE's design principles for teacher education reform.

The RAND Corporation and the Manpower Demonstration Research Corporation (MDRC) jointly received funding from the Rockefeller, Ford, and Nellie Mae Education Foundations to conduct a study of TNE. RAND and MDRC followed and evaluated the TNE initiative from October 2002 to September 2005. This monograph presents the findings to date from that study.

This monograph has two main purposes: (1) to place TNE in the larger context of teacher education reform and to critically examine the process by which reform will result in caring, competent, and highly qualified teachers capable of producing improvements in student learning and (2) to examine TNE's contributions to the grantee institutions' teacher education programs and culture and to assess the sustainability of TNE beyond the life of the grant. This monograph should be of interest to educational researchers, funders interested in K–12 education, and education policymakers at the national, state, and local levels who are struggling with issues of teacher quality and how to improve learning for all students.

This research was conducted within RAND Education and reflects RAND Education's mission to bring accurate data and careful, objective analysis to the national debate on education policy.

The principal author of this work may be contacted by email at Sheila_Kirby@ rand.org or by phone at 703-413-1100, x5322. For more information on RAND Education, contact the Acting Director, Susan Bodilly. She can be reached by email at Susan_Bodilly@rand.org, by phone at 703-413-1100, x5377, or by mail at the RAND Corporation, 1200 South Hayes St., Arlington, VA 22202-5050. More information about RAND is available at www.rand.org.

Contents

Figures

Tables

Summary

Schools of education and teacher preparation programs have been under attack for decades. On the one side, opponents of traditional teacher preparation programs and state certification requirements argue for reducing or doing away with those requirements, reducing the number of education courses, and increasing the number of alternative certification programs that can prepare students for teaching in a shorter period of time without overloading them with education courses. On the other side, proponents of teacher education programs call for greater professionalization of the teaching profession through a variety of means—by defining the knowledge and skills that teachers must possess to teach effectively, by using accreditation of teacher education programs to ensure that the programs are transmitting the necessary knowledge and skills, and by testing and certification to ensure that teachers do in fact have the knowledge and skills.

In summer 2001, Carnegie Corporation of New York (hereafter Carnegie) took on the challenge of reforming teacher education and launched an ambitious initiative called Teachers for a New Era (TNE), which is aimed at bringing about radical changes in the way that teachers are prepared for their profession. RAND and the Manpower Demonstration Research Corporation (MDRC) followed and evaluated the initiative for a period of three years (October 2002 through September 2005). This monograph presents the results to date of that study.

The Teachers for a New Era Initiative

The ultimate goal of the TNE initiative is to improve kindergarten through twelfth grade (K–12) student outcomes by improving the quality of the teachers in K–12 schools. TNE seeks to do this by stimulating construction of excellent teacher education programs at selected colleges and universities; in turn, these programs would become exemplars for other institutions and would offer lessons learned about best practices, thus improving the quality of teacher graduates produced by a broad range of institutions of higher learning.

To assist institutions in this endeavor, Carnegie, joined by the Annenberg and Ford Foundations, awarded $5 million over a period of five years to each of several selected colleges and universities. The first round of awards was announced in April 2002. The first four grantees were Bank Street College of Education in New York City; California State University, Northridge (CSUN); Michigan State University (MSU); and the University of Virginia (UVa). The second round of awards to an additional seven institutions was announced in summer 2003; those institutions are Boston College (BC), Florida A&M University (FAMU), Stanford University, the University of Connecticut (UConn), the University of Texas at El Paso (UTEP), the University of Washington (UW), and the University of Wisconsin-Milwaukee (UWM). The grantees were chosen to be representative of the various types of institutions that prepare teachers—public and private institutions, large research universities, comprehensive education universities, stand-alone colleges of education, urban universities, institutions preparing large numbers of minority teachers, and small and large producers of teachers.

In 2002, the Rockefeller Foundation asked RAND and MDRC to conduct an evaluation of the implementation of TNE at the first four sites—Bank Street, CSUN, MSU, and UVa. In 2004, the Nellie Mae Education Foundation, primarily because of its regional interest in institutions in the Northeast corridor, asked RAND and MDRC to include BC and UConn from the second cohort of grantees in the evaluation. In December 2005, the Ford Foundation asked RAND and MDRC to extend the evaluation to include two other sites—FAMU and UTEP—because these two institutions are large producers of minority teachers.

While the long-term objective of the evaluation is to provide evidence of whether the initiative has been "successful," both from the individual institutions' point of view and from that of the TNE funders, in the short-term, the evaluation seeks to examine the extent to which the grantees are implementing Carnegie's TNE design principles and to understand the factors that foster or hinder implementation.

This monograph, which builds upon an earlier RAND report (Kirby et al., 2004) that examined first-year implementation in the first cohort of grantees, seeks to place the TNE initiative in the larger context of the current politics surrounding teacher education and other education reform efforts, to understand the evidence base underlying the principles that TNE espouses, and to provide an overview of the sites' progress in implementing the three major TNE design principles:

- A teacher education program should be guided by a respect for evidence.
- Faculty in the arts and sciences disciplines must be fully engaged in the education of prospective teachers.
- Teaching should be recognized as an academically taught clinical-practice profession.

We also address the question of sustainability of TNE and its likely long-term legacy to the field of teacher education, although the findings are necessarily speculative, given that these questions can be addressed only in the long-term.

This monograph is based primarily on information collected during an annual site visit to the eight sites whose evaluations were funded by sponsors, and it draws from the sites' annual reports, TNE renewal application materials, literature reviews, and Web site searches. At each site, we interviewed various faculty members and administrators working on TNE issues—university leaders, TNE leadership teams, arts and sciences faculty, teacher education faculty, and new faculty hired specifically under TNE, among others. Because we are simply tracking process implementation, we report on activities and initiatives under way at the sites as reported by TNE participants during our site visits.

The latest round of site visits was conducted from September 2005 through January 2006, although due to FAMU's organizational changes and delays in getting funding, we were unable to conduct the first site visit at FAMU by the time of this writing. For the remaining three institutions whose evaluations were not funded (Stanford, UW, and UWM), we collected data from the site's individual TNE Web sites and/or materials from the TNE project director at each site.

As of September 2005, the first cohort had been implementing TNE for three years, and the second cohort had been implementing TNE for two years.

Theory of Change

As Weiss (1972) explained, it is important to know not only *what* a program expects to achieve but also *how* and *why* it will achieve certain goals. We developed the logic model, or "theory of change," used in this study in three stages: we (1) delineated the assumptions underlying TNE and examined their validity, (2) listed enabling factors that need to be aligned for the reform to be implemented, and (3) determined the potential outcomes that are likely to occur in the short term and long term, if the theory is well-implemented.

The TNE prospectus (Carnegie Corporation of New York, no date [n.d.]) outlines three broad design principles that the TNE funders believe characterize excellent teacher education programs and to which the selected institutions are expected to adhere:

1. A teacher education program should be guided by a respect for evidence. A culture of research, inquiry, and data analysis should permeate the program. Attention needs to be paid to pupil-learning gains accomplished under the tutelage of teachers who are graduates of the program.

2. Faculty in the disciplines of the arts and sciences must be fully engaged in the education of prospective teachers, especially in the areas of subject matter understanding and general and liberal education.

3. Teaching should be recognized as an academically taught clinical-practice profession. Adherence to this principle requires close cooperation between colleges of education and actual practicing schools, appointment of master teachers as clinical faculty in the college of education, and a two–year residency induction period for graduates of a teacher education program.

The guiding themes or design principles espoused by TNE are remarkably similar to those of several other reform efforts and teacher education accreditation organizations, suggesting a consensus in the field regarding the themes that should govern best practices in teacher education. However, while the principles themselves pass the test of logical reasonableness and draw from a variety of literature, the evidence supporting the principles is mixed at best. This does not necessarily negate the principles' validity—we simply point out that evidence does not exist or seems to be weak with respect to the assumed effect of some of the elements of the theory of change underlying TNE, and this may have an impact on TNE's desired outcomes.

TNE's thesis is that adoption and implementation of these design principles will result in an "excellent" teacher education program, whose teacher graduates will be well trained, capable, and qualified. Teachers trained by institutions that are well aligned with the TNE principles will be "high-quality" teachers, whose quality is measured by the learning gains made by their pupils. However, TNE is a complex initiative that requires institutional and cultural changes for it to succeed. It is designed to introduce fundamental changes to two institutions (universities and schools) and requires them to work collaboratively. Earlier reform efforts, most notably the work of the Holmes Group (1986, 1990, and 1995), have shown that these interorganizational collaborations are challenging to maintain. These efforts (and education reform efforts more generally) have highlighted the importance of several factors in implementation of teacher education reform—university-wide commitment; strong, stable leadership and depth of leadership; high-quality and committed faculty; high-quality students; strong partnerships with K–12 schools; and supportive policy environments. The policy environment—which is largely exogenous to the reform—is particularly important because, although TNE is looking for out-of-the-box thinking, these institutions still have to comply with state rules and regulations governing teacher licensure and certification.

TNE[1] builds on lessons learned from previous reform efforts in several ways. First, it recognizes that a complex program of reform requires both substantial funding and external technical assistance, and TNE provides both. Second, to ensure that the

---

[1] References to "TNE" in this report are to both the initiative itself and the TNE funders. The architect of TNE, the design of which is discussed in depth in subsequent chapters, is Carnegie Corporation of New York.

participating sites are best positioned to undertake such a reform, TNE selected institutions that were considered among the best in their "class" of institution and placed the grant in the provost's office rather than in a school of education. Third, support for TNE efforts is being fostered by informational sessions to educate policymakers about the initiative and engage them in it.

A national evaluation of a program of this magnitude and complexity faces several challenges, chief among them that the outcomes of interest—e.g., effectiveness of teachers as measured by students' learning gains and teacher retention—are not likely to be seen or measured until several years after the initiative ends. In the short run, we are limited to tracking implementation and some of the in-program outcomes.

"Value-Added" of TNE

Overall, the TNE design principles fit well with the culture and mind-set of the TNE sites, partly because the sites were chosen for their pre-TNE alignment with these principles, and because many of these institutions have tried to implement various versions of these principles as members of other reform networks. This section covers the value added by TNE through the three major design principles.

Decisions Driven by Evidence

All the TNE sites reported that participating in TNE has led to a growing respect for evidence-based decisionmaking across the institution.

First, TNE has brought about a new emphasis on collecting reliable, valid, and multiple measures of teacher education program effectiveness in schools of education, including pupil-learning gains made under the tutelage of program graduates, and using such evidence for program improvement. However, the sites are also aware of the complexity of using standardized test scores to provide valid evidence of the value added by the teacher education program. Many sites struggle to obtain data linking K–12 pupils to their teachers due to limitations in state and district data systems and privacy regulations. Even in cases in which such data are available, it is unclear how these data could and should be used to inform teacher education program improvement due to problems of attribution—i.e., being able to link teacher-related effects to particular elements of a program. Further, some TNE sites simply have small sample sizes that would not allow them to make inferences with any degree of confidence.

Second, TNE has resulted in a cultural shift across these institutions, with a new emphasis on evidence and assessment permeating many departments, not just the teacher education program.

Third, TNE has forced a new realization of the need to develop and implement integrated data systems capable of housing linked data elements, tracking student progress over time, and being updated and expanded on a regular basis as new data are collected or new data-collection efforts are undertaken.

Engagement of Arts and Sciences Faculty

TNE funds have enabled new and increased participation in teacher education by those in the arts and sciences. While participation of arts and sciences faculty is strongest in departments with historical ties to teacher education, the sites report an overall deepening of these relationships and new participation from other arts and sciences departments. Faculty members participating in TNE noted that working together on a common project has led education and arts and sciences faculty to have a greater understanding of each other's motivations and goals, greater respect for one another, and recognition by arts and sciences faculty that many of their students are future teachers. Many education faculty members, after an initial period of resistance, are increasingly seeking out arts and sciences colleagues for collaboration and to discuss issues concerning teacher candidates' content knowledge.

TNE has made arts and sciences faculty more aware of how they can contribute to the preparation of future teachers and, at some sites, has involved them in teacher education program planning and evaluation, joint development of teaching and knowledge standards, joint advising, team-teaching, study groups, and developing courses or sections aimed at future teachers. This is not to suggest that many of these activities were not occurring pre-TNE but simply that the sites report a more systematic cross-discipline involvement in teacher education and a greater recognition of the need for collaboration in this effort across departments.

Some sites have hired new arts and sciences faculty with ties to teacher education. These faculty members are placed within their disciplinary departments but, by contract, are required to spend some amount of time working on teacher education issues or acting as liaisons between their department and the teacher education program. Some of these faculty members are on joint appointments.

Junior faculty working on TNE expressed the concern that, given the responsibilities of TNE, they may not have sufficient time to meet their requirements for scholarship and publishing and, as such, may be disadvantaged when it comes time for promotion and tenure decisions. When these issues are raised, the TNE leadership teams have had several responses: They provide ample assurances that research and publications on education issues will count toward promotion and tenure; they point to the new and exciting possibilities for joint research that exist in schools ("a natural lab"); or they simply acknowledge that junior arts and sciences faculty need to be less involved in TNE and will have those individuals work for only short periods of time on TNE activities or will have senior faculty involved in the TNE work instead. The sites will need to continue working on this issue to ensure that TNE faculty are fully accepted by their peers and are successful in their positions.

Teaching as an Academically Taught Clinical-Practice Profession

Involvement of K–12 Faculty. While all the TNE sites recognize the importance of developing strong relationships with K–12 schools, and some are attempting to develop professional development schools at some clinical sites (classrooms in which student teaching and education research is done), the TNE sites have not been uniformly successful in implementing this principle to the degree that the TNE creators envisaged. Developing clinical sites is useful in the sense that those sites provide model laboratories to distill best practices and enhance conversations among partners in teacher education, but scaling up clinical sites is time-consuming and expensive.

Most of the sites have some K–12 representatives on their TNE teams, selected in consultation with leaders of the schools, but the degree to which K–12 faculty are involved varies considerably by site and across TNE teams. In terms of hiring teachers in residence, some sites have been successful, while others have not, for a variety of reasons largely having to do with problems in hiring away experienced teachers from secure and relatively well-paid positions, reluctance on the part of school districts to release teachers for temporary university assignments, university-district pay differentials, and lack of clarity about the roles and expectations of teachers in residence.

Induction. The induction component of TNE (a two-year "residency" period for graduates of teacher education programs, during which teacher graduates would be provided with various supports during the crucible years of teaching) was hailed as one of the most innovative of the TNE elements, but it has proven to be the most difficult to implement in practice. Because the induction concept was new to many of the sites, they initially struggled to define their role in this effort and to find induction activities that they could actually implement and sustain. Some TNE sites have moved ahead with developing Web sites to provide a variety of online induction help, developing stronger relationships with the school districts, setting up small model induction programs in cooperating districts, and institutionalizing induction by creating master's degree programs linked to induction. Other sites reported that they do not believe they have enough staff to provide such support and continue to struggle with this piece of the design. Almost all the sites agree that involving arts and sciences faculty in direct induction activities—or indeed, in supervision of student teaching—is a real challenge.

In addition, the state and school district policy environment has been a barrier to implementing university-based induction programs. The sites are seriously concerned about whether there is or will be a demand for university-based support and whether new teachers will be willing to pay for such programs, because these factors will determine the sites' ability to sustain such programs in the long run. This concern arises for several reasons. First, most states and some districts have mandated induction programs for beginning teachers, many of which are provided to teachers free of charge. Second, in some instances, programs or courses designed by the sites have not been endorsed by the state and, therefore, do not count toward continuing education or for permanent licensure. Third, the sites are finding that new teachers are overwhelmed with the realities of the classroom and their state or district induction requirements, and, as such, feel that they are unable to participate in additional activities. Fourth, sites are also finding it difficult to track their graduates; state-maintained teacher databases may offer the best means of tracking graduates, but getting access to those databases can be difficult.

Those sites that have been successful in offering or piloting induction programs have collaborated with and sought to fulfill the needs of the local districts.

Thinking About Sustainability

When asked about sustainability of TNE, the sites reported that many of the changes occurring at the sites are likely to become institutionalized over time. First, apart from TNE, a confluence of other factors, such as accreditation requirements and the new demand from policymakers, parents, and students for accountability for teacher education, is forcing all institutions to build comprehensive databases on teacher education students, collect evidence of student learning, and track students to gather outcome data farther "downstream" from a student's graduation date to prove effectiveness of teacher education. However, it is important to note that a wide chasm exists between collecting and analyzing data and actually using the data for program improvement. Organizations often emphasize the collection of data to convey "an illusory sense of rationality," in which the purportedly rational and deliberate activity to collect data masks the fact that they fail to actually use these data to make decisions.

Second, part of this new push to collect and evaluate evidence will require arts and sciences faculty to become involved in ensuring that students get a good undergraduate liberal education. Thus, the discussions and partnerships between education and arts and sciences faculty—particularly faculty in those departments that historically have had ties to teacher education—are likely to deepen and to continue. As new TNE arts and sciences faculty with an interest in or ties to teacher education become more accepted and more numerous, they will help to sustain a culture of involvement in teacher education by those in the arts and sciences.

Third, if the TNE induction programs can work with the states and school districts to provide or to extend the induction offerings in ways that the state is willing to endorse and that the states and districts can financially support, the induction programs and support systems for graduates that are being designed now are likely to endure.

Likely Legacy of TNE

TNE has taken an ambitious and well-funded approach to what has been called an intractable problem—the reform of teacher education. Ultimately, TNE will be judged by its long-term impact on the field of teacher education, and, more importantly, by its impact on the quality of teaching and learning in the nation's schools. Thus, to evaluate TNE's legacy, we need to examine what has been or will be the likely impact on the quality and retention of new teacher graduates being produced by these institutions, how that impact will translate into improvements in pupil learning, and how these new and improved methods of preparing teachers will be disseminated across the nation.

Thus far, the actual changes in the teacher education programs at the TNE sites appear to be small and incremental. This is not surprising, given that these institutions were selected because they were among the best in their "class" of institutions. However, the process by which these incremental changes to a program will result in highly qualified, competent teachers who will be markedly "better" than the graduates before them is not well defined.

Under the TNE design, the grantees would become exemplars for other institutions, which would learn from the grantees and seek to emulate their TNE programs in part or in whole and thus extend the reach of TNE and its impact on the field of teacher education. But these anticipated outcomes are based on several assumptions that may not hold. First, the evidence regarding the effect of the changes adopted or proposed by the sites on the quality of teacher graduates will accumulate only over a very long period of time and will require substantial effort to assemble. Second, earlier reform efforts have shown that institutions are slow to emulate others, even when faced with evidence of successful changes. Third, a key premise of TNE is that it takes substantial amounts of money to reform a teacher education program. Thus, how are the peer institutions expected to successfully transform themselves, absent this level of funding? Even with the funding, the changes seen so far in the teacher education programs at TNE sites are small, piecemeal, and incremental. Fourth, it is not clear that TNE constitutes a coherent reform program that can simply be ported to peer institutions for adoption. Fifth, the question of attribution is a tricky one. Even if one observed non-TNE institutions adopting principles that seem to resemble those of TNE, how can such a change be attributed to TNE? After all, several reform efforts and accreditation bodies share the same principles, particularly the emphasis on the "culture of evidence." From the point of view of correctly identifying the legacy of TNE, this question remains the thorniest one of all.

Like every reform effort, TNE has several goals. Given that among its goals are changing institutional culture, bringing new awareness of the role that all faculty play in preparing teachers, and helping to make teacher education a priority for institutions of higher learning, the TNE initiative is likely to be a success. The goal of improving teaching more generally across a college or university and improving the quality of general and liberal education that undergraduates receive may also be met. But these successes cannot be attributed solely to TNE, given the political, economic, and social forces also driving change. With respect to whether TNE's other goals will be met—radical changes in the way teachers are prepared, evidence that these changes will produce high-quality teachers capable of bringing about marked improvements in pupils' learning, and clear guidance for peer institutions to adopt and to adapt the TNE program design principles, the answers are less clear, and, given the less-than-stellar history and cyclical nature of past teacher education reform efforts, perhaps less optimistic.

Acknowledgments

We thank the three sponsors of this work—the Rockefeller Foundation, the Nellie Mae Foundation, and the Ford Foundation—for their interest in and support of the TNE evaluation. We are particularly grateful to the TNE sites for their participation in the evaluation. They generously provided us with materials, hosted us for site visits, and shared their thoughts, successes, and concerns with us. We appreciate their honesty and their hospitality. We also thank Daniel Fallon of Carnegie Corporation (the architect of TNE) and Michael Timpane for useful conversations on the reform initiative and its progress.

We especially thank our reviewers, Susan Moore Johnson of Harvard University and Henry (Hank) Levin of Teachers College, Columbia University, for their critical and constructive reviews. Their suggestions and comments greatly added to the substance and clarity of this document. We also thank our RAND colleagues, Sue Bodilly and Catherine Augustine, for providing useful comments on an earlier version of this report. Finally, we thank Nancy DelFavero for her thorough and careful editing and for her patience.

Acronyms

AACTE	American Association of Colleges of Teacher Education
AC	alternative certification
ACT	Accelerated Collaborative Teacher Preparation Program
AED	Academy for Educational Development
AERA	American Educational Research Association
AOI	Action-Oriented Inquiry
A&S	Arts & Sciences (University of Virginia)
ASSIST	Advocating Strong Standards-Based Induction Support for Teachers
ASTEC	Arts and Sciences Teacher Education Collaborative
B.A.	bachelor of arts
BC	Boston College
BEST	Beginning Educator Support and Training
B.I.S.	bachelor of interdisciplinary studies
BPS	Boston Public Schools
B.S.Ed.	bachelor of science in education
CBEST	California Basic Educational Skills Test
CPRE	Consortium for Policy Research in Education
CRESST	Center for Research on Evaluation Standards and Student Testing
CSU	California State University
CSUN	California State University, Northridge
DAF	digital assessment file
DPS	Detroit Public Schools

FAMU	Florida A&M University
ELL	English-language learner
FTCE	Florida Teacher Certification Examination
FYI	Four-Year Integrated Teacher Credential Program
GE	general education
GPA	grade point average
GRE	Graduate Record Examinations
HBCU	Historically Black Colleges and Universities
HLM	hierarchical linear modeling
IB/M	Integrated Bachelor's/Master's Program
INTASC	Interstate New Teacher Assessment and Support Consortium
IR	institutional research
ITEP	Integrated Teacher Education Program
K–12	kindergarten through grade 12
LAUSD	Los Angeles Unified School District
LSOE	Lynch School of Education
M.A.T.	master of arts in teaching
MDRC	Manpower Demonstration Research Corporation
M.Ed.	master of education
M.I.T.	master in teaching
MKT	Mathematical Knowledge for Teaching
MPS	Milwaukee Public Schools
M.S.	master of science
M.S.Ed.	master of science in education
MSP	Math Science Partnership
M.S.T.	master of science in teaching
MSU	Michigan State University

M.T.	master of teaching
NBPTS	National Board for Professional Teaching Standards
N–8	nursery school through grade 8
NCATE	National Council for Accreditation of Teacher Education
NCTAF	National Commission on Teaching and America's Future
n.d.	no date
NNER	National Network for Educational Renewal
NTC	Santa Cruz New Teacher Center
P–12	preschool through grade 12
P–16	preschool through baccalaureate
PACT	Performance Assessment for California Teachers
PCK	pedagogical content knowledge
PDS	professional development school
PRS	personal response system
RAC	Research Advisory Council
RFP	request for proposal
SFC	Bank Street School for Children
SOL	Standards of Learning
SOLO	Structure of the Observed Learning Outcome
STEP	Stanford Teacher Education Program
TCPCG	Teaching Certification Program for College Graduates
TEAC	Teacher Education Accreditation Council
THEA	Texas Higher Education Assessment
TIR	teacher in residence
TKS	teacher knowledge standards
TNE	Teachers for a New Era
TQM	Total Quality Management

TRG	The Renaissance Group
TVAAS	Tennessee Value Added Assessment System
UConn	University of Connecticut
UNITE	Urban Network to Improve Teacher Education
UTEP	University of Texas at El Paso
UTLA	United Teachers Los Angeles
UVa	University of Virginia
UW	University of Washington
UWM	University of Wisconsin–Milwaukee
VAM	value-added modeling

CHAPTER ONE

Introduction

Schools of Teacher Education: Defending the Ramparts

Schools of education and teacher education programs have been under attack for decades. They have been portrayed as "intellectual wastelands," decried as "impractical and irrelevant" by practitioners, and cited as the root cause of bad teaching and inadequate learning (Labaree, 2004; Cochran-Smith and Zeichner, 2005). On the one side, opponents of traditional teacher preparation programs and state certification requirements argue for reducing or doing away with certification requirements, reducing the number of education courses, and increasing the number of alternative certification programs that prepare teachers in a shorter time period and without overloading them with education courses. This viewpoint is exemplified by former Secretary of Education Rodney Paige, who in his first annual report to Congress on teacher quality (U.S. Department of Education, 2002) painted a picture of low standards, heavy emphasis on pedagogy in education courses, and burdensome state regulations regarding certification requirements:

> There is little evidence that education school coursework leads to improved student achievement . . . The data show that many states mandate a shocking number of education courses to qualify for certification . . . These burdensome requirements are the Achilles heel of the certification system. They scare off talented individuals while adding little value. Certainly, some of the required courses might be helpful, but scant research exists to justify these mandates (U. S. Department of Education, 2002, pp. 19, 31).

Paige's report also stressed the importance of several alternative certification programs, such as Teach for America, in dealing with shortages of qualified teachers and teacher candidates.

More recently, columnist George Will in a January 16, 2006, *Newsweek* column, ridiculed the focus on "professional disposition" in today's schools of education. In that piece, Will cited an article titled "Why Johnny's Teacher Can't Teach" (MacDonald, 1998):

The surest, quickest way to add quality to primary and secondary education would be addition by subtraction: Close all the schools of education . . . Many education schools discourage, even disqualify, prospective teachers who lack the correct "disposition," meaning those who do not embrace today's "progressive" political catechism . . . Today's teacher-education focus on "professional disposition" is just the latest permutation of what MacDonald calls the education schools' "immutable dogma," which she calls "Anything But Knowledge" . . . MacDonald says, "The central educational fallacy of our time," which dates from the Progressive Era of the early 20th century, is that "one can think without having anything to think about."

On the other side, proponents (including groups such as the National Council for Accreditation of Teacher Education [NCATE], Interstate New Teacher Assessment and Support Consortium [INTASC], National Board for Professional Teaching Standards [NBPTS], and National Commission on Teaching and America's Future [NCTAF]) call for greater professionalization of the teaching profession through defining the kinds of knowledge and skills teachers should have in order to teach effectively; the use of program accreditation to ensure that programs are indeed transmitting these skills and knowledge; and testing and certification to ensure that teachers do possess these skills and knowledge. NCATE President Arthur Wise, in a sharply worded retort to the George Will column, invited Will to "get outside the Beltway and visit the real world, including today's universities that prepare teachers" and pointed out that teacher candidates major in the disciplines they are preparing to teach and take the same courses and same exams as other students take.

The lines are sharply drawn, and neither side appears willing to concede that the other may have a valid point. As Labaree concluded, "Balance, it seems, is unwelcome on both sides of this debate" (Labaree, 2004, p. 171).

Spurred by the scathing criticisms leveled at teacher education and undaunted by the fact that most funders interested in improving kindergarten through grade 12 (K–12) education have come to regard teacher education as a "black hole," Carnegie Corporation of New York (hereafter, Carnegie) took on the challenge of reforming teacher education and launched an ambitious reform initiative, called Teachers for a New Era (TNE),[1] in summer 2001 with the goal of radically transforming how teachers are prepared for

---

[1] References to "TNE" in this report are to both the initiative itself and to the TNE funders. The TNE reform, the design of which is discussed in depth in subsequent chapters, was created by Carnegie Corporation of New York.

their profession. The RAND Corporation and the Manpower Demonstration Research Corporation (MDRC)[2] followed and evaluated the TNE initiative for three years (October 2002 to September 2005). This monograph presents the results to date of that study.

In the next section, we present a brief overview of the initiative, which is drawn largely from the TNE prospectus,[3] before turning to the work RAND has done as part of the national evaluation of TNE.

The Teachers for a New Era Initiative

The ultimate goal of the TNE initiative is to improve K–12 student outcomes by improving the quality of teachers in K–12 schools. TNE proposes to do this by stimulating construction of excellent teacher education programs at selected colleges and universities, with the idea that these programs will become exemplars for peer institutions. In its TNE prospectus, Carnegie made clear that it was seeking "a catalytic revision of teacher education led by colleges and universities committed to a new future for teaching and learning in the nation's schools" (Carnegie Corporation of New York, n.d.). To assist institutions in this endeavor, Carnegie planned to make awards in the amount of $5 million over a period of five years to six to eight institutions of higher education. Two other foundations—the Annenberg Foundation and the Ford Foundation—joined Carnegie in the first year in funding the TNE initiative, allowing a larger number of institutions (11 in all) to be funded. The primary funder remains, however, Carnegie Corporation of New York—the TNE initiator and designer.

TNE is currently administered by the Academy for Educational Development (AED), which provides hands-on technical assistance to the TNE institutions and monitors their implementation progress for the TNE funders.

TNE Rationale and Goals

Carnegie Corporation offered a rationale for its focus on improving teacher education:

> New and convincing evidence that teaching is more important for schoolchildren than any other condition has been stunning in its clarity and exciting in its implications . . . Now, recent research based upon thousands of pupil records in many different cities and states establishes beyond doubt that the quality of the teacher is the most important cause of pupil achievement. Excellent teachers can bring about

---

[2] Created in 1974 by the Ford Foundation and federal agencies, MDRC, with offices in New York and Oakland, California, is best known for conducting large-scale evaluations of policies and programs targeted to low-income people. MDRC's studies have expanded to public-school reform and other policy areas (see http://www.mdrc. org/).

[3] The prospectus (Carnegie Corporation of New York, no date [n.d.]) can be found at http://www.carnegie. org/sub/program/teachers_prospectus.html.

remarkable increases in pupil learning even in the face of severe economic or social disadvantage. Such new knowledge puts teacher education squarely at the focus of efforts to improve the intellectual capacity of schoolchildren in the United States. More than ever, the nation needs assurance that colleges and universities are educating prospective teachers of the highest quality possible (Carnegie Corporation, n.d.).

The ultimate goal of the TNE initiative is both bold and ambitious. The TNE prospectus further states:

> At the conclusion of the project, each of these institutions should be regarded by the nation as the locus for one of the best programs possible for the standard primary route to employment as a beginning professional teacher. The benchmarks of success for this effort will be evident in the characteristics of the teachers who graduate from these programs. They will be competent, caring, and qualified, will be actively sought by school districts and schools, and will be known for the learning gains made by their pupils (Carnegie Corporation, n.d.).

Carnegie also made it clear that it is expecting radical changes in the way institutions organize themselves academically, allocate resources, evaluate participating faculty, and partner with K–12 schools. Although not specified in the prospectus, these radical changes might include a greater awareness and understanding of the role of all faculty in preparing teachers; new partnerships and collaborations among arts and sciences, teacher education, and K–12 faculty; higher priority being placed on teacher education; and acknowledgment of the contributions of faculty to teacher education in promotion and tenure decisions.

TNE Site Selection Process

Early in fall 2001, Carnegie appointed a National Advisory Panel to help select institutions that would be invited to submit proposals for funding under the terms of the TNE initiative. Carnegie then asked RAND to provide analytic assistance to the panel and to Carnegie during the selection process. Carnegie asked panel members to consider the following criteria for selection:

- the quality of the teacher education program currently in place at the institution
- the capacity of the institution to serve as an exemplar or model for other institutions
- the effects of the institution on the enterprise of teacher education
- the local or regional public policy environment that most directly affects the institution
- the capacity of the institution to engage in leadership activities to persuade other institutions to adopt successful features of the TNE design principles

- the quality of the faculty and administration
- other criteria that were deemed relevant.

After a considerable amount of discussion, such criteria as depth and breadth of leadership, stability of leadership, and commitment to change were included in the list of criteria to be considered during the selection process. In addition, Carnegie and the panel representatives were sensitive to the importance of selecting a group of institutions that represented the wide variety of institutions and programs that prepare teachers. The panel members and representatives from Carnegie and other foundations identified several teacher education institutions as meeting all or some subset of the criteria listed above. RAND developed comparable profiles of these institutions based on publicly available data. Based on these data and on their own judgment, panel members and foundation representatives selected seven institutions as candidates for funding in the first year. Carnegie representatives, panel members, RAND, and, in some cases, other foundation members made site visits to these seven institutions early in 2002. Based largely on the data gathered during the site visits, panel members and foundation representatives ranked the institutions.

Originally, Carnegie planned to fund six to eight institutions. The Annenberg and Ford Foundations later joined Carnegie in funding TNE; as a result, the total number of institutions funded by TNE increased to 11.

The first round of awards was announced in April 2002. The first four grantees were Bank Street College of Education; California State University, Northridge (CSUN); Michigan State University (MSU); and the University of Virginia (UVa).

The second round of awards to an additional seven institutions was announced in summer 2003. In the second round, institutions were also asked to submit short preliminary proposals, and the quality of these proposals was included as part of the selection criteria. The seven additional grantees were Boston College (BC), Florida A&M University (FAMU), Stanford University, University of Connecticut (UConn), University of Texas at El Paso (UTEP), University of Washington (UW), and University of Wisconsin–Milwaukee (UWM).

Each institution was funded for three years initially and is expected to submit a renewal application and undergo a site visit at the end of that period to receive the next two years of funding in the five-year funding period.

TNE National Evaluation

In December 2002, the Rockefeller Foundation asked RAND and MDRC to conduct an evaluation of the implementation of TNE at the first four sites—Bank Street College of Education; CSUN; MSU; and UVa. In August 2004, the Nellie Mae Education Foundation, primarily because of its regional interest in institutions in the Northeast corridor, asked RAND and MDRC to include BC and UConn from the second cohort of grantees in the evaluation. In December 2005, the Ford Foundation asked RAND

and MDRC to extend the evaluation to include two other sites—FAMU and UTEP—because these two institutions are large producers of minority teachers.

The long-term objectives of the evaluations are (1) to provide evidence of whether the TNE initiative has been "successful"—both from the individual institutions' point of view and from the funders' point of view; (2) to identify factors that foster or hinder the implementation of reform of teacher education programs at the program, institution, district, and state levels; (3) to promote an understanding of the many factors and actors that need to be aligned to successfully reform teacher education and improve student learning; and (4) to evaluate the overall contribution of TNE to teacher education reform in the country, states, and school districts. Some of these questions can be answered only in the long term, after several cohorts of students have graduated from the newly designed programs and have been in the labor force for some time and after peer institutions have had a chance to adopt and adapt the TNE design. Some, perhaps, will never be fully answered. Nonetheless, these are appropriate research questions for the longer-term evaluation.

In the short term, the evaluation seeks to address the following two research questions:

- To what extent did the grantees implement Carnegie's three major design principles and other principles outlined in the prospectus? What did the grantees attempt to do with the Carnegie funds?
- What factors fostered or hindered implementation?

Answering these questions is crucially important to the evaluation. If implementation is weak or fails to occur, then examining longer-term outcomes becomes pointless to a large extent.

The TNE grant requires each institution to set aside funds for a local site evaluation to be conducted by an agency external to the teacher education program. The site evaluations—unlike the national evaluation—are site specific and, at this stage, are designed to provide formative feedback, in some cases on specific issues, to the institutions as they implement the initiative. The national evaluation encompasses a cross-site design and is intended to draw lessons learned from attempting to implement the design principles outlined by Carnegie in its prospectus (Carnegie Corporation of New York, n.d.) in various institutions, cultures, and environments. Both the short-term research (process evaluation) and longer-term research (summative evaluation) should be useful for policymakers struggling with improving the quality of the nation's teachers and schools; for schools and districts attempting to hire, train, and retain teachers; for institutions preparing teachers; and for any future initiatives aimed at reforming teacher education.

Purpose of This Monograph

This monograph reports on the progress in implementation of TNE at the following 11 sites as of September 2005:

- Cohort I grantees—Bank Street, CSUN, MSU, and UVa
- Cohort II grantees—BC, FAMU, Stanford, UConn, UTEP, UW, and UWM.

As of that date, the first cohort of grantees had been implementing TNE principles for three years, while the second cohort had been implementing TNE principles for two years. This monograph, which builds on and extends an earlier report (Kirby et al., 2004) that examined first-year implementation in the first cohort of grantees, has four main purposes:

- To place the TNE initiative in the larger context of the current politics surrounding teacher education and other reform efforts
- To understand the evidence base underlying the principles that TNE espouses
- To provide an overview of the progress in implementing the three major design principles (described in the next chapter) across the sites, with a view to highlighting interesting and innovative ideas and activities currently under way in these institutions and the challenges the institutions face in implementation
- To use cross-site observations to assess what is new and different in these institutions and, more important, what is likely to be sustained over the longer term.

While it may be somewhat premature, we also offer some thoughts on the likely legacy of TNE in terms of its larger impact on the field of teacher education and the quality of teaching and learning in the nation's schools.

Data Used in This Study

As we mentioned above, the TNE initiative had received funding to track the progress of TNE implementation at eight of the 11 TNE institutions—Bank Street, CSUN, MSU, UVa, BC, FAMU, UConn, and UTEP. However, with sponsor approval, we were able to use a small amount of funding to undertake some limited data collection at the remaining three institutions (Stanford, UW, and UWM), which allowed us to present a national picture of the reform. The findings on these sites (included in the appendices) are necessarily more limited than those of the other institutions, but they do help to provide a coherent picture of the kinds of activities all the institutions are undertaking as part of the TNE reform.

The findings in this monograph are based primarily on data collected during annual two-day site visits to seven of the sites (Bank Street, BC, CSUN, MSU, UConn,

UTEP, and UVa). We did not conduct site visits to the three institutions for which we had limited funding for data collection, and we did not conduct site visits to FAMU for the reasons discussed below. The site visits took place in the fall of each year. The latest round of site visits was conducted from September 2005 through January 2006.

Site visits encompassed interviews with the project officer, president or provost, deans of the arts and sciences and education departments, faculty from the arts and sciences and education departments who are involved in teacher education and TNE, and supervisors of clinical sites (classrooms in which student teaching and education research is done), and interviews or focus groups with principals and teachers in partner K–12 schools. These interviews used semi-structured protocols that were shared with the sites prior to the site visit. In addition, each site was asked to review RAND's summary site-visit notes each year and was given an opportunity to make factual corrections.

Due to organizational changes at FAMU, we were unable to conduct the first FAMU site visit by the time of this study. Further, FAMU has undergone a number of changes in its leadership since the inception of the TNE-grant process. Changes have occurred in the Offices of the President, Provost and Vice President for Academic Affairs, Vice President for Finance and Administrative Affairs, and Vice President for Research. As a result of these and other personnel changes, there have been delays in the grant approval process. The TNE grant agreement for FAMU was not finalized until May 2005. While FAMU received preliminary funding for TNE in the amount of $110,000 in April 2004, the first regular reimbursement of university costs for grant activities was in September 2005. Consequently, although we provide a brief overview of FAMU's TNE activities in Appendix E, we rely on data from the other sites in presenting cross-site trends.

For the remaining three institutions (Stanford, UW, and UWM), we collected data from their individual TNE Web sites (see Appendix A for a list of those sites), we requested additional materials from the TNE project director at each site, and/or we conducted brief interviews with the TNE leadership teams.

The process outcomes reported here are based on self-reports and materials provided by the sites, with no further validation, including annual progress reports and, in the case of the first cohort, the detailed third-year applications submitted by the sites to the funders for renewal of the grant. Cross-site observations are gleaned from an examination of findings from all the sites but depend more heavily on the detailed case studies. In addition, we conducted an extensive literature review to map TNE's "theory of organizational change," and we collected data from Web sites on other reform efforts.

We also conducted interviews with the architect of TNE—Daniel Fallon, Chair, Education Division, Carnegie Corporation of New York—and education expert Michael Timpane, a member of the advisory team overseeing TNE.

Organization of This Monograph

Chapter Two describes the major design principles of TNE and then places TNE in the context of the various efforts aimed at reforming teacher education, while pointing to similarities and differences among these reform efforts. Chapter Three presents TNE's theory of organizational change and examines the evidence base for the underlying principles of TNE. It highlights the number of actors and factors that need to be aligned for the TNE theory to work and for its goal of improving teaching and pupil learning to come to fruition.

In Chapters Four and Five, our focus turns to the TNE sites and implementation of TNE. Chapter Four provides a brief profile of each institution, while Chapter Five examines cross-site trends in implementing the three major design principles: (1) decisions driven by evidence; (2) engagement of arts and sciences faculty in teacher education; and (3) teaching as an academically taught clinical practice profession (encompassing both increased involvement of K–12 faculty in teacher education and a two-year residency program through which graduates are provided support and mentoring). Chapter Five also presents comments from participants regarding the contributions made by TNE to the institutions' programs and cultures and the sustainability of TNE beyond the life of the grant. The chapter concludes with comments from funders regarding the progress of the reform and its sustainability. Chapter Six provides our conclusions and thoughts on the likely legacy of TNE to the larger field of teacher education.

Appendix A lists the institutions' TNE-specific Web sites and other Web sites of interest. Appendices B, C, and D provide an overview of implementation of the three design principles in the first and second cohort of grantees. Appendix E presents a brief summary of the activities undertaken by Florida A&M University.

CHAPTER TWO

TNE in the Context of the Broader Teacher Education Reform Effort

This chapter sets TNE in the context of the broader teacher education reform efforts in the nation. We first describe the design principles that TNE espouses; these become the focus of our later chapters on the progress of TNE implementation. We next provide a brief overview of other initiatives aimed at reforming teacher education. In particular, we focus on (1) the revamping of standards for accreditation by the two major teacher education accreditation bodies and (2) five major reform initiatives that are representative of the myriad reform efforts in the country and that encompass several higher-education institutions, much as TNE does. A final section highlights the similarities and differences between the TNE design principles and those underpinning these other teacher education reform efforts.

TNE Design Principles

The TNE prospectus (Carnegie Corporation of New York, n.d.) outlines three broad design principles that the funders believe characterize excellent teacher education programs and to which the selected institutions are expected to adhere:

1. A teacher education program should be guided by a respect for evidence. A culture of research, inquiry, and data analysis should permeate the program. Attention needs to be paid to pupil learning gains accomplished under the tutelage of teachers who are graduates of the program.
2. Faculty in the disciplines of the arts and sciences must be fully engaged in the education of prospective teachers, especially in the areas of subject-matter understanding and general and liberal education.
3. Teaching should be recognized as an academically taught clinical-practice profession. Adherence to this principle requires close cooperation between colleges of education and actual practicing schools, appointment of master teachers as

clinical faculty in the college of education, and a two–year residency induction period for graduates of a teacher education program (Carnegie Corporation of New York, n.d.).

The following paragraphs, with material quoted from the prospectus, briefly describe what TNE expects under each of these design principles:

First, a teacher education program should be evaluated against the credible evidence of best practices and program design, and changes to the design should be informed by qualitative, quantitative, and/or experimental research. "An exemplary teacher education program should begin with a persuasive scholarly discussion of what constitutes excellence in teaching . . . [and] the means by which teaching effectiveness can be increased . . . Working continually with evidence and evaluations of research, however, is an efficient means for clarifying our observations and building our confidence in practice. It builds a culture that justifies ongoing redesign of work as the program learns from the very steps it takes to improve." The prospectus emphasizes that gains in pupil learning must be an essential criterion by which to judge the effectiveness of teacher graduates. While recognizing that this is difficult and will entail collecting data over a longer period of time, the prospectus insists that sites describe the "method by which such measures will necessarily in due course assume their proper role in validating the design . . . In addition to this long-term consideration of the role of pupil learning, attention to the assessment and measurement of pupil learning will be an integral element of the teacher education program, especially gaining attention during the student teaching component."

Second, each site is required to ensure that teacher candidates have deep "subject matter understanding and general and liberal education, whose domains lie principally within the core competencies of faculty in the arts and sciences." Because the professional authority of teachers derives from their being perceived as educated persons, "Teacher candidates must be expected to know more in the way of subject matter than just what they are charged with teaching." Thus, arts and sciences faculty are expected to work with teacher education faculty with respect to the design of academic majors in the arts and sciences and/or the program of general and liberal education to ensure that the teacher candidates possess integrative knowledge of the nature, premise, modes of inquiry, and limits of various disciplines. In addition, "(S)ome faculty in the arts and sciences will be expected to participate in the supervision of teacher candidates in clinical settings." Deans, department chairs, and colleagues in the disciplines are expected to collaborate in these efforts.

Third, excellent teacher education programs conceptualize teaching as a clinical practice profession and make this concept an integral part of the program design. Thus, the program should ensure that its teacher graduates are able to (1) assess what pupils know and can do as the point of departure for new learning; (2) develop a rigorous curriculum that engages pupils, builds on their prior knowledge, and fosters deep understanding of content; (3) collaborate with colleagues and families to ensure coherence and ongoing success with pupils; and (4) build a repertoire of teaching strategies to accommodate a range of learning styles, abilities, and cultural backgrounds. In addition, "(A)n exemplary teacher education program will develop close functional relationships with a number of practicing schools . . . Faculty from the university or college will be actively involved in arranging, supervising, and teaching teacher candidates in the clinical setting of the classrooms of the practicing schools . . . (E)xperienced excellent teachers should be recognized as faculty colleagues."

The prospectus further emphasizes that programs should take responsibility for the teacher candidate's first two years of full-time regular service in the teaching profession. During this time, "faculty from the higher-education institution, inclusive of arts and sciences faculty, will confer with the teacher on a regular basis, arrange for observation of the teacher's clinical practice, and provide guidance to improve practice." Further, teacher graduates need to understand the importance of engaging in regular professional development activities to sustain and further develop the skills of clinical practice.

In addition to these three major design principles, the TNE prospectus emphasizes a number of other areas that teacher education programs need to address as part of their program redesign:

- **Pedagogical Content Knowledge.** Faculties from both arts and sciences and education need to work together to ensure that teachers have both a deep understanding of subject matter and pedagogical content knowledge (PCK)[1] that would allow them to teach imaginatively and productively.
- **Literacy and Numeracy Skills.** The program should ensure that teacher candidates acquire and demonstrate mastery of literacy and numeracy skills, and that they are prepared to teach them, irrespective of the level at which they will be teaching.
- **Academic Concentration of Elementary and Middle School Teachers.** Attention needs to be paid to the question of an appropriate academic concentration for a candidate intending to become an elementary-school teacher (and perhaps a middle-school teacher). This question should be addressed in a rigorous way, with close attention to credible evidence from the research literature, to ensure that elementary-school teachers learn the core structure of multiple disciplines and are prepared to teach content knowledge in a variety of subjects.

---

[1] Pedagogical content knowledge is the combination of understanding content and how best to translate that content knowledge to students through appropriate lessons and pedagogy.

- **Use of Technology.** Knowing how to evaluate and use new technologies to facilitate teaching and learning is an essential skill in the teacher's repertoire; therefore, programs need to integrate instruction about technology throughout the curriculum.
- **Cultural Considerations and Minority Recruitment.** Given the demographic and cultural composition of the nation's students, teachers need to be taught basic elements of the cultures in which students live and how sensitivity to culture works as an ally to effective teaching. In addition, there is an especially pressing need for teacher candidates who represent minority communities, particularly in the areas of science and mathematics. Teacher education programs need to find ways to recruit more students from groups that are underrepresented in teaching.
- **Late Deciders.** Some students decide to become teachers late in their undergraduate careers and/or transfer in from community colleges. Therefore, specific provisions need to be developed within the program to ease the entry of qualified candidates who come to the program later than the normally indicated point of admission.

Many of these issues are central components or concerns of many teacher education programs, and TNE recognizes their importance and requires that attention be paid to them. However, TNE expects that each institution will resolve these issues in a manner best suited to its environment and goals; the major design principles—evidence-based decisionmaking, rigorous content and pedagogical content knowledge, and an integrated clinical component—need to form the core of the program and to underpin other goals and components.

TNE's thesis is that adoption and implementation of these design principles will result in an "excellent" teacher education program, whose teacher graduates will be well trained, capable, and qualified. Teachers trained by institutions well aligned with the TNE principles will be "high-quality" teachers, whose quality is measured by the learning gains made by their pupils.

TNE also makes it clear that it is expecting teacher education to be a university-wide commitment. To ensure that the institutional leadership is fully engaged in the reform effort, the TNE award is made to an officer in the president or provost's office whose administrative authority extends throughout all academic units of the institution, rather than to a school, college, or dean.

Institutions selected for awards are expected to become national exemplars of best practice in the field of teacher education. To fulfill this responsibility, they are expected to widely disseminate information about lessons learned, successful innovations, and difficulties encountered.

National Accreditation Organizations

Two organizations—NCATE and the Teacher Education Accreditation Council (TEAC)—act as national accreditation agencies for teacher education programs. NCATE (http://www.ncate.org/public/aboutNCATE.asp), founded in 1954, accredits schools, colleges, and departments of education (professional education units) in U.S. colleges and universities. NCATE currently accredits 614 colleges of education, and nearly 100 more are seeking NCATE accreditation.

TEAC (http://www.teac.org/) was founded in 1997 partly in response to attacks on the quality of teacher education programs. It bills itself as an alternative approach to accreditation of teacher education, focusing on verifiable evidence of teacher candidates' learning, and it accredits teacher education *programs*, not the college, school, department, or other administrative unit. Since NCATE revised its standards in 2000 to also focus on evidence, the principles of the two organizations—though not their methods—are substantially similar. Currently, teacher education programs at 15 institutions have TEAC accreditation status.

We next outline the standards adopted by NCATE and TEAC for accreditation before moving on to discuss other teacher education reform efforts. As we point out later in this chapter in a section comparing these reform efforts and TNE, the accreditation standards are very similar to the TNE design principles.

National Council for Accreditation of Teacher Education Standards

NCATE believes every student deserves a caring, competent, and highly qualified teacher. NCATE has six standards it uses to judge the ability of teacher education departments (or units, as NCATE refers to them) to create such teachers (National Council for Accreditation of Teacher Education, 2002):

> **Standard 1:** Candidates' Knowledge, Skills, and Dispositions. Candidates preparing to work in schools as teachers or other professional school personnel know and demonstrate the content, pedagogical, and professional knowledge, and the skills and dispositions necessary to help all students learn. Assessments indicate that candidates meet professional, state, and institutional standards.
> **Standard 2:** Assessment System and Unit Evaluation. The unit has an assessment system that collects and analyzes data on applicant qualifications, candidate and graduate performance, and unit operations to evaluate and improve the unit and its programs.
> **Standard 3:** Field Experiences and Clinical Practice. The unit and its school partners design, implement, and evaluate field experiences and clinical practice so that teacher candidates and other school personnel develop and demonstrate the knowledge, skills, and disposition necessary to help all students learn.
> **Standard 4:** Diversity. The unit designs, implements, and evaluates curriculum and experiences for candidates to acquire and apply the knowledge, skills, and

disposition necessary to help all students learn. These experiences include working with diverse higher education and school faculty, diverse candidates, and diverse students in [preschool through grade 12] P–12 schools.

Standard 5: Faculty Qualifications, Performance, and Development. Faculty are qualified and model best professional practices in scholarship, service, and teaching, including the assessment of their own effectiveness as related to candidate performance. They also collaborate with colleagues in the disciplines and schools. The unit systematically evaluates faculty performance and facilitates professional development.

Standard 6: Unit Governance and Resources. The unit has the leadership, authority, budget, personnel, facilities, and resources, including information technology resources, for the preparation of candidates to meet professional, state, and institutional standards.

Teacher Education Accreditation Council

TEAC's accreditation process requires each education program to present evidence that it prepares competent, caring, and qualified professional educators. The accreditation process examines and verifies the evidence. The quality principles and capacity standards on which it judges education programs are as follows (Teacher Education Accreditation Council, 2004):

> **Quality Principle I: Evidence of Student Learning.** The core of TEAC accreditation is the evidence that the program faculty provides in support of its claims about students' learning and understanding of the professional education curriculum, especially subject-matter knowledge and teaching skill. This includes crosscutting liberal-education themes: learning how to learn, multicultural perspectives and accuracy, and technology.
>
> **Quality Principle II: Valid Assessment of Student Learning.** TEAC expects program faculty to provide (1) a rationale justifying that the assessment techniques it uses are reasonable and credible and (2) evidence documenting the reliability and validity of the assessments.
>
> **Quality Principle III: Institutional Learning.** TEAC expects that a faculty's decisions about its programs are based on evidence, and that the program has a quality-control system that (1) yields reliable evidence about the program's practices and results and (2) influences policies and decisionmaking.
>
> **Standards of Capacity for Program Quality.** TEAC defines a "quality" program as one that has credible evidence that it satisfies the three quality principles. However, TEAC also requires the faculty to provide independent evidence that the program also has the capacity—curriculum, faculty, resources, facilities, publications, student support services, and policies—to support student learning and program quality.

Major National Reform Efforts

TNE is one in a long line of reform efforts seeking to change and improve teacher education. In this section, we examine six reform efforts:

- The National Network for Educational Renewal (NNER)
- The Holmes Group/Holmes Partnership
- Arts and Sciences Teacher Education Collaborative (ASTEC) Project 30 Alliance
- The Renaissance Group
- Urban Network to Improve Teacher Education (UNITE)
- The BellSouth Foundation initiative ReCreating Colleges of Education.

We selected the first five reform efforts because they involve a number of institutions (including some TNE institutions) across the nation and have goals and principles similar to those of TNE, although, unlike TNE, the impetus for these efforts originated in large part from the institutions themselves rather than from an outside funder. The sixth reform effort—that of the BellSouth Foundation—is similar to TNE in that the impetus and funding for the effort came from a foundation.

The National Network for Educational Renewal

NNER (http://depts.washington.edu/cedren/nner/) was launched in 1986 as a national laboratory to implement and test the ideas that are at the core of the Agenda for Education in a Democracy (The Agenda), a comprehensive education-renewal initiative launched by noted education expert John I. Goodlad and others. The Agenda addresses how best to prepare teachers and students in a social and political democracy. The Agenda's strategy has focused on the simultaneous renewal of schooling and teacher education for the well being of children and youth. The Agenda adopted 20 "postulates" that guide its work (Agenda for Education in a Democracy, n.d., citing Goodlad, 1994). These postulates include many ideas aligned with the TNE design principles, such as emphasizing literacy and critical-thinking abilities for teachers, educating teachers so that they inquire into the nature of teaching and schooling throughout their careers, and establishing links to teacher education graduates for the purposes of evaluating and revising the teacher education program and easing teachers' transition into teaching.

NNER is a membership network dedicated to the simultaneous renewal of schools and the institutions that prepare teachers. NNER's mission includes providing equal access to quality learning for all students, promoting responsible stewardship of schools and universities, improving teaching and learning through pedagogy that nurtures and challenges all learners, and providing students with the knowledge, skills, and disposition to become fully engaged participants in a democratic society.

NNER's primary strategy is to create school/university partnerships in which currently enrolled P–12 students and future teachers receive quality educational experiences. NNER believes that collaborative policies and practices between school districts and institutions of higher education are necessary to advance this work. In fact, NNER believes that university faculty in the arts and sciences, faculty members in education, and faculty in public schools should be equal partners who are collectively responsible for the Agenda.[2]

The Holmes Group/Holmes Partnership

The Holmes Partnership is a nationwide network of more than 70 partnerships between major research universities and local K–12 schools and seven national partner organizations involved in the reform of teacher education. The Holmes Partnership traces its roots to the Holmes Group, a coalition formed in the late 1980s of deans and other chief academic officers of schools of education at more than 100 major research universities from all 50 states. Concerned about the low status and quality of teacher preparation programs in higher education, the Holmes Group focused on the reform of the K–12 system through the improvement of teacher quality and teacher preparation programs. The group's goals addressed issues including teacher education curricula, testing and certification requirements, teaching career paths, the relationship between institutions of higher education and K–12 schools, and the quality of the teaching workplace. Among its major accomplishments is the publication of three reports that have had a lasting influence on the teacher education policy arena: *Tomorrow's Teachers* (The Holmes Group, 1986), *Tomorrow's Schools* (The Holmes Group, 1990), and *Tomorrow's Schools of Education* (The Holmes Group, 1995).

In 1996, the members of the Holmes Group, recognizing that universities alone could not accomplish the task of improving teacher quality, joined forces with a number of other national organizations involved in teacher education reform. In addition, group members sought to partner with local P–12 schools. The Holmes Partnership, as the new group was named, strives to enact the vision for teachers, schools, and teacher education laid out in its three reports, with a special emphasis on teacher education research. The partnership's goals include high-quality professional preparation for teachers; simultaneous renewal of public schools and teacher education programs (transformational change of the schools to help them improve at the same time that the teacher education programs are being transformed); equity, diversity, and cultural competence; scholarly inquiry and programs of educational research; faculty development for future professors of education; and teacher education policy analysis and development.

---

2   See the NNER "Mission Statement" Web page, http://depts.washington.edu/cedren/nner/about/index.htm.

Arts and Science Teacher Education Collaborative Project 30 Alliance

ASTEC Project 30 was originally conceived as a three-year teacher education reform initiative sponsored by Carnegie Corporation and directed by an arts and sciences representative, Daniel Fallon, now at Carnegie, and an education representative, Frank Murray, who later founded TEAC. Projects were initiated at 30 representative colleges and universities in 1988. Project 30 identified five themes as being important to providing a context for the development of teaching as a profession, which were to be considered jointly by institutions' education and arts and sciences faculties: Subject Matter Understanding; General and Liberal Education; Pedagogical Content Knowledge; International, Cultural, and Other Human Perspectives; and Recruitment of Underrepresented Groups into Teaching. In 1991, when the original initiative ended, the participating schools incorporated as the ASTEC Project 30 Alliance in order to continue the work. The alliance focuses on the same intellectual agenda for teacher education that requires the full collaboration of arts and sciences faculty and faculty in education.

The Renaissance Group

The Renaissance Group (TRG) (http://education.csufresno.edu/rengroup/) began in 1989 when a small group of presidents, provosts, and deans of education met to discuss the current state of national reform efforts to improve teacher education and what institutions could do to further these efforts. It currently is a national consortium of 39 colleges and universities with a major commitment to teacher education. TRG's principles include the importance of the education of teachers as an all-campus responsibility, a campus culture that values and models quality teaching, creation of partnerships with practicing professionals, extensive use of field experiences in diverse settings, adherence to high standards and accountability, a focus on student learning, effective use of technology, and development of teachers as creative and innovative leaders. TRG currently has action groups focused on the following issues: assessing teacher education programs, supporting best practices, support for achieving National Board Certification, distance learning, and clinical experiences.

In 1999, 11 member universities, along with their partner schools, were awarded a Teacher Quality Enhancement Project grant under the Renaissance Partnership. The partnership's two primary goals include being accountable for the impact of teacher graduates on the pupils they teach and institutionalizing reforms in preparation programs. As part of this effort, the 11 project sites developed data-management systems that enabled universities to collect, analyze, and report performance data on their graduates; used teacher work samples to measure the impact of teacher candidates on pupils' learning; and developed team mentoring of teacher education candidates by teacher educators, arts and sciences faculty, and school practitioners.

Urban Network to Improve Teacher Education

UNITE (http://www.urbannetworks.net/index.cfm?contentID=7) is a collaboration between university and P–12 schools in urban areas dedicated to the study of unique challenges faced by urban teachers and ways to improve the teachers' preparation and support system. UNITE was initiated in 1993 by nine member schools. The three-year "UNITE I" project focused on study and analysis of urban schools, teachers, communities, and students. The project was incorporated into the Holmes Partnership in 1998 and now consists of 31 local partnerships across the country. "UNITE II" emphasized the redesign of teacher preparation and induction. As stated on the UNITE Web site, this redesign was characterized by

- a coherent all-university approach to teacher education
- continuing engagement with key understandings and skills needed to develop classroom and school learning communities as the bedrock for effective learning in content areas.
- a structured and sustained form of professional and interprofessional socialization designed to enable both a collaborative school culture and effective cooperation with other youth and family services in the community
- an expanded vision of what constitutes a Professional or Interprofessional Development School for urban learning communities.
- the seamless extension of preservice teacher education into the induction years or first years of teaching.

UNITE entered its third cycle (UNITE III), and its current goal is to develop a knowledge base for urban teacher education theory and practice. It is focusing on developing and publicizing best practices from each UNITE partner in the areas of urban teacher preparation, recruitment, and induction.

BellSouth Foundation's ReCreating Colleges of Education Initiative

In 1997, the BellSouth Foundation began a five-year initiative to assist eight colleges and universities in the Southeast to recreate their teacher education programs in the hope of spurring a renaissance in teacher preparation in the region. BellSouth sent out a request for proposals (RFP) to 300 colleges of education in the Southeast. The RFP stressed diversity, good teaching, university commitment to teacher education, use of technology to enhance teaching, student learning and assessment, and the immediate and compelling need to change the teaching practice. Given these parameters, each institution created its own design and plan for reforming its teacher education program.

After identifying promising proposals from the 75 that were submitted, 12 institutions were invited to the foundation's offices for a half-day of discussion and interviews. Each institution's president or provost, dean of education, and key faculty members were in attendance at each session. Eight institutions were then selected: Berry College, East Carolina University, Fort Valley State University, Furman University,

University of Alabama–Birmingham, University of Florida, University of Louisville, and Western Kentucky University. Grants awarded to each institution ranged from $150,000 to $250,000. Each institution was required to allocate institutional matching funds after the first year of funding. The initiative ended in 2001. While the institutions made some progress in reforming their teacher preparation programs, none succeeded in achieving a complete transformation.

Comparisons Between TNE Principles and Accreditation and Other Teacher Education Initiatives

The guiding themes and program design principles of teacher education reform programs initiated by the teaching field and those initiated by accreditation organizations are remarkably similar, suggesting a consensus among teacher education reformers regarding the themes that should govern best practices for teacher education (although, as we show later, the evidence base for these principles is mixed at best). The Carnegie TNE prospectus echoes several of these principles. In this section, we highlight the similarities and differences in the three major design principles across the reform initiatives and note some differences that set TNE apart from the other reform efforts.

Similarities

A teacher education program should be guided by a respect for evidence. The idea that teacher education programs should use research-driven practices and base their reforms on evidence on the effectiveness of teacher education curricula and graduates in the teaching field is central to many reform efforts. The Holmes Partnership, for example, includes the promotion of scholarly inquiry and programs of educational research among its five main goals. NNER emphasizes the need for research-based practice in several of its postulates and, in fact, its member sites were intended to be the testing ground for the ongoing research and inquiry conducted by the Agenda's Institute for Educational Inquiry. One of TRG's major activities is to measure the effectiveness of teacher education programs in using research to inform program renewal.

Further, the accreditation organizations also emphasize evidence of student learning in their standards. For example, as stated earlier, institutions seeking NCATE accreditation must provide evidence that teacher candidates know and demonstrate the content, pedagogical, and professional knowledge, the skills, and the dispositions necessary to help all students learn. Primary sources of evidence of these characteristics are candidates' performance data on certification examinations. Candidates are expected to demonstrate positive effects on student learning, and institutions are expected to measure these effects during clinical practice (i.e., student teaching, when students go out into real schools and teach, under supervision). Thus, program documentation required by NCATE for accreditation includes internal performance-assessment data and external data, such as results on state licensing tests and other assessments outside of the teaching institution. NCATE also requires institutions to provide evidence that they have a unit assessment and evaluation system that collects and analyzes data to improve the unit and its programs. NCATE looks for indications that teacher education programs use multiple assessments to evaluate candidates; use information from external sources, such as state licensing exams, evaluations during induction or mentoring,[3] employers' reports, and follow-up studies; establish procedures to ensure credibility of assessments; and use results from assessments of candidates to evaluate and make improvements in the unit's programs, courses, teaching, and clinical experiences.

TEAC places an even heavier emphasis on evidence of student learning—encompassing subject-matter knowledge, pedagogical knowledge, "caring," and teaching skills—as a requirement for accreditation. Institutions must demonstrate the link between assessments of student learning and program goals and requirements. Evidence can be qualitative and/or quantitative and may include such data as student grades, standardized test scores (e.g., on teacher licensure tests), faculty evaluation, student self-reports, and surveys of graduates and employers. TEAC also requires institutions to include evidence that the assessments are valid and reliable and that the conclusions drawn from those assessments are appropriate. Faculty must commit to using several measures that are valid, reliable, and indicate true student learning. Further, TEAC requires institutions to demonstrate that decisions regarding program structure and coursework are based on evidence of student learning.

Faculty in the disciplines of the arts and sciences must be fully engaged in the education of prospective teachers, especially in the areas of subject-matter understanding and general and liberal education. All of the reforms described above address the need for teacher education to be a university-wide commitment that engages arts and sciences colleagues in preparing teachers.

The Holmes Group report *Tomorrow's Schools* argues that teacher education reform, both in creating curricular change and in promoting quality teaching, should be a university-wide process:

> Members of the faculty of the university—education professors and arts and sciences faculty—and of the school should collaborate as colleagues meeting regularly and intensively on the whole range of tasks (Holmes Group, 1990, p. 45).

Even more explicitly than the Holmes Partnership as a whole, UNITE emphasizes "a coherent all-university approach to teacher education" as one of its five principles. Project 30 prides itself on the full engagement of faculty members in the arts and sciences in the task of teacher education reform and was founded as a joint venture between arts and sciences and education faculty. As described earlier, NNER believes

---

[3] Some states and districts mandate induction programs in which new teachers are required to participate to obtain a full teaching license. Some assign mentors to work with new teachers.

that university faculty in the arts and sciences, faculty members in education, and faculty in the public schools should be equal partners who are collectively responsible for the Agenda for Education in a Democracy.

The emphasis on university-wide commitment is one of the cornerstones of TRG, and university presidents and deans were key players in TRG's founding. For example, TRG's principles include the following:

> The education of teachers is an all-campus responsibility . . . The initial preparation of teachers is integrated throughout a student's university experience and includes a general education program, in-depth subject matter preparation, and both general and content-specific preparation in teaching methodology (The Renaissance Group, 2005–2006).

Lastly, the BellSouth Foundation's RFP for its ReCreating Colleges of Education initiative stressed a university-wide commitment to teacher education.

Teaching should be recognized as an academically taught clinical-practice profession. The third TNE design principle encompasses five subparts: the importance of pedagogy, the use of schools as clinical sites for teacher education programs, the appointment of practicing K–12 teachers to university faculty, support of graduates through a residency for two years after graduation, and preparation of teacher education candidates for continuous professional growth. Other reform efforts include many of these TNE principles in their work. For instance, the Holmes Partnership publications address each of these five subparts:

- **Pedagogy.** *Tomorrow's Teachers* (The Holmes Group, 1986) and *Tomorrow's Schools* (The Holmes Group, 1990) both advocate the development of new and better means to assess teacher knowledge.
- **Use of schools as clinical sites.** *Tomorrow's Schools* develops the notion of "professional development schools" as, among other things, clinical learning environments.
- **Teachers given university faculty appointments.** *Tomorrow's Teachers* and *Tomorrow's Schools* call for stronger relationships between university faculty and master teachers in the schools, to include the development of "career professionals" or "clinical professors."
- **Residency period for education graduates.** TNE's call for provisional certification and close supervision of beginning teachers is reminiscent of *Tomorrow's Teachers'* distinction between "instructors" and "professional teachers."
- **Preparation of candidates for professional growth.** *Tomorrow's Schools* emphasizes that professional development schools should promote continuous learning for all adult staff, including experienced teachers, teacher educators, and administrators.

NCATE's third standard for accreditation requires teacher education units to offer partner-school experiences and appropriate field experiences, while UNITE lists improving teacher induction services as one of its five principles. TRG's principles include the creation of partnerships with practicing professionals, the extensive use of field experience in diverse settings, and the development of teachers as creative and innovative leaders. Further, as mentioned above, two of TRG's current action groups are focused on issues of clinical experiences and on providing support for teachers applying for National Board Certification.

NNER's postulates include educating teachers such that teachers continue to inquire into the nature of teaching and schooling throughout their careers and establishing links to teacher education graduates to ease graduates' transition into teaching. NNER's primary strategy to improve teacher education is to engage in school/university partnerships.

Differences

Emphasis on External Resources as a Catalyst for Change. A key difference between TNE and other reform efforts is the belief underlying the TNE prospectus that substantial external resources and technical assistance are needed for reform to be successful; the TNE initiative is structured to provide both.

TNE is providing $5 million per institution and is expecting institutions to provide matching funds ($3 million of which must be placed in an endowment to support sustainability), for a total of $10 million per institution. This level of funding is unprecedented in the history of teacher education reform. By comparison, the BellSouth initiative provided universities grants of $150,000 to $250,000.

In addition, the Academy for Educational Development was asked by the TNE funders to provide hands-on technical assistance to the TNE sites and to monitor their progress—a role that requires a balancing act between being a "critical friend" to the sites and being alert for early problems and issues to address as an agent of the sponsor. Each institution is monitored against its own goals and work plan. AED stays in close contact with the sites and ensures that they remain focused on their teacher education reform effort and make progress as expected. AED also helps to develop solutions to address problems as they arise. A problem would have to be intractable before AED would ask Carnegie to address it formally. AED does, nevertheless, keep Carnegie informed of progress on a regular basis.

Emphasis on Measuring Pupils' Learning Gains. TNE's "thesis" is that adoption and implementation of its key design principles will result in an "excellent" teacher education program whose graduates will be "high-quality" teachers. While TNE accepts other forms of measuring the learning gains made by pupils under the tutelage of its grantees' education graduates, it requires the institutions to measure pupils' learning through standardized achievement tests—tests that are increasingly valued by policymakers.

TRG is also working on measuring the impact of teachers on student learning, but it primarily uses a work-sample methodology. TNE is the first teacher education reform initiative to insist on formal evidence that a training program is effective in producing teachers who can improve student learning relative to teachers who have not participated in the program.

Emphasis on Providing Formal Residency Programs. As discussed earlier, most reform efforts call for some sort of induction support for new teacher graduates. TNE takes this support one step further by requiring its grantees to establish a two-year residency program, roughly following the model for medical clinicians. Teacher graduates must be tracked and offered a variety of support and assistance—e.g., courses, workshops, mentoring, and online help—during the residency. Further, arts and sciences faculty should be partners in designing and offering such support.

Notable Shortcoming: Limited Number of Objective Evaluations

Our review of teacher education reforms shows that considerable thought and effort have been devoted to reforming those programs. However, our review also revealed a notable shortcoming: While rife with rhetoric and innovative ideas, teacher education reform is sadly short on objective evaluations. Of the reform efforts we cover in this chapter, only the Holmes Group and BellSouth Initiative efforts have been subject to a third-party evaluation. However, those two evaluations sound a note of caution on being overly optimistic about the long-term impacts of teacher education reform efforts.

Evaluation of The Holmes Group

The Rise and Stall of Teacher Education Reform (Fullan et al., 1998)—an evaluation of the Holmes Group—examines the appropriateness of the goals and vision of the group, the impact of its agenda at member schools, and its broader legacy to the field. Based on survey questionnaires sent to deans and education faculty at member schools, interviews with key stakeholders, and site visits to five member institutions, the authors assessed reform from 1985 to 1995 and offered a vision of and recommendations for reform for the new millennium.

In examining the appropriateness of the Holmes Group's goals, the authors reported that such notions as more-differentiated career ladders for teachers, better program exit assessments that are more carefully linked to the actual knowledge requirements of teaching, professional development schools (PDSs),[4] and stronger links between colleges and universities and P–12 schools appeared to have widespread currency among schools of education and other reformers.

The actual influence of the Holmes Group agenda at individual member institutions was less clear. Generally, Fullan et al. observed that while the Holmes Group did provide an important "kick start" to universities already in the process of rethinking their teacher education programs, the group's agenda had only a moderate influence on the particulars of newly redesigned programs. More specifically, only 50 percent of member universities attempted to formulate a five-year teacher education program, as the Holmes Group initially advocated. The most significant reforms across all universities included the development of overarching conceptual frameworks for curriculum guidance, the introduction of more-rigorous program entry standards, and the development of improved preservice assessments. The universities were less successful in articulating learning goals for teacher education candidates, emphasizing research and inquiry throughout the program, and evaluating teacher education programs internally. Overall, 40 percent of the member institutions credited the Holmes Group as providing the impetus for their program reforms.

Fullan et al. found that 75 percent of member institutions had significant involvement in local P–12 school improvement and had partnered with P–12 teachers in teacher education activities. Furthermore, all member institutions had developed at least one PDS. The quality of the university/P–12 relationship and the function of the PDS, however, often left something to be desired. A few universities seemed to view their PDS as more of a "trophy" than as a functioning educational opportunity. Even for universities that took their PDS more seriously, a number of challenges stood between fulfilling the Holmes Group's vision and the reality of PDSs. First, Fullan et al. noted a lack of genuine collaboration between university faculty and P–12 teachers. They reported that while school personnel were somewhat involved in the day-to-day operation of teacher education in PDSs, program design and decisionmaking remained the sole province of the university faculty. Furthermore, the lack of tenure or promotion opportunities in PDS work meant that university faculty had little incentive to invest their already limited time and energy resources in the work of the schools. The authors also noted that the emphasis on medical school–style clinical professorships seemed to diminish the research aspects of the PDS concept, making the schools primarily focused on practice and clinical work with little to offer in research or continu-

---

[4] Professional development schools are institutions formed through partnerships between professional education programs and P–12 schools. PDS partnerships have a four-fold mission: the preparation of new teachers, faculty development, inquiry directed at the improvement of practice, and enhanced student achievement. PDSs are often compared to teaching hospitals. The teaching hospital was designed to provide clinical preparation for medical students and interns; PDSs serve the same function for teacher candidates and in-service faculty. Both settings provide support for professional learning in a real-world setting in which practice takes place (National Council for Accreditation of Teacher Education, 1997–2006).

ing professional development for faculty members. Finally, and most discouraging, the authors found that despite the grand intentions of their designers, PDSs showed no scale-up or networking abilities to influence other schools without direct ties to universities.

Fullan et al. turned to the Holmes Group's wider influence on non-member institutions and other teacher education reform efforts. They credited the organization with playing a highly influential role in shaping and lending legitimacy to the debate over teacher education in the late 1980s and noted how widespread many of the group's goals and ideas had become.

Still, they pointed out a few shortcomings. First, the fact that the membership group consisted of prestigious major research universities proved to be both a blessing and a curse: a blessing in the credibility it lent to the effort and a curse in the resentment it engendered among nonmembers, especially when those institutions failed to live up to the group's ideals.

Second, the Holmes Group has been widely critiqued as "all talk and little action." Although the organization's role as an agenda setter has been an important one, it has been left to other groups, such as NNER, to serve as agenda implementers. The group suffered a marked loss of momentum in the early 1990s when the time came to put into action the ideas the group had spent the previous five years developing.

Third, Fullan et al. noted that the Holmes Group failed to make any systematic attempt to change the national, state, or local policies that often hampered its members' reform efforts.

Evaluation of the BellSouth Initiative

A qualitative evaluation of the BellSouth initiative concluded that, although almost all the institutions made important strides in their teacher education reform work, none achieved the complete transformation envisioned at the start of the initiative (Wisniewski, n.d.). All the colleges substantially increased their collaborative working relationships with schools, sought new ways to work with arts and sciences partners, and moved toward longer and more intensive practical experiences for teaching candidates. They also struggled with how to reward faculty members who were working more closely with schools than were other faculty members. However, the scope of the work and commitment that was required was greater than any of the institutions had realized, and some institutions faced challenges related to lack of support and turnover in university leadership.

TNE and the Current Evaluation

As mentioned earlier, RAND has been tracking the first cohort of TNE grantees since the inception of the initiative and has been tracking a subset of the second cohort for a shorter period of time. Because it is still early in the reform effort, we have qualitative data based on self-reports on the implementation of TNE in these sites.

The longer-term—and ultimately the more important—questions of whether the reform will succeed in transforming teacher education at these institutions, whether the sites will be able to successfully prove that their teachers are indeed adding value to student learning, whether the sites will be able to sustain the reform effort after the grant has ended, and whether the sites will have an impact on peer institutions are unlikely to be answered for several years. Answers to these questions will be particularly important to funders because of their substantial investment—approximately $70 million in both direct funding and technical assistance over the course of the five years—in a small number of institutions that seem to hold promise for radical and transformative change.

CHAPTER THREE

TNE's Theory of Change: Assumptions, Enabling Factors, and Potential Outcomes

This chapter delineates the "theory of change" underpinning TNE and the possible outcomes that would result if the theory proves to be valid and its assumptions are met. The final section of this chapter takes a more detailed look at the proximal outputs and activities that one should observe at the TNE sites as they implement TNE. This chapter sets the context for Chapter Five, which reports implementation progress at the individual sites.

Any new program or project can be thought of as representing a theory, in that a program decisionmaker hypothesizes that a particular treatment will cause certain predicted effects or outcomes. We use a "theory-approach" logic model (W.K. Kellogg Foundation, 2004) to link theoretical ideas, underlying program assumptions, and desired outcomes. As Weiss (1972) explained, it is important to know not only *what* the program expects to achieve but also *how* and *why* it will achieve certain goals. We develop the logic model, or theory of change, in three stages: (1) delineate the assumptions underlying TNE and examine their validity; (2) list the enabling factors that need to be aligned for the reform to be implemented; and (3) determine the potential outcomes that are likely to occur in the short term and long term, if the theory is well-implemented.

Assumptions Underlying TNE

Table 3.1 lists the major assumptions underlying the TNE initiative. TNE starts with three overarching beliefs. The first—not universally shared among educators—is that university-based ("traditional") teacher preparation programs can improve teacher quality and provide guidance on the best way to prepare teachers. The second belief is that developing such innovative reform models cannot be undertaken without substantial outside resources—i.e., funding and technical assistance. The third belief is, "If you build it, they will come"—i.e., given sufficient evidence, other institutions will emulate the TNE grantees and will reform their own teacher education programs.

Table 3.1
Key Assumptions of TNE

Overarching Beliefs
- Traditional, university-based teacher preparation programs can improve teacher quality.
- Substantial external resources (funding and technical assistance) are needed to produce radical change.
- Other institutions will follow the example of the TNE institutions, given sufficient evidence.

Decisions Driven by Evidence
- Quality teacher education programs will seek to continuously improve by using research-based evidence.
- Evidence should include the quality of teacher education graduates.
- Teacher quality can and should be measured through pupils' learning gains, and such evidence should be used in making program improvements.

Engagement of Arts and Sciences Faculty in Teacher Education
- Teachers' inadequate knowledge of content has a negative impact on pupil learning; thus, improving content knowledge improves student learning.
- The best way of improving the content knowledge of new teachers is by involving arts and sciences faculty in the teacher education program.

Teaching as an Academically Taught Clinical-Practice Profession
- An integrated clinical component improves the quality of teacher graduates.
- Involvement of K–12 teachers in teacher education programs improves teacher education faculty and teacher candidates' knowledge and understanding of "real" schools and classrooms.
- New teachers in the first two years of teaching are novices in their profession and need support during this induction period.
- Support for new teachers is best provided by the teachers' education institutions.
- New teachers need support in teaching content, and this support can best be provided by involving arts and sciences faculty in the induction program.

The TNE prospectus (Carnegie Corporation of New York, n.d.) outlines several key principles that characterize "excellent" teacher education programs, including (1) decisions driven by evidence, (2) engagement of arts and sciences faculty in teacher education, and (3) an integrated clinical component that includes involvement of K–12 faculty in the program and establishment of a two-year residency induction program. Table 3.1 presents the major assumptions on which TNE rests, grouped under these three categories.

In support of the TNE design principles, the TNE prospectus states that

> The principles have been shown in most cases by credible evidence to contribute to increases in teaching effectiveness. When the empirical evidence is weak, they represent consensus views of leading researchers and practitioners, based upon experience and reason, about a secure base for building teacher effectiveness (Carnegie Corporation of New York, n.d.).

However, no documentation of such evidence is provided in the prospectus to help readers evaluate this claim. Indeed, it is not clear that there is such a thing as "consensus views" on a "secure base" for teacher effectiveness. Cochran-Smith and Fries (2005b, pp. 37–38) note the following:

Sometimes the same research [is] cited to support conflicting positions. Sometimes close scrutiny reveal[s] that particular studies provided no clear evidence for the claims being made . . . . There are also more claims than ever before about the relationships that do and do not exist among teacher qualifications, the policies and practices governing teacher preparation, teaching performance, and educational outcomes.

Wading through the competing claims of researchers and advocates alike regarding the evidence on how best to build an effective teacher education program is a challenging proposition. Fortunately, several reviews of research in teacher education (Allen, 2003; Wilson, Floden, and Ferrini-Mundy, 2001; Cochran-Smith and Zeichner, 2005) provide a broad view of the available evidence on the factors that contribute to quality teacher preparation. All three reviews seek to identify the most rigorous, original, peer-reviewed empirical studies of teacher education in the United States over the past several decades to provide an even-handed analysis of what the evidence says and does not say about a variety of topics related to teacher education. We used these reviews as a framework to help us to focus on the best available evidence to support the assumptions implicit in Carnegie's TNE design.

Overarching Beliefs
Traditional, university-based teacher preparation programs can improve teacher quality. Unlike the several calls for dismantling teacher education schools (as mentioned at the top of Chapter One), TNE starts with the assumption that university-based preparation programs can improve the quality of teachers, and that this assumption can be proven through the collection of rigorous evidence. As stated earlier, reform of university-based teacher preparation programs has a long history, but it is short on evidence that the changes from reform have substantially improved the quality of teacher graduates and the learning that pupils gain under the tutelage of these teachers.

The past three decades have seen a proliferation of routes by which individuals can enter teaching and/or obtain licensure; currently, 45 states and the District of Columbia offer such alternative routes. "Alternative certification" (AC) encompasses all "nontraditional venues that lead to teacher licensure" (Mikulecky, Shkodriani, and Wilner, 2004). These programs are generally geared to aspiring teachers who already have a baccalaureate degree and vary considerably with respect to requirements, sophistication, and rigor. Often, institutions that offer traditional university-based teacher preparation programs also offer AC programs.

Debate over the quality of teachers prepared through alternative routes and through traditional programs has been fierce and continues unabated. Surveys of the literature show few studies that meet minimum methodological standards—for example, studies that are peer-reviewed, use longitudinal student-level achievement data, and control for student background (Podgursky, 2004; Wayne and Youngs, 2003; Mayer et al., 2003; Allen, 2003; Wilson, Floden, and Ferrini-Mundy, 2001). All of these authors conclude that the findings on the relative performance in the classroom of AC graduates versus traditionally prepared graduates is decidedly mixed. Mayer et al. (2003, p. A-20) point out,

> To evaluate programs of alternative certification with greater precision, a study would need to focus on a few clearly defined alternatives, with detailed components and requirements. However, the study would also need to be large enough to detect reasonably sized impacts and broad enough to provide insight into implications for educational policy.

It is interesting to note in passing that Carnegie funded a study of alternative certification programs by SRI International concurrently with its funding of the first cohort of TNE grantees. The aim of that study was to explore the components of various alternative routes to teacher certification and their relative effectiveness in preparing teachers for the classrooms. The study summed up as follows:

> Beyond the obvious conclusion that alternative certification programs and participants defy simplistic characterizations, our research suggests [that] . . . teacher development in alternative certification appears to be a function of the interaction between the program as *implemented,* the school context in which the on-the-job training occurs, and the career trajectory of the individual participant . . .
>
> This more complex view of alternative certification should lead researchers away from simplistic comparisons between alternative and traditional certification programs. Our early findings suggest that failure to disaggregate program participants into subgroups can lead to outcome studies with the wrong unit of analysis and the kind of inconsistent findings that currently dominate the literature (Humphrey et al., 2005, pp. 29–30).

More recently, Lee Shulman, president of the Carnegie Foundation for the Advancement of Teaching, voiced a similar sentiment:

> Teacher education does not exist in the United States. There is so much variation among all programs in visions of good teaching, standards for admission, rigor of subject matter preparation, what is taught and what is learned, character of supervised clinical experience, and quality of evaluation that, compared to any other academic profession, the sense of chaos is inescapable. The claim that there are "traditional programs" that can be contrasted with "alternative routes" is a myth . . . It should not surprise us that critics respond to the apparent cacophony of pathways and conclude that it doesn't matter how teachers are prepared (Shulman, 2005).

Ultimately, then, the underlying belief that traditional, university-based programs can improve teacher quality (presumably over and above what other programs can achieve) by adopting the TNE design principles is simply that—an article of faith, rather than a tenet based on rigorous, long-term evidence.

Substantial external resources (funding and technical assistance) are needed to produce radical change. Fundamentally changing the behaviors and tasks of an existing organization is one of the most difficult reforms to accomplish. This is especially true when significantly different behaviors are called for, when the tasks and behaviors are those of a large and diverse group, and when those in the group have varying incentives to change (Mazmanian and Sabatier, 1989). These factors all apply to the TNE initiative. Implementation of a design created by an external agent involves students, faculty, and administrators across the institution; faculty and administrators at the K–12 level; federal, state, and local governments; funders and their agents; and multiple other individuals. The radical changes expected by TNE could be expected to require significantly different sets of behaviors on the part of all these individuals and entities, all of which respond to and are driven by many varying incentives, rules, and regulations inherent in the infrastructure of universities and schools (Cuban, 1984; Gitlin and Margonis, 1995; Huberman and Miles, 1984). Many previous studies of implementation of school reform in K–12 schools offer some important lessons learned regarding successful implementation of a reform being driven from the top. In the words of one study,

> Policy makers can't mandate what matters most: local capacity and will . . . Environmental stability, competing centers of authority, contending priorities or pressures. and other aspects of the social-political milieu can influence implementor willingness profoundly (McLaughlin, 1987, pp. 172–173).

TNE is looking to the implementation sites to adapt the design principles to best fit their individual circumstances and policy environment. However, others have found that adaptation of reform designs does not always lead to enhancement of original policy or necessarily promote the desired performance outcomes; researchers refer to these unanticipated consequences as policy "disappearance," policy erosion, policy dilution, policy "drift," or simply poor or slowed implementation (Cuban, 1984; Daft, 1995; Sabatier and Mazmanian, 1979; Pressman and Wildavsky, 1973; Weatherley and Lipsky, 1977; Yin, 1979). It is often the case that these undesirable outcomes occur because the support mechanisms that are necessary to help an external agent implement an intervention are not in place. McDonnell and Grubb (1991) make clear that successful implementation of any educational mandate, whether by an external agent or by the institution itself, requires the support of the implementers, capacity on the part of implementers to follow the mandate, and enforcement or incentives to support compliance. The building of capacity requires infusion of resources—time, funding, and information—either social or intellectual. These resources are often referred to in the education field as "slack resources" or "slack," without which reform cannot be successfully undertaken. Capacity cannot be mandated; it must be built with slack resources.

The education literature (e.g., McLaughlin, 1990) points to important "supports" that often lead to implementation that more closely approaches that expected by policymakers (i.e., fidelity):

- Funding to get an initiative under way and at a level that indicates the initiative's importance
- Clear communication to promote an understanding by stakeholders and implementers of the intervention and its intended effects
- Special attention from funders and other leaders and assistance with implementation.

In designing TNE, Carnegie paid particular attention to the lessons learned about support for an initiative from past reform efforts. Thus, TNE rests on the crucial assumption that *substantial* external resources and technical assistance are needed for the reform to be successful in changing the way that teachers are prepared in institutions. As stated earlier, the TNE initiative is structured to provide both substantial funds ($5 million per institution, which is expected to be matched by the institution itself, for a total of $10 million for TNE) and considerable facilitation and monitoring by AED.

Other institutions will follow the example of the TNE institutions, given sufficient evidence. TNE's goals require teacher education programs to take a step up—to go from being "excellent" at what they do to becoming "exemplary." Once these institutions know what works, it is incumbent upon them to help other institutions to adopt similar programs, in part or in whole. Ultimately, the legacy of the TNE initiative will be judged by whether the reform efforts last and to what extent they are emulated across the nation.

To this end, AED and Carnegie and other funders are publicizing the reform effort widely through professional meetings and the establishment of a TNE Learning Network in which 30 institutions have been invited to participate. The institutions will have access to the TNE Web site and electronic publications, attend workshops and conferences, share reports and information, and receive invitations to TNE-related sessions at annual meetings of the American Association of Colleges for Teacher Education, the American Educational Research Association, and other national meetings ("TNE Widens the Circle," n.d.).

TNE grantees are also provided a limited amount of partnership funds to encourage them to develop relationships with peer institutions, community colleges, and/or K–12 schools or districts.

Despite these efforts, there is little evidence to suggest that reforms are willingly embraced by peer or partner institutions. Even within networks, some institutions are more likely to embrace and implement the reform more faithfully than others. An evaluation of the Holmes Group (Fullan et al., 1998) suggests that the influence of earlier reform efforts on member and nonmember institutions is uncertain:

> The much-vaunted "prestige" of the Holmes Group has been a double-edged sword throughout the decade of its life. There is no doubt that the prestige of a group whose membership included leading American universities lent credibility to its suggested reforms . . .

On the other hand, an air of exclusionary elitism was associated with the Holmes Group, a situation that created some resentment. Such resentment increased as it became clear that not all Holmes members were committed to acting on the Holmes agenda for reform, while many non-Holmes institutions were working hard to improve their teacher preparation programs (Fullan et al., 1998, pp. 37–38).

Decisions Driven by Evidence

Quality teacher education programs will seek to continuously improve by using research-based evidence. Implicit in the first TNE design principle is the assumption that quality teacher education programs will seek to continuously improve by using research-based evidence. This idea is gaining increasing prominence in education more broadly and "data-driven decisionmaking" have become buzzwords in the field. Notions of data-based decisionmaking and continuous improvement in education are modeled largely on successful practices from industry and manufacturing, especially Total Quality Management (TQM) and Organizational Learning, which emphasize that organizational improvement is enhanced by responsiveness to performance data (e.g., Deming, 1986; Juran, 1988; Senge, 1990a; Senge, 1990b). Schmoker (1996) applies these theories to the educational context, arguing that attention to short-term, measurable results will lead to long-term school improvement.

TQM is commonly associated with the work of W. Edwards Deming, a mathematical physicist and statistician whose ideas on quality control are credited with revolutionizing the manufacturing industry in Japan before gaining prominence in the United States. He argued that organizations should operate as scientists do by formulating theories, developing hypotheses, designing and conducting experiments, and collecting and analyzing data (the so-called Deming Cycle of Plan, Do, Check, Act). Notably, experimentation ("do") is based on theory and existing evidence ("plan"), but "act" follows after and is dependent on monitoring and systematic measurement of processes and outcomes in the "check" phase. The cycle is a continual loop, in which the completion of one pass through the loop brings the organization back to another round of planning. Senge (1990a; 1990b) is often credited with popularizing the idea of the "learning organization," although subsequent researchers have added considerably to the theory of organizational change and learning. Barnett (n.d.) defines organizational learning as "an experience-based process through which knowledge about action-outcome relationships develops, is encoded in routines, is embedded in organizational memory, and changes collective behavior." Collecting, retrieving, analyzing, and learning from information helps organizations to study their environment and to adapt to change, thus ensuring organizational survival (deGues, 1988; Drucker, 1999; Nonaka, 1991; Schein, 1993; Senge, 1990a, 1990b).

Still, the theories of organizational learning and TQM are not without complexities. Total Quality Management has come under scrutiny in recent years as some researchers have documented significant implementation problems and lower-than-projected results (e.g., Ernst and Young, 1992; Harari, 1993; Pfeffer, 1994; Powell, 1995; Szwergold, 1992). Overall, the research on the efficacy of TQM has been decidedly mixed (Choi and Behling, 1997; Eskildson, 1994; Fisher, 1992; Gilbert, 1992; Mohrman et al., 1995; Powell, 1995; Westphal, Gulati, and Shartell, 1997; Wruck and Jensen, 1994).

A number of studies in the field have focused on understanding why organizations often fail to use information to produce learning and improved outcomes. Several researchers have suggested that data and information tend to have low relative importance in organizational decisionmaking due to the highly politicized nature of most decisions. Instead, ideology and vested interests tend to take precedence over information (Markus, 1983; Weiss, 1983; Ostrom, 1990; Simon, 1991; Dean and Sharfman, 1993). Feldman and March (1981) suggest that the role of information is primarily symbolic, because organizations advance the collection of data to convey the illusory sense of rationality but do not use data as a basis for actual decisionmaking (see Wise [1979] for an interesting discussion of how a focus on results in the schools, especially expected results defined from on high, at the school district or state level, can lead to even more bureaucratic, top-down control, which can work against other reforms).

More recently, some researchers have focused on the types of decisions that tend to lend themselves to information use and organizational learning and have found that decisionmakers are most likely to use information in contexts where problems are highly structured. When problems are difficult to define, possible solutions are not well known, and the certainty of outcomes is low, decisionmakers tend to rely on tacit, intuitive knowledge instead of data (Choo, 1998; Daft, 1998; Daft and Macintosh, 1981; Turban, McLean and Wetherbe, 1998). Others have suggested that organizational learning has as much to do with the culture of an organization as it does with the structures and processes put into place to promote learning.

Evidence should include the quality of teacher education graduates. The idea that teacher education programs should base their program improvements on evidence of the quality of their teacher graduates has not been tested empirically. As we pointed out earlier, TNE is one in a long line of reform efforts calling for teacher education programs to pay closer attention to measures of the quality of their graduates. The 1998 reauthorization of Title II of the Higher Education Act established a reporting system for states and institutions of higher education to collect information on the quality of their teacher training programs, including information on state teacher certification requirements, the performance of prospective teachers on state licensure tests, and the number of teachers hired with temporary or emergency certificates. "Teacher warranty" programs instituted at the state level in Georgia and Kentucky and at the institutional level at universities (including TNE recipients UVa and UConn) in 20 other states require teacher education programs to assume responsibility for the classroom performance of their graduates.[1]

The idea that organizational improvement should include attention to final outcomes certainly passes the test of logical reasonableness. However, the theory and history of the quality movement in industry offer a caution that exclusive focus on final outcomes can actually be a barrier to effective improvement. Among the primary innovations of the quality movement was the idea that "inspecting in" quality at the end of production was too late; rather, post-war quality advocates such as Deming (1986), Crosby (1979), and Juran (1988) focused on prevention of errors through process analysis and monitoring that would lead to actions that would minimize the possibility of unacceptable products in the first place.

To the extent that evidence on the final classroom outcomes produced by teacher education graduates are used to inform and improve the "production processes" of teacher preparation, TNE's focus on the quality of teacher graduates is appropriate and useful. However, if the focus on the quality of teacher education graduates becomes disconnected from the study of the processes that led to that quality (or lack thereof), then it may run counter to the continuous-improvement models that provide the theoretical underpinnings for TNE's emphasis on evidence-based improvement.

Teacher quality can and should be measured through pupils' learning gains. The emphasis on evaluating teacher education programs by the effect the programs' graduates have on the learning of the pupils they teach is another contentious aspect of the TNE design. Generally referred to as "value-added modeling" (VAM) in education, this approach has received increasing attention in recent years as a strategy for determining the effectiveness of teachers and/or schools while theoretically factoring out the influence of home and community environments or of different levels of achievement at the start of schooling. Several different models for assessing the

---

[1]   Teacher warranties are agreements between teacher preparation institutions and the employing school districts that obligate the institutions to provide additional course work, counseling, or other support for a new teacher who is not meeting school or district standards. This remediation is provided at no cost to the teacher or district. In some cases, institutions limit their warranty to those teachers who are teaching in their field of certification and study, or who are teaching in-state or within a reasonable distance from their institution's campus. Some states and university systems have established quality-assurance guarantees as part of a more extensive P–16 (preschool through baccalaureate) education reform effort. For example, the University System of Georgia established a policy that the system universities will guarantee the quality of their teacher graduates. In 1997, Alabama mandated a teacher warranty program that was implemented in most institutions in the state. However, a survey done by the American Association of Colleges of Teacher Education in 2000 showed relatively few requests from districts to provide warranty-type assistance to teacher graduates (Earley, 2000).

effectiveness of individual teachers have been specified (e.g., McCaffrey et al., 2004; Rowan, Correnti, and Miller, 2002; Sanders, Saxton and Horn, 1997). Models have also been specified for school-level evaluation (e.g., Adcock and Phillips, 2000; Bryk et al., 1998), and several states have begun considering the use of value-added methods in their state school accountability systems under the No Child Left Behind Act (e.g., Pennsylvania Department of Education, n.d.).

The use of value-added assessment to evaluate teacher education programs is less common, although not unprecedented. Researchers at Louisiana State University have been working since 2003 to develop value-added methodologies for assessing the effectiveness of Louisiana's teacher education programs. In two initial one-year pilot studies, Noell (2004, 2005) found differential growth rates for pupils taught by recent graduates of different teacher preparation programs and identified one outlier program in particular whose recent graduates had pupils who showed learning gains exceeding those of pupils in classrooms taught by more-experienced teachers. Obviously, one needs to be cautious about interpreting these outcomes to be program effects, if selection effects are not fully taken into account.

However, concerns remain about the feasibility of value-added methodologies and the validity and reliability of their results. In their review of current value-added techniques, McCaffrey et al. (2004) identify a number of complexities in the estimation of teacher effects, including problems with incomplete data, omitted variables, changing test construction, and differing modeling assumptions, and they note that the sensitivity of value-added estimates to many of these factors is currently unknown, making accurate and precise estimation of teacher effects a challenging undertaking. They conclude that "VAM-based rankings of teachers are highly unstable, and only large differences in estimated impact are likely to be detectable," and, as a result, "interpretations of differences among teachers based on VAM estimates should be made with extreme caution" (McCaffrey et al., 2004, p. 113).

In addition, several researchers have noted that the link between teacher preparation and pupil achievement may prove too challenging to measure. As the American Educational Research Association's (AERA's) Panel on Research and Teacher Education stated,

> This kind of research depends on a chain of causal events with several critical links: empirical evidence demonstrating the link between teacher preparation programs or structures and teacher candidates' learning (i.e., candidates' knowledge growth, skills, and dispositions); empirical evidence demonstrating the link between teacher candidates' learning and their practice in actual classrooms; and empirical evidence demonstrating the link between the practices of graduates of teacher preparation programs and what their pupils learn. Individually each one of these links is complex and challenging to estimate. When they are combined, the challenges are multiplied . . . Unraveling the complicated relationship between and among these variables and the contexts and conditions in which they occur is

exceedingly complex, and of course this entire enterprise assumes in the first place that there is consensus about appropriate and valid outcome measures, an assumption that is arguable (Cochran-Smith and Zeichner, 2005, p. 3).

Furthermore, even if this link can be made, some researchers on the AERA panel have questioned how useful and important the outcomes would be to actual policy and practice in teacher education. In this regard, the AERA Panel said,

> (I)t is not research that determines "who wins" that is most important, but research that helps to identify and explain what the active ingredients are in teacher preparation programs whose graduates have a positive impact on pupils' learning . . . and the conditions and contexts in which they are most likely to be present (Cochran-Smith and Zeichner, 2005, p. 4).

Engagement of Arts and Sciences Faculty in Teacher Education

Teachers' inadequate content knowledge has a negative impact on pupils' learning; thus, improving content knowledge improves learning. Studies examining prospective teachers have found deficiencies in the kind of deep subject matter understanding that many experts believe is necessary for effective teaching. For example, Holt-Reynolds (1999) found limited conceptual knowledge of literature among most prospective high school English teachers who were studied; Kennedy (1998) found that many prospective teachers lacked knowledge of the underlying principles behind the rules of grammar; Stoddart et al. (1993) found that the prospective science teachers they studied had knowledge of science phenomena, such as weather, that was no more extensive than that of the elementary school students they would be teaching; and Wilson and Wineburg (1988) found that prospective high school history teachers who were studied lacked an accurate understanding of history as a field of study. A host of studies has documented deficiencies related to a number of topics in the conceptual knowledge of prospective math teachers, including deficiencies in knowledge of division of fractions, the nature of functions, and the real-number system (e.g., Adams, 1998; Ball, 1990a; Ball 1990b; Borko et al., 1992; Graeber, Tirosh, and Glover, 1989; McDiarmid and Wilson, 1991; Simon, 1993; Stoddart et al., 1993; Tirosh and Graeber, 1989; Wilson, 1994).

As Wilson, Floden, and Ferrini-Mundy (2001) note after reviewing the available evidence, "The subject-matter preparation that prospective teachers currently receive is inadequate for teaching toward high subject-matter standards, by anyone's definition." Thus, improving teachers' content knowledge should improve their ability to teach content to their pupils.

The best way of improving the content knowledge of new teachers is by involving arts and sciences faculty in the teacher education program. The assumption that these deficiencies in content knowledge can best be addressed by involving arts and sciences faculty more deeply in the teacher education program is largely untested, although it does have significant historical precedence. As early as the first half of the 20th century, critics were charging that the capabilities of university "educationists" were questionable when compared with the "academic" professors of the arts and sciences and were calling for changes in how and where teacher education took place (Lagemann, 2000; Lucas, 1999). As Cochran-Smith and Fries (2005b, p. 74) observed,

> Extremists on one side proclaimed that teachers were being taught how to teach but not what to teach; extremists on the other side claimed that if one really knew how to teach, one could teach anything.

In the 1960s, the Carnegie Corporation of New York funded a study by James Conant (1963) that recommended greater emphasis on liberal arts and humanities in teacher preparation and less emphasis on pedagogy. More recently, in 1998, U.S. Secretary of Education Richard Riley recommended the end of education degrees (Zumwalt and Craig, 2005). In response, 39 states (including the ten states where TNE grantees are located) now require a content degree for prospective teachers, which in most cases means more arts and sciences study (U.S. Department of Education, 2004). However, despite this past research, the value of greater arts and sciences involvement in teacher education, particularly in the way that TNE envisions it, is largely unstudied.[2]

One line of research that provides some evidence on the value of greater arts and sciences involvement has addressed the impact of arts and sciences coursework or majors on teachers' content knowledge and/or their pupils' achievement. For example, several studies using large-scale assessment and survey data have found that middle school and high school students whose math teachers held a bachelor's or master's degree in mathematics performed better on mathematics achievement tests than did other students (Goldhaber and Brewer, 2000; Hawkins, Stancavages, and Dossey, 1998; Rowan, Chiang, and Miller, 1997; Wenglinsky, 2002). Two of these studies (Goldhaber and Brewer and Hawkins, Stancavages, and Dossey,) specifically found higher pupil achievement for teachers with mathematics majors than teachers with education majors. Other subjects have been less well studied; one study found no similar effect on achievement for teachers with a science major (Goldhaber and Brewer, 2000), although there is some mixed evidence that for some grade levels and some fields (e.g., physical science), science coursework may have a positive impact on student achievement (Druva and Anderson, 1983; Monk, 1994; Monk and King, 1994). Looking at teachers' subject matter knowledge in particular, Cornett (1984) found that recent college graduates with arts and sciences majors scored slightly better on state certification tests measuring content knowledge than did graduates with educa-

---

[2] Apart from the evidence about arts and sciences coursework for teacher trainees, the implementation of this principle is likely to prove problematic for those institutions whose students receive all or a major bulk of their arts and sciences coursework at other institutions. This would happen if the teacher education program is a graduate program or if it receives a substantial number of transfers from community colleges.

tion majors. Once again, one needs to be cautious in interpreting these results if there is a selectivity bias among the students who opt for an arts and sciences major versus an education major.

However, an arts and sciences degree does not seem to guarantee adequate content knowledge for teaching; several other studies of prospective teachers' content knowledge found that even after completing a full arts and sciences content major, many prospective teachers still lacked deep conceptual knowledge in their teaching field (Ball, 1990a; Ball, 1990b; Borko et al., 1992; Holt-Reynolds, 1999; McDiarmid & Wilson, 1991).

What little evidence exists on the impact of a subject major on elementary students' learning, however, suggests that there is no similar effect for younger students for math (Hawkins, Stancavages, and Dossey, 1998) or reading (Rowan, Correnti, and Miller, 2002). Indeed, the latter study found a negative impact on elementary student achievement for teachers holding an advanced degree in mathematics. The authors hypothesize that for elementary teachers, a math degree may

> . . . somehow interfere with effective teaching, either because it substitutes for pedagogical training in people's professional preparation, or because it produces teachers who somehow cannot simplify and clarify their advanced understanding of mathematics for elementary school students (Rowan, Correnti, and Miller, 2002, p. 1541).

A second line of research regarding the potential for arts and sciences involvement in teacher education to improve teachers' content knowledge focuses on outcomes associated with specific individual arts and sciences courses. Many of these studies look at courses featuring innovations akin to arts and sciences activities at some TNE institutions, such as small-group discussion of content (Civil, 1993); integrated lecture and laboratory experiences (Fones, Wagner, and Caldwell, 1999); emphasis on creating a culture of mathematical inquiry (McNeal and Simon, 2000); and emphasis on prospective teachers' scientific practices and discourse (Smith and Anderson, 1999). All of these studies found positive effects from the courses in question on such outcomes as prospective teachers' confidence, attitude, self-reported knowledge, and speech patterns. None, however, examined changes in teachers' actual knowledge or the impact of these courses on teachers' effectiveness, and only one (Fones, Wagner, and Caldwell, 1999) included a comparison of outcomes between teachers who had innovative courses and those who had more-traditional courses.

In sum, the evidence base provides some support for the notion that arts and sciences coursework has a positive impact on teacher effectiveness at the secondary level, particularly in mathematics. However, the weight of the evidence does not necessarily lead to the conclusion that more arts and sciences involvement in teacher education will result in better teacher content knowledge or greater teacher effectiveness. In particular, content knowledge is no guarantee of one knowing how to teach content—pedagogical content knowledge is critical to being an effective teacher. Several studies also highlight the value of coursework in math education or math pedagogy, which may be taught by education faculty as opposed to arts and sciences faculty, and field experiences in K–12 schools in increasing prospective teachers' pedagogical content knowledge (Gess-Newsome and Lederman, 1993; Grossman and Richert, 1988; Malone, Jones, and Stallings, 2002; Valli and Agostinelli, 1993). Indeed, one study provides evidence that such coursework may actually have an even greater positive effect on teachers' effectiveness than regular mathematics coursework taught by arts and sciences faculty (Monk, 1994).

Finally, the existing evidence on the effects of arts and science coursework on teacher effectiveness is associational, but not necessarily causal, because it fails to take into account the differences among prospective teachers who choose to pursue different levels of mathematics study. It might be the case, for example, that teachers who are inclined to take a greater number of math classes enjoy math more or are better at it than those who chose to take fewer math classes; higher pupil learning gains might be attributable to these preexisting characteristics rather than to knowledge added through teachers taking math classes.

In weighing all of the existing evidence on arts and sciences coursework for new teachers, the AERA Panel concluded that

> support for arts and sciences requirements and for foundations based on arts and sciences work . . . appears to depend less on an evidentiary base than does support for the courses seen as the province of "educationists" (Floden and Meniketti, 2005, p. 282).

Teaching as an Academically Taught Clinical-Practice Profession

An integrated clinical component would improve the quality of teacher graduates. Numerous studies suggest potential benefits from some sort of clinical experience for prospective teachers. In many ways, the real issue pointed out by the TNE prospectus has less to do with the existence of field experiences within a teacher education program than with the integration of the clinical experience with the program. (Some form of fieldwork and/or student teaching is the norm in almost all teacher education programs, including for all 11 TNE grantees.) The issue of integration has been less well studied than the effects of field experiences in general, perhaps because the notion of integration is multifaceted and thus is difficult to clearly define and measure across studies of various programs. Clearly, in an ideal situation, a well-integrated clinical component would include several elements—observation, assessment, supervision, feedback, intervention, and reassessment.

The literature on specific types of field experiences in sites known as professional development schools (PDS) offers one potential avenue for understanding the effect of the integration of clinical components on the quality of the graduates of teacher education programs. Modeled in part after medical teaching hospitals, the PDS concept generally links universities with one or more K–12 school sites to create a collaborative research and learning environment for pre-service teachers, university faculty, and K–12 educators. The relationship should be collaborative and the benefits reciprocal for all parties involved. The PDS idea has been advocated by several previous high-profile teacher education reform efforts. For example, John Goodlad (1994) and the NNER advocate "centers of pedagogy" involving partnerships between schools and universities dedicated to teacher preparation and the improvement of pedagogy, while the Holmes Group (1990) outlined its vision of the PDS concept in *Tomorrow's Schools*. Notable in the PDS concept is the close integration of the field experience placement sites with the university teacher education program.

Several studies have compared prospective teachers who student teach in PDS sites with those who complete more-traditional, and presumably less-well-integrated, student teaching placements and have found a variety of favorable outcomes for the PDS programs including higher confidence (Blocker and Mantle-Bromley, 1997; Connor and Killmer, 2001; Sandholtz and Wasserman, 2001; Wilson, 1996); higher program satisfaction (Blocker and Mantle-Bromley, 1997); higher expectation of remaining in teaching (Reynolds, Ross, and Rakow, 2002); and better self-perceived skills, knowledge, and interactions with their pupils (Connor and Killmer, 2001; Yerian and Grossman, 1997). Notably, however, none of these studies attempted to examine the effects of PDS experiences on student teachers' actual teaching performance or on their effectiveness in terms of raising student achievement. Reynolds, Ross, and Rakow (2002) examined principals' evaluations of teacher graduates from PDS and non-PDS programs at one university and found no difference between the two groups after individual differences had been accounted for. One negative outcome reported in several PDS studies was a higher level of stress for student teachers at PDS sites (Hopkins, Hoffman and Moss, 1997; Blocker and Mantle-Bromley, 1997).

However, while the research to date on PDS sites and other field experiences provides some suggestions of the potential benefit of integrated clinical components in teacher education, the evidence is far from conclusive. Allen (2003) provides a strong critique of the research in this area. First, the field experiences that were studied vary considerably from one another on a number of dimensions, so it is difficult to generalize them. Most of these studies are descriptive and small scale, and few include comparisons with other programs, so conclusions about the benefits of clinical practice relative to other possible activities are unsupportable. Furthermore, the outcomes studied almost never include measures of actual teacher practice or teacher effectiveness, so it is unclear whether the documented changes in attitudes and beliefs actually make a difference in teacher quality. Finally, as Allen (2003) notes, the bulk of the research on PDS sites and other field experiences has been conducted by individuals who are involved in the program being studied and who are often active advocates of the PDS concept, which leads to a potential conflict of interest. This echoes the concerns of Wideen, Mayer-Smith, and Moon (1998) that researchers' commitment to the PDS concept and the unbalanced power relationships between researchers (often professors) and participants (often the professors' students) are often problematic and seldom fully disclosed in this line of research. As a result of these concerns, Allen concludes that the evidence on the effect of field experiences and PDS sites on teacher quality is inconclusive.

In sum, the current research base related to integrated clinical practice components in teacher education programs provides mixed evidence at best that field experiences lead to positive changes in prospective teachers' attitudes and beliefs, and no studies provide evidence on the link between these changes and teaching performance or student achievement. The majority of this research is too methodologically problematic to draw any strong conclusions about the efficacy of integrated clinical practice in improving teacher quality. While this idea may seem to pass the test of logical reasonableness, it cannot be said that it is grounded in a firm base of evidence.

Involvement of K–12 teachers in teacher education programs improves teacher education faculty and teacher candidates' knowledge and understanding of real schools and classrooms. K–12 teachers have long been involved in teacher education programs during teacher candidates' clinical experiences, acting as mentors and supervisors of student teachers. Anecdotal evidence exists on the importance of good mentors and candidates' frequent exchanges with K–12 faculty to bring a dose of realism to a teacher education program. Unfortunately, there is evidence to suggest that many teachers are averse to being observed by teacher candidates, so it is difficult to get a true measure of their teaching style and ability, and candidates may be placed with teachers who are ill-suited to the purpose of mentoring.

TNE asks its grantees to think about ways in which K–12 teachers could be fruitfully involved with the program, especially as teachers in residence (TIRs) at the university. The question of selection of TIRs is an important one. Anecdotal evidence suggests that these appointments sometimes are made as political favors to certain teachers and that unions are allowed to select teachers based on seniority, not merit. Clearly, a careful selection and vetting process is needed to ensure that teachers involved with the teacher education program are indeed master teachers capable of modeling best practices and being mentors to teaching candidates.

The literature that speaks to these issues is somewhat sparse and draws largely from the PDS literature. For example, in one study, student teachers in PDS sites increased their awareness of systemic issues in education and gained a greater "career" perspective (as opposed to a "job" perspective) (Walling and Lewis, 2000). Another study (Tabachnik and Zeichner, 1984) also found that student teaching helped candidates gain a more realistic view of teaching. One study of six PDS sites (Button, Ponticell, and Johnson, 1996) found that K–12 faculty served as important resources for university professors, while faculty members in another PDS site were influenced by the school's focus, needs, and practices in revising the teacher education curriculum (Allexsaht-Snider, Deegan, and White, 1995). In a fourth study, teacher educators in a PDS site credited that experience with helping them to learn to work collabora-tively (Hudson-Ross, 2001); however, Gill and Hove's (2000) study of several PDS sites linked to West Virginia University's teacher education program found that collabora-tive research between university and K–12 faculty happened in only a few cases.

While there is limited evidence suggesting that university faculty may benefit from PDS experiences, most research in this area points out the difficulties in estab-lishing a trusting and productive PDS partnership. Wiseman and Nason (1995), for example, document the slow development of trust in one PDS site between university faculty and K–12 practitioners over two years. Allexsaht-Snider, Deegan, and White (1995) also note that collaboration took considerable time to develop and required improvements in communication and a reconceptualization of roles in another PDS.

New teachers in the first two years of teaching are novices in their profession and need support during this induction period. There is broad consensus in education that new teachers are novices and in need of support during the early "crucible" years of teaching. Given the existing structure of the educational system, in which teach-ers in their independent classrooms tend to be shut off from one another, new teach-ers often find themselves isolated and alone. In addition, assuming full responsibility for an entire school year for a classroom of students tends to be a huge jump in duties from the duties of a student-teaching placement. As Ingersoll and Kralik (2004) said, "Critics have long assailed teaching as an occupation that 'cannibalizes its young' and in which the initiation of new teachers is akin to a sink or swim, trial by fire, or boot camp experience." Furthermore, as Zumwalt and Craig (2005, p. 139) report, "New teachers are more likely to find their first jobs in harder-to-staff, lower-performing rural and central schools with high proportions of minority and low-income students," which tend to make the first years of teaching even more challenging.

One major concern is that new teachers may be less effective in the classroom than more experienced teachers. For example, O'Connor, Fish, and Yasik (2004) found that novice teachers' classrooms had significantly lower levels of classroom com-munication and flexibility than did the classrooms of experienced teachers. Other studies have found that, compared with more senior teachers, novice teachers are less flexible and responsive to student needs (Cleary and Groer, 1994; Leinhardt, 1989; Livingston and Borko, 1989; Westerman, 1991); have less understanding of classroom phenomena (Carter et al., 1988; Peterson and Comeaux, 1987; Sabers, Cushing, and Berliner, 1991); and display shallower conceptual understanding (Gallagher, 1994; Weinert, Shrader, and Helmke, 1990). Teaching experience has also been included in a number of studies examining the impact of school resources on school outcomes (e.g., Fetler, 1999; Ferguson, 1991; Greenwald, Hedges, and Laine, 1996; Hanushek, 1992; Hanushek, Kain, and Rivkin, 1998; Rowan, Correnti, and Miller, 2002), which found that classroom experience is positively associated with student achievement. These results would tend to suggest that teachers in their first years in the classroom are less effective than more experienced teachers. Furthermore, some researchers have suggested that new teachers' experiences in their first years in the classroom have a formative effect that influences their effectiveness and attitudes over their entire teaching career (McDonald, 1980; Bush, 1983); however, there is very little empirical evidence on the long-term development of teachers.

A second concern is the retention of new teachers. A number of studies of teacher retention have found that teachers are most likely to leave teaching in their first year in the classroom and that the risk remains relatively high for the first four or five years of their career, after which the risk declines significantly (Boe et al., 1997; Hanushek, Kain, and Rivkin, 2001; Kirby, Berends and Naftel, 1999; Murnane, 1984; Murnane et al. 1991; Singer and Willett, 1988; Stinebrickner, 1999). Given these findings, policymakers and researchers have hypothesized that providing additional support to new teachers during the critical first years might increase the likelihood they will remain in the profession and thus enhance the quality of the teaching force as a whole.

Research examining the reasons for teacher attrition does raise some concerns as to the potential impact of induction programs on retention rates. One body of work suggests that financial concerns play a significant role in teachers' decisions to remain in teaching (e.g., Grissmer and Kirby, 1997; Imazeki, 2002; Ingersoll, 2001; Kirby and Grissmer, 1993; Murnane and Olson, 1989, 1990; Rickman and Parker, 1990; Shen, 1997; Stinebrickner, 1998, 2001a, 2001b). Other research suggests that working conditions, including class size, teaching load, and school characteristics, may play a significant role in teacher retention (Falch and Strom, 2002; Hanushek, Kain, and Rivkin, 2001; Mont and Rees, 1996; Shen, 1997). The relative importance of these factors, which induction programs cannot address, and other factors that can be ameliorated through first-year support systems is unclear; however, the more important that financial considerations and working conditions are, the less effect induction programs would likely have in reducing new-teacher attrition.

Unfortunately, the empirical research base on new-teacher induction is limited in regard to the question of the effectiveness of induction programs in enhancing retention and student achievement. Ingersoll and Kralik (2004) identified more than 150 studies of induction and mentoring programs and found that only ten of them met criteria for rigor, such as the use of quantitative data, evaluation of clearly defined outcomes, and comparison of teachers in induction programs with teachers who did not participate in such programs.

Nevertheless, a handful of studies do suggest potential benefits in teacher retention from induction and mentoring programs. Odell and Ferraro (1992) found that the retention rates among two cohorts of teachers in New Mexico who had received mentoring four years earlier were better than the statewide average rate, although they do not offer details on the conditions of the schools or districts in which these teachers were teaching or whether they differed from the state average in other ways. Henke, Chen, and Geis (2000) examined data from the national Baccalaureate and Beyond Survey and found that teachers who reported participation in an induction program had lower attrition than other teachers, although, again, there were no controls for other school and district characteristics that might affect attrition. In their analysis of the national Schools and Staffing Survey data, Ingersoll and Smith (2004) found that teachers who received no induction support left teaching at a higher rate than did teachers who received some form of induction support, controlling for teacher and school characteristics; furthermore, the greater the number of types of support offered (e.g., mentoring, peer collaboration, teacher network), the less likely teachers were to leave. Finally, Fuller (2003) and the Charles A. Dana Center (2002) found that Texas teachers who participated in a statewide induction program had lower attrition in the first three years of teaching than did teachers who did not participate in the program; this effect held for high-poverty and high-minority schools and across school levels. Strong (2005) reported positive effects on retention from California's Beginning Teacher Support and Assessment program.

Empirical evidence on the effects of induction programs on a beginning teacher's effectiveness is even more limited. Michael Strong and colleagues at the New Teacher Center have begun some exploratory work on the relationship between induction and student achievement, and have reported some initial positive findings. For example, Strong (1998) reports that students of new teachers participating in the Santa Cruz New Teacher Project scored as well as students of experienced teachers on the SAT9 reading assessment; however, no comparison group of non-supported new teachers was included. Fletcher, Strong, and Villar (2005) used hierarchical linear modeling methods and student-level data linked to teachers in three California districts to show that new-teacher support may be associated with gains in reading achievement for elementary school students, although there seem to be differences related to the intensity of the induction support provided. This work remains in its infancy, however, and should be considered suggestive at best.

Nonetheless, despite the limited evidence on their effects, induction programs for new teachers are becoming increasingly popular in school districts across the country.

Support for new teachers is best provided by the teachers' educational institution. TNE's focus on university-provided induction support is impossible to evaluate on the basis of existing empirical research. Allen (2003) found from his review of the literature that the evidence on what makes induction programs successful is "inconclusive." The limitations of the research base on the effectiveness of induction in general have already been discussed; the enormous variety of induction programs studied and the fact that many programs have not been adequately described in the research makes drawing research-based conclusions about the most effective forms of induction nearly impossible.

Furthermore, research regarding the characteristics of effective professional development suggests that the TNE model of universities providing induction services for their own teacher graduates, regardless of where the graduates are teaching, may be suboptimal. Garet, Porter, and Desimone (2001) examined professional development in a national sample of teachers and identified features that were particularly effective in improving the practice of teaching, including collective participation of groups of teachers from the same school, department, or grade level and the coherence of the professional development activities with teachers' other experiences and development opportunities. Under the TNE model, however, the induction services offered to graduates are likely to be separate from the context of each new teacher's school and experience and, therefore, may be less effective than locally provided services, unless the TNE services and the local district services are closely linked and developed in collaboration.

Despite the paucity of evidence, Carnegie and TNE are not alone in asking teacher education programs to provide support for their new teacher graduates. Earley (2000) reports that ten institutions that are members of the American Association of Colleges of Teacher Education (AACTE) offered in-service support to all their new teacher graduates. Also increasing in prominence in recent years are teacher warranty programs (discussed above), which require teacher education programs to provide follow-up remediation services at no cost for teachers whose classroom performance do not meet the standards of their hiring schools and districts. As Allen (2003) reports, institutional warranties imply that the responsibility of teacher preparation institutions for their students does not end once students graduate but also extends to the in-service development of teachers. Unfortunately, no evidence on the effects of these programs currently exists.

New teachers need support for teaching content, and this support can best be provided by involving arts and sciences faculty in the induction program. As we discussed earlier, a number of studies have identified significant deficiencies in the content knowledge of teachers, both new teachers and experienced ones. The extent to which new teachers need content knowledge support, however, is less clear. Some researchers suggest that new teachers face a number of challenges in "survival skills," such as classroom management, which new teachers regard as a far-more-pressing concern than issues of content knowledge. Fuller (1969), for example, posited that new teachers pass through several stages of development, beginning with an initial concern about personal adequacy, before they are able to focus on teaching performance and student learning. Veenman (1984) cites student discipline and motivation, individualizing instruction, assessment, and dealing with parents as new teachers' most-pressing concerns. A series of in-depth case studies of first-year teachers by Bullough (1987, 1989, 1990) also found that issues of classroom management overwhelmed new teachers, such that teachers were able to attend to pupil learning and instructional issues only after they had established routines and procedures for resolving control problems. From her review of the literature on new-teacher development, Kagan concluded that

> until novices have established standard routines and resolved their images of self
> as teacher, they will be obsessed with discipline and class control . . . . Attempts to
> force a different focus may be misguided (Kagan, 1992, p. 163).

This line of research suggests that support in areas other than the teaching of content may be more important to new teachers, at least initially.

Furthermore, even when teachers are ready to focus on instructional issues and pupil learning, it is not clear that arts and sciences faculty members are the best source of support. As we discussed earlier, there is some evidence that arts and sciences coursework may be associated with teacher effectiveness in secondary mathematics, but the conclusion that additional involvement of arts and sciences faculty in the development of new teachers will by itself improve teachers' content knowledge is not well supported. Looking at university-provided professional development in particular, Desimone, Garet, and Birman (2003) found that professional development programs run by mathematics and science departments were less likely than those run by education departments to have features that have been shown to be most effective in improving teacher learning, such as strong coordination with the school district, a long time span over which activities continue, many hours of contact between teachers and professional developers, and strategies for feedback and continuous program improvement.

In the previous section, we examined the research evidence supporting the TNE design principles. It is clear that while the principles themselves pass the test of logical reasonableness and, in fact, draw from a variety of literature, the evidence supporting the principles is mixed at best. However, this does not necessarily negate their validity—we simply point out that evidence does not exist or seems to be weak with respect to the assumed effect of some the elements of the theory behind the TNE design principles and that the theory of change may not bring about the desired outcomes. Regardless, these principles form the foundation of TNE's theory of organizational change, so we now turn to examining several factors and actors that need to be aligned for the theory to work in practice.

Enabling Factors

Several conditions must be fulfilled before a major reform effort seeking a substantial departure from the status quo will achieve its objectives (Sabatier and Mazmanian, 1979). These "enabling factors" were included in the TNE prospectus and in the TNE-grantee selection process, and have been shown to be important in several studies of implementation of reform.

Figure 3.1 depicts the TNE theory of change. The center box lists the design principles that TNE believes characterize excellent teacher education programs.

The box on the left lists factors and actors that need to be aligned for coherent and effective implementation of the theory of change. The right side of the figure links well-trained, competent, and qualified teachers to student learning and achieve-

Figure 3.1
Theory of Change Underlying the TNE Initiative

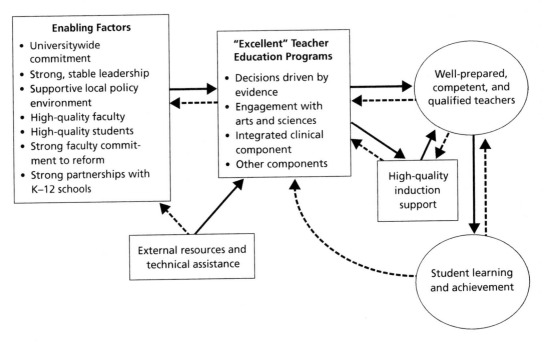

NOTE: Dashed lines indicate feedback loops.

ment, as envisioned by TNE. The dashed lines represent the feedback loops into the program—which are necessary if program improvement is to be evidence-based. (The theory of change is discussed in greater detail in Kirby et al., [2004].)

TNE emphasizes university-wide commitment by insisting that the TNE grants be administered out of the institutions' provost's office and not the institutions' department of education, enabling TNE to be seen as a university endeavor, resulting in greater faculty buy-in. Other factors (see Figure 3.1) that have been shown to be important in implementing radical change are strong, stable leadership and depth of leadership (Elmore, 2000); high-quality and committed faculty (Fullan, 1991; Mazmanian and Sabatier, 1989; Weatherly and Lipsky, 1977); high-quality students (Ehrenberg and Brewer, 1995; Ferguson, 1991; Ferguson and Ladd, 1996; Greenwald, Hedges, and Laine, 1996; Kain and Singleton, 1996); and strong partnerships with K–12 schools (see the discussion in Chapter Two on calls by the Holmes Group and Holmes Partnership for establishing professional development schools and NNER's call for simultaneous renewal of schooling and teacher education).

Impact of Policy Environment and Trends in Teacher Supply

The policy environment is particularly important because although TNE is looking for out-of-the-box thinking, the TNE institutions still have to comply with state rules and regulations governing teacher licensure and certification. These and other regulations may act to inhibit entry into the new TNE programs or limit the ability of the programs to substantially change teacher education in some areas. For example, states often mandate specific course work for certification (Prestine, 1991; Walsh, 2001), adopt different types of licensure tests with different passing scores (National Research Council, 2001), and mandate induction requirements.

One important point to note is that the conditions of teacher demand and supply in states and districts might lead to various strategies that run counter to or undermine an institution's efforts at reform. For example, alternative certification programs or emergency credentialing may seem to be easier routes into teaching for qualified candidates who do not wish to commit the time or the financial resources required in a more rigorous, structured program. A recent report by the Education Commission of the States (Mikulecky, Shkodriani, and Wilner, 2004) noted that these programs seem to be more successful than traditional programs in attracting minorities and males into teaching and staffing hard-to-fill schools or critical shortage areas. For example:

- In Texas, 9 percent of all teachers are minorities, while 41 percent of those who prepare for a teaching career through alternative routes are minorities.
- In New Jersey, 9 percent of all teachers are minorities, while 20 percent of alternatively certified teachers are minorities.
- In the Troops to Teacher program, 90 percent of participants are male, compared with 26 percent of teachers nationwide, and 30 percent are minorities compared with 10 percent nationwide.
- Twenty-nine percent of teachers who came to teaching through alternative routes end up teaching math.
- Twenty-four percent who took alternative routes teach in the sciences.
- Eleven percent who took alternative routes teach special education.
- Twenty-five percent who took alternative routes teach at inner-city schools, compared with 16 percent overall (i.e., all new teachers who graduate).

As Mikulecky, Shkodriani, and Wilner (2004, p. 3) summarized,

> With federal programs providing increasing support and oversight, and organizations such as NCATE accrediting community college programs, alternative certification programs are not only evolving, but also gaining wider acceptance.

TNE explicitly recognizes the importance of the state and local policy environment in its criteria for selecting TNE institutions, while acknowledging that the policy environments might change over time. Carnegie Corporation of New York, the main driving force behind TNE, contracted with the Consortium for Policy Research in Education (CPRE) (http://www.cpre.org/Research/Research_Project_Carnegie_TNE.htm) to examine the policy environments in the ten states in which the TNE grantees are located. Carnegie asked CPRE to investigate two critical questions:

- What policy changes may be needed to ensure implementation, continuation, and dissemination of these reforms in teacher education?
- What actions may be taken to bring about these changes?

Apart from the policy environment itself, the trends in teacher supply seem to suggest that many new teachers are nontraditional entrants into teaching in the sense that they are older and making a mid-life career switch from other careers into teaching. For example, a survey of a random sample of new teachers in seven states revealed a very high proportion of mid-career entrants into teaching, ranging from 28 percent to 47 percent of all new entrants into teaching. These mid-career switchers are less likely than their first-career counterparts to enroll in a time-consuming and costly teacher-preparation program (Johnson et al., 2004). This sort of reluctance combined with the negative views on the part of policymakers and others of the value and quality of a traditional university-based teacher preparation program may make the TNE programs a hard sell, regardless of their quality and evidence base.

Potential Outcomes and Impacts of the TNE Initiative

TNE is a complex initiative that requires radical institutional and cultural changes. A national evaluation of an initiative of this magnitude and complexity faces several challenges, chief among them that the outcomes of interest are not likely to be seen or measured until several years after the initiative ends. As we mentioned in Chapter One, the long-term objectives of the evaluation are: (1) to provide evidence of whether the TNE initiative has been "successful"—both from the individual institutions' point of view and from the funders' point of view; (2) to identify factors that foster or hinder the implementation of reform of teacher education programs at the program, institution, district, and state levels; (3) to promote an understanding of the many factors and actors that need to be aligned to successfully reform teacher education and improve student learning; and (4) to evaluate the overall contribution of TNE to teacher education reform in the country, states, and school districts. Achieving these objectives requires that several kinds of outcomes and impacts (referred to as "outcomes" for the sake of brevity) be tracked and measured over time as the initiative unfolds. As Kirby et al. (2004) point out, it is useful to categorize these outcomes as in-program outcomes, intermediate outcomes, and final outcomes (see Figure 3.2).

Figure 3.2
Potential Outcomes of TNE

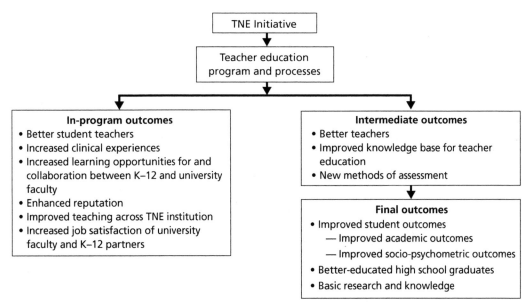

In-Program Outcomes

In-program outcomes can be thought of as those affecting various stakeholders because of the stakeholders' direct participation in the TNE programs. For example, the changes in teacher education program content and structure should improve the quality of student teachers, and this improvement should in turn directly benefit the teacher education students themselves (greater confidence in the classroom), the teacher education program (decreased need for counseling, assistance, or intervention, and greater ability to provide productive supervision), the partner K–12 schools (increased ability to provide quality instruction and to provide targeted assistance to K–12 students), and the TNE funders (who emphasize close relationships between universities and schools and integrated clinical [i.e., student teaching] experiences). As another example, the TNE institutions plan to hold workshops with and disseminate their findings regarding effective teaching to faculty members not directly involved in the initiative, which could bring about improved teaching across the institutions. This would benefit the institutions' faculty as well as teacher education students and possibly non–teacher education students, TNE funders (who value effective teaching), and institutions of higher education—both partner institutions (those who are participating in TNE but are not fully funded TNE grantees) and non-TNE institutions—if knowledge on how to bring about more effective teaching were widely disseminated.

Intermediate Outcomes

Intermediate outcomes can be thought of as benefits that accrue later in the process and that are valuable in and of themselves, but are not regarded as final outcomes. We define three types of intermediate outcomes.

The first intermediate outcome of the TNE programs is "better" teachers, who are defined as competent, caring, and well-educated, with strong self-confidence and a belief they can succeed and strong knowledge of content and pedagogy, and who are likely to be sought after by districts and schools. There is the assumption that these higher-quality teachers will enter and remain in teaching—a strong and perhaps overly optimistic assumption, given that earlier research has shown that higher-aptitude students either do not choose teaching as a profession or, once in the profession, do not remain in it long (Hanushek and Pace, 1995; Henke, Chen, and Geis, 2000; Lankford, Loeb, and Wyckoff, 2002; Murnane and Olsen, 1990; Murnane, Singer, and Willett, 1989; Stinebrickner, 2001a and 2001b).

The second intermediate outcome is an improved knowledge base for teacher education. Each of the TNE institutions is making an effort to review the research base of teacher education and to collect evidence on what works and what does not work. This effort presumably is likely to benefit a wide range of stakeholders—e.g., teacher education faculty, who can use this evidence to improve their programs; partner institutions, to whom this knowledge is disseminated; non-TNE teacher-preparation institutions that could use the information to develop evidence-based teacher education programs; and TNE funders, who may be interested in seeing such knowledge developed and disseminated.

The third intermediate outcome is the development of new assessment methods. Because assessment is a key component of the TNE initiative, each of the TNE institutions is examining various methods of teacher education assessment and thinking about developing new ones. These would be used to assess their teacher candidates and graduates and to improve the program. In addition, the institutions are looking to develop or improve diagnostic assessments that could be used to monitor progress of K–12 students and to improve classroom instruction. These new assessments will add to the general knowledge base of teacher education and could benefit a wide range of non-TNE institutions and students.

Final Outcomes

Final outcomes are the end results of the institutional change process outlined by TNE. The ultimate goal of the TNE initiative is, of course, to improve student outcomes (both academic and socio-psychometric), but this final outcome is likely to also have longer-term and broader benefits. Better teaching and a more supportive class environment are likely to lead to improved conditions of learning and teaching in classrooms and schools. This could foster a greater interest in learning, a higher level of student engagement, and a greater respect for cultural differences.

Academic outcomes would include improved content knowledge, retention in school, and, eventually, better-educated high school graduates. Evidence of these outcomes might be fewer special-education referrals, fewer students retained in grade, and higher numbers of high school graduates. Students could also meet proficiency standards sooner, thus freeing up their schedules to take more advanced and enrichment courses. This latter academic outcome is contingent on the other outcomes taking place, i.e., students are indeed learning more, performing better, and have fewer behavioral problems.

In addition, recent research has emphasized the importance of non-cognitive (i.e., sociological and psychological) outcomes. In particular, Heckman (2006) argues persuasively that

> environments that do not cultivate both cognitive and noncognitive abilities (such as motivation, perseverance, and self-restraint) place children at an early disadvantage . . . Noncognitive ability is neglected in many public policy discussions, yet it is a major determinant of socioeconomic success. Cognitive ability and noncognitive ability are both important in explaining schooling attainment, participation in crime, and a variety of other outcomes. Moving persons from the bottom to the top of either cognitive or noncognitive distributions has equally strong effects on many measures of social and economic success.

Thus, improving the non-cognitive as well as the cognitive outcomes of students is likely to have payoffs in terms of persistence, high school graduation, and productivity.

Having better-educated high school graduates, another final outcome, has benefits across the board—it would benefit all institutions of higher learning in that they would have better-educated freshmen, and future employers would benefit by having a higher-quality workforce. These benefits may in fact be reflected in potential cost savings.

Another final outcome consists of a codified knowledge base of what teachers need to teach students at all ability levels—similar to clinical practice guidelines in medicine. This outcome, too, would have broader benefits if the knowledge and research are disseminated to other institutions and K–12 schools and districts.

The ultimate outcome measure defined by TNE is the measure of gains in pupils' learning. However, improving student outcomes depends on more than just teacher quality—federal, state, and district policies; the principal's leadership; school contexts; and the level of community support all influence student learning. The list of factors influencing student learning is overwhelming, and even the best-prepared teachers could be stymied by an unsupportive school or home environment, poor or unstable school or district leadership, and policies that could result in little or no learning being accomplished in their classrooms. The effect of teacher quality on student achievement will need to be measured carefully to account for these many factors. In this respect, the VAM statistical techniques offer a potentially useful method for isolating teacher effects, but great care must be taken in including the proper controls and in making inferences from the analyses. McCaffrey et al. (2004) warn that the magnitude of some of the effects reported in the literature are overstated and that reported teacher effects are sensitive to assumptions underlying the statistical models, but they note that this issue has been largely ignored in the literature. Kupermintz (2003) examined the validity of teacher evaluation measures produced by the Tennessee Value Added Assessment System (TVAAS). He pointed out several issues affecting the validity of the TVAAS teacher evaluation information, including the importance of correctly accounting for the ability and background characteristics of students.

None of the intermediate or final outcomes can be measured in the early years of the reform effort. In the short run, we are limited to tracking implementation and some of the in-program outcomes. However, as we pointed out earlier, this kind of process evaluation offers valuable data and insights that can inform a longer-term, summative evaluation of TNE and provide formative feedback to assist the TNE sites.

Going from the Broad Overview to "Nuts and Bolts": Activities and Outputs

Our examination of TNE implementation and outcomes to this point has been fairly broad-based and somewhat theoretical. As a lead-in to some implementation specifics, it is useful to examine the kinds of activities and outputs one would expect to see as the TNE design principles are translated into practice. The following definitions (from W.K. Kellogg Foundation, 2004) are of terminology used in logic models:

> **Activities** are the processes, techniques, tools, events, technology, and actions of the planned program. These may include products—promotional materials and educational curricula; services—education and training, counseling, or health screening; and infrastructure—structure, relationships, and capacity used to bring about the desired results.
>
> **Outputs** are the direct results of program activities. They are usually described in terms of the size and/or scope of the services and products delivered or produced by the program. They indicate if a program was delivered to the intended audiences at the intended "dose." A program output, for example, might be the number of classes taught, meetings held, or materials produced and distributed; program participation rates and demography; or hours of each type of service provided.
>
> **Outcomes** are specific changes in attitudes, behaviors, knowledge, skills, status, or level of functioning expected to result from program activities and which are most often expressed at an individual level.
>
> **Impacts** are organizational, community, and/or system-level changes *expected to result* from program activities, which might include improved conditions, increased capacity, and/or changes in the policy arena.

We focus on activities and outputs, rather than final outcomes and impacts, because TNE is still in its early years. Table 3.2 lists the activities and outputs related to the three major TNE design principles. These few examples illustrate the kinds of activities one would expect to see at the sites.

To implement evidence-based decisionmaking, the leadership team must determine the kind of data that are needed to inform decisions about the program (e.g., data on teacher candidates, teacher graduates, and pupils), how best to collect such data, and how to make decisions based on these data. As such, the outputs resulting from such activities are the development and implementation of a comprehensive data base, well-defined indicators that drive the data being collected, an established frequency with which these data are collected, numbers of faculty who use such data to make course decisions, numbers of courses and improvements to those courses based on evidence, and a process for reviewing these data.

For engagement of arts and sciences faculty, the activities would include the active involvement of arts and sciences faculty in the teacher education program—advising candidates and graduates in clinical settings; articulating teaching standards and goals, including both subject-area content knowledge and pedagogical content knowledge; and creating or revising courses to match those standards and goals. These activities would result in improved subject-area content knowledge or pedagogical content knowledge, increased contact with teacher education students and graduates, and frequent and trusted interactions between teacher education faculty and arts and sciences faculty.

Similarly, for the integrated clinical component activities, one should see increased involvement of K–12 faculty in program decisionmaking, team teaching, development of courses, and participation in research; appointment of K–12 teachers as university faculty; university faculty spending time in schools on both teaching and research; varied and frequent clinical experiences for students, and frequent feedback during those sessions.

Most of these activities are occurring at the TNE sites, suggesting that the sites are implementing TNE principles and/or adapting them to fit their own circumstances and environments. The larger question of whether (and how) the intensity, frequency, and magnitude of these activities and outputs imply "deeper" implementation and, therefore, will lead to "better" outcomes is a difficult one to address and remains largely unanswered. For example, how frequently should arts and sciences faculty and teacher education faculty interact to qualify as "high" implementation? In a large university, should 10 percent of arts and sciences faculty be involved? Or is 20 percent a better number? Should one K–12 teacher be hired as a teacher in residence, or should more be hired? What if district policy makes it unfeasible to hire such teachers? Should changes be observed in one, two, or more courses?

The fact that the TNE sites were selected largely because they already ranked high on several TNE selection criteria suggests that large and "radical" change in teacher education at these institutions is unlikely; given the glacial pace of change at universities, it may be difficult to point to anything other than incremental changes as evidence of implementation, and it may be a long time before any real impact on teacher candidates, their learning, and their experiences is seen.

Table 3.2
Example Activities and Outputs Related to the Three Major TNE Design Principles

Activities	Outputs
Decisions Driven by Evidence	
Leadership determines the data that are needed to inform program decisions about program prerequisites, program requirements, individual courses, and clinical experiences.	Data system in place
	Number of faculty who make course decisions based on evidence
Leadership establishes a process for systematically collecting and analyzing program data.	Number of course decisions based on evidence
	Number of courses affected (could include new courses)
Leadership establishes a system for gathering K–12 pupil-learning data.	Number of programmatic decisions made (could include changes to prerequisites; course sequencing)
Leadership collects data on students as they progress through the program (including quality, retention, placement).	Number of times faculty receive new data from the data collection/analysis system
Leadership collects data on graduates, including K–12 pupil-learning data, retention in teaching, characteristics of schools where graduates are teaching.	Amount and type of data collected by the program
	Frequency of data collection
	Quality and diversity of students attracted to the program
Leadership establishes a process for making program decisions.	Retention of students in the program
Faculty/leadership engage in data collection.	Placement of students in the program
Faculty/leadership analyze data.	
Faculty/leadership make decisions based on data.	
Faculty/leadership implement decisions.	
Engagement of Arts and Sciences	
Institution develops arts and sciences partners who are actively involved in the teacher education program.	Regular interactions between teacher education faculty and arts and sciences faculty about content knowledge and pedagogical content knowledge
Arts and sciences faculty collaborate with teacher education faculty to	Regular interactions between teacher education candidates/graduates and arts and sciences faculty about content knowledge and pedagogical content knowledge
provide expert advice to teacher education faculty on content knowledge needed by candidates and graduates	Improved content knowledge and pedagogical content knowledge in courses taken by teacher education candidates
advise candidates and graduates in clinical settings	before program
	during program
articulate teaching standards and goals that include content knowledge and pedagogical content knowledge	Use of induction activities by graduates to enhance content knowledge and pedagogical content knowledge
create/revise courses and clinical experiences to match teaching standards and goals, including teacher education courses, academic-major courses, and general- and liberal-education courses.	Requests from graduates for assistance with content knowledge and pedagogical content knowledge
	Research on K–12 schools and collaborative activities aimed at improving teaching and learning

Table 3.2—Continued

Activities	Outputs
Engagement of Arts and Sciences—Continued	
create induction experiences to match teaching standards and goals	Improved teaching in arts and sciences courses for all students
conduct research on K–12 schools and the processes of teaching and learning.	
Arts and sciences faculty develop understanding of how to improve their own teaching.	
Teaching as an Academically Taught Clinical-Practice Profession	
Teacher education program actively seeks to engage K–12 faculty by	Greater number of K–12 faculty involved in the program through
including K–12 faculty in making programmatic decisions	guiding clinical experiences
creating strong relationships with clinical sites (schools)	teaching courses
	participating in research activities
appointing K–12 teachers as faculty members in teacher education	Increased training provided to clinical supervisors
seeking expert advice from K–12 faculty regarding clinical experiences, pedagogy, and teacher professionalism.	Implementation of a clearly-defined, rigorous, and well-understood system for clinical experiences that includes observation, monitoring, feedback, intervention, and reevaluation
The institution seeks to appoint K–12 faculty as faculty in arts and sciences departments.	Varied clinical experiences for teacher education candidates
The teacher education program	Use of pupils' assessments to measure student learning and as a diagnostic tool for clinical experiences
develops standards for clinical experiences, including a rigorous system of observation, monitoring, feedback, intervention, and reevaluation	Regular feedback provided by K–12 and university faculty during clinical experiences
reviews clinical experiences and makes changes as needed	Implementation of a structured induction program
	Participation of graduates in an induction program
develops relationships with districts and the state to understand induction requirements and programs	Survey of teacher graduates to collect data that could inform induction offerings and program revision
develops induction programs and offers them to new teacher graduates	Feedback loop to revise induction offerings
involves arts and sciences faculty in these programs to offer advice on content	Link to district and state induction requirements and programs
tracks graduates and surveys them to understand what they need in the first two years of teaching	
develops materials and workshops/courses tailored to these needs.	

CHAPTER FOUR

Profiles of the TNE Institutions

As described in Chapter One, Carnegie selected the TNE institutions based on a set of criteria, including the institutions' alignment with the TNE design principles. Table 4.1 provides an overview of the institutions at baseline (i.e., pre-TNE). The table shows that Carnegie purposefully selected a diverse array of institutions in terms of their location, type, mission, and racial-ethnic diversity of the student body. Of the TNE grantees, three are private institutions, one of which, Bank Street, is unique in that it is a stand-alone college of education. The institutions are spread across six regions of the United States.

State teacher education policies mandate the type of degrees that will lead to initial certification, and some states do not allow undergraduate degrees in education. Four of the TNE institutions (BC, Stanford, UVa, and UConn) offer a five-year, integrated bachelor of arts (B.A.)/master of teaching (M.T.) program in which students obtain an undergraduate degree, a master's degree in teaching, and teaching certification.

Only one institution, CSUN, produces a very large number of new teacher graduates per year (approximately 1,550). The number of teacher graduates at the other institutions ranges from 50 to approximately 600 per year.

While all the institutions value diversity, they vary in the actual diversity of the student body, with UTEP and CSUN producing large numbers of Hispanic teachers and FAMU producing large numbers of African-American teachers.

The sections that follow provide brief profiles of the TNE grantee institutions at baseline. While the institutions have several other education degree programs (e.g., Ph.D., M.A. in Education Leadership), we focus on the teacher education programs that lead to initial teaching credentials.

Bank Street College of Education

Bank Street College of Education in New York City is an independent, private institution devoted entirely to improving the education of children and their teachers and administrators. Bank Street comprises three divisions: Children's Programs, which runs the School for Children and the Family Center; the Division of Continuing

Table 4.1
Characteristics of TNE Grantees at Baseline

	Region	Type of Institution	Approximate Annual Number of Teacher Education Graduates	Teacher Education Degree Programs Leading to Initial Certification	Diversity of Student Body
First Cohort of TNE Grantees					
Bank Street College of Education	Northeast	Private, stand-alone college of education	250	Graduate	African-American: 14% Hispanic: 9% Asian: 3%
California State University–Northridge	West	Public university	1,550	Undergraduate; post-baccalaureate	African-American: 2% Hispanic: 25% Asian: 6%
Michigan State University	Midwest	Public university	560	5-year undergraduate; post-baccalaureate	Non-white: 8%
University of Virginia	Southeast	Public university	100	5-year B.A./M.T.; graduate	Non-white: 10%
Second Cohort of TNE Grantees					
Boston College	Northeast	Private college	270	Undergraduate; 5-year B.A./M.T.; graduate	Non-white: 17%
Florida A & M University	Southeast	Public university	175	Undergraduate; graduate; post-baccalaureate	African-American: 78%
Stanford University	West	Private university	50	5-year B.A./M.T.; graduate	African-American: 5% Hispanic: 11% Asian: 27%
University of Connecticut	Northeast	Public university	100	5-year B.A./M.T.; graduate	African-American: 1% Hispanic: 3% Asian: 1%
University of Texas at El Paso	Southwest	Public university	500	Undergraduate; post-baccalaureate	Hispanic: >50%
University of Washington	Northwest	Public university	160	Graduate	Non-white: 20%
University of Wisconsin–Milwaukee	Midwest	Public university	570	Undergraduate; post-baccalaureate	Non-white: 10–12%

Education; and the Graduate School of Education, which is devoted entirely to the professional education of educators. The Graduate School offers master of science (M.S.) and master of science in education (M.S.Ed.) degrees, and it offers initial and continuing New York State teaching and administrative certification through a number of programs that can be completed in as little as 12 to 15 months, although two years to completion is most typical.

All applicants must have completed a bachelor's degree prior to their acceptance into Bank Street. Bank Street generally wants candidates with a minimum grade point average (GPA) of 3.0 out of 4.0, although admissions officers may accept some candidates with lower GPAs who show other evidence of the requisite academic strength. In 2000–2001, 1,022 graduate students were enrolled in courses at Bank Street. Of these, 89 percent were women, 14 percent were black, 9 percent were Latino/Latina, and 3 percent were Asian. Bank Street graduates approximately 250 teachers per year from programs leading to initial certification.

Boston College

BC is a private university that upholds its Jesuit Catholic heritage. The Lynch School of Education (LSOE) at BC offers teacher education programs for both undergraduate and graduate students. It offers B.A., master of education (M.Ed.), master of arts in teaching (M.A.T.), and master of science in teaching (M.S.T.) degrees, all of which lead to an initial teaching license. The Fifth-Year Program allows Boston College undergraduates with arts and sciences majors to earn their bachelor's and master's degrees and teaching certification in five years. Students in the undergraduate program typically earn a second major in a subject discipline in arts and sciences or in an interdisciplinary field, in addition to the major in education. Elementary and early childhood education majors also have the option of having a second LSOE major, such as human development.

Students entering the undergraduate program meet all of BC's general entry requirements. To officially declare a teacher education major, students must have at least a 3.0 out of 4.0 GPA. BC enrolled 500 undergraduate and 300 graduate students in teacher education programs in 2002–2003. Approximately 83 percent of teacher education students were women, 17 percent were minorities, and less than 3 percent were international students. BC graduates approximately 270 teacher education students per year

California State University, Northridge

CSUN is a public university located in Los Angeles's San Fernando Valley and is a member of the California State University System. CSUN offers multiple pathways for obtaining elementary, secondary, and special education teaching credentials, including undergraduate programs offered jointly by the College of Education and arts and sciences colleges (the Integrated Teacher Education Program [ITEP] and the Four-Year

Integrated Teacher Credential Program [FYI]). In addition, it offers three versions of credentialed, post-baccalaureate programs: a traditional program, an internship program, and the Accelerated Collaborative Teacher (ACT) Preparation Program.

Candidates for the ITEP and FYI programs must meet the requirements for entry into CSUN and pass the Entry Level Mathematics Examination and the English Placement Test. Post-baccalaureate candidates must have a grade point average of 2.67 out of 4.0, have passed the California Basic Educational Skills Test (CBEST), and have verified subject-matter competency by completion of an approved college or university subject-matter program or passage of a state-approved subject-matter test. Internship candidates must also be full-time teachers in a self-contained classroom within the CSUN geographical area.

CSUN's teacher education program is quite large and accounts for more than 10 percent of CSUN's overall enrollment. In 2000–2001, CSUN issued 1,554 initial credentials. Approximately half of teacher education graduates were white, 25 percent were Hispanic, 6 percent were Asian, 2 percent were African-America, and 15 percent were classified as Other/Unknown.

Florida A&M University

FAMU is a public university in Tallahassee, Florida, that is also one of the Historically Black Colleges and Universities.[1] Through the teacher education program, FAMU offers the bachelor of science degree, master's degrees, and a post-baccalaureate program for students to complete requirements for certification.

Prospective teachers generally apply to the program at the end of their sophomore year at FAMU or at the end of their second year of community college. Criteria for admission are a GPA of 2.5 out of 4.0 or higher for the general-education component of undergraduate studies or a completed baccalaureate degree with a 2.5 GPA; a FAMU cumulative GPA of 2.5; grades of C or better on all required general-education classes; passing scores on the Florida Teacher Certification Examination (FTCE) General Knowledge Test; passing scores on all four components of the College Level Academic Skills Test (the basic skills test for Florida); a pre-admission interview with the College of Education Admissions Committee; a criminal background check; and satisfaction of all of Florida's "Gordon Rule" requirements, which require basic competency in math, reading, and composition.

---

[1]   The Higher Education Act of 1965, as amended, defines an HBCU as "[A]ny historically black college or university that was established prior to 1964, whose principal mission was, and is, the education of black Americans, and that is accredited by a nationally recognized accrediting agency or association determined by the Secretary [of Education] to be a reliable authority as to the quality of training offered or is, according to such an agency or association, making reasonable progress toward accreditation."

In 2000–2001, 644 students were enrolled in teacher preparation programs at FAMU. Of these, 70 percent of undergraduates and 76 percent of graduate students were women, and 89 percent of undergraduate and 78 percent of graduate students were African-American.

Michigan State University

MSU is a public university in Lansing, Michigan. MSU's primary teacher education program is a five-year route to a bachelor's degree and a Michigan teaching certificate. The Department of Teacher Education also offers an 18-month certification program for post-baccalaureate applicants. Candidates for secondary education credentials complete a major in an academic discipline, while candidates for elementary education credentials may complete an integrated teaching major offered by the College of Education, two teaching minors, or a major in an academic discipline.

Students are admitted to the College of Education in the junior year. All applicants must have a 2.5 out of a 4.0 cumulative GPA and have passed all sections of the Michigan Test of Teacher Certification in Basic Skills. In practice, the limitation on enrollments has led to a marked increase in the mean GPA of admitted students. The college admitted 610 students to the teacher education program in fall 2001. Of these, 8 percent were minorities. At baseline, MSU prepared approximately 550 to 600 teachers a year.

Stanford University

Stanford University in Stanford, California, is a private university. Stanford offers two paths to a teaching credential: a 12-month master's program that culminates in a secondary teaching credential and the master of arts in education, and a fifth-year Coterminal Stanford Teacher Education Program. Graduates of the Coterminal program receive a bachelor's degree in one of Stanford's undergraduate departments, a master's degree in education, and a State of California preliminary teaching credential in either secondary or elementary education. Approval of the student's undergraduate department and of the School of Education is required for admission into the Coterminal program.

Criteria for admission into the graduate program include a bachelor's degree from an accredited college or university with a cumulative GPA of at least 3.0 out of 4.0 and Graduate Record Examinations (GRE) results. The School of Education does not have a cutoff GRE score requirement. The evaluation of each applicant is based on all the materials in the file and is not exclusively based on test scores. From 1999 to 2002, the average GPA of admitted students has been between 3.10 and 3.26, while the average GRE of admitted students has been between 560 and 571 on the verbal section, 613 and 653 on the quantitative section, and 618 and 658 on the analytical section.

At baseline, Stanford graduated approximately 50 teachers per year. Of these, in 2000-01, 5 percent of graduates were African-American, 27 percent were Asian-American/Pacific Islander, 11 percent were Hispanic, 2 percent were Native-American, 45 percent were white, and 10 percent declined to answer.

University of Connecticut

UConn, in Storrs, Connecticut, is a public university. The Neag School of Education offers two programs leading to teaching certification: the Integrated Bachelor's/Master's Program (IB/M) and the Teaching Certification Program for College Graduates (TCPCG).

Students apply for admission to the IB/M teacher education program in the spring of their sophomore year. Admission is limited to 40 students in elementary education, 20 in comprehensive special education, and 15 for each of the subject-area programs, for a total of approximately 130 students in each cohort.

Applicants are required by the state to pass the Praxis I Pre-Professional Skills Test and to have previous experience working with children. The Connecticut Board of Education requires that students entering a teacher education program have at least a B minus average in their undergraduate courses, but most Neag School programs are more competitive than that.

Admission to the TCPCG program leading to the master of arts in education requires submission of an application in the spring of senior year. Candidates are expected to have maintained a 3.0 out of 4.0 cumulative GPA for all four years of undergraduate work. At baseline, UConn graduated a little more than 100 teacher education students per year. Approximately 94 percent of UConn's teacher education students are white. The TCPCG program, though initially quite small, tends to be more diverse. The TCPCG program had grown over time and had enrolled approximately 60 students in summer 2005.

University of Texas at El Paso

UTEP is a public university located near the U.S.-Mexico border. More than 70 percent of the student body is Hispanic; 83 percent come from El Paso County and 9 percent are Mexican nationals. The majority are first-generation college students. The College of Education offers undergraduate and post-baccalaureate teacher education programs leading to initial teacher certification. Undergraduates seeking elementary certification complete a bachelor of interdisciplinary studies (B.I.S.) degree offered in the College of Education. Students who wish to become secondary-school teachers complete a bachelor's degree outside the College of Education. These students major in the subject area they wish to teach and complete a minor in secondary education.

To be admitted to the teacher education program, undergraduates must fulfill the following requirements: complete the required English, communications, and math courses with grades of C or better; provide passing scores on the Texas Higher Education Assessment (THEA) in reading, writing, and mathematics; and complete 60 hours of college work with a cumulative GPA of 2.5 or better. At baseline, the university prepared approximately 500 candidates for initial certification each year. More than half of those teachers were Hispanic.

University of Virginia

UVa is a public university in Charlottesville, Virginia. At UVA, the Curry School of Education and the College of Arts and Sciences offer a five-year integrated Teacher Education Program, the culmination of which leads to both a B.A. and M.T. degree. In addition, the Curry School of Education offers a two-year master's program in which students with a completed bachelor's degree in a non-educational field earn an M.T. degree under the post-graduate (PG)/MT program. The Commonwealth of Virginia mandates a liberal arts degree for all teachers within the state. Hence, all teacher education students must have academic majors in the College of Arts and Sciences, with the exception of health/physical education students, who receive a bachelor of science in education (B.S.Ed.) degree in the undergraduate component of the program.

To be accepted into Curry, students are expected to have a combined SAT or GRE score of 1000 or higher, an overall GPA of 2.7 out of 4.0, and a 3.0 GPA in their major. In practice, most students exceed these standards. Between 1990 and 2001, UVa graduated approximately 100 teachers per year. Approximately 10 percent of those teacher education candidates were non-white.

University of Washington

UW, in Seattle, is a public university. The College of Education offers a master in teaching (M.I.T.) degree, which also leads to initial teaching certification.

Students applying to the M.I.T. program must have a bachelor's degree, a minimum of 60 hours of documented experience (observation and participation) with the age level the student wishes to teach, and a 3.0 GPA. Students must have completed a certain number of credits in three broad areas of knowledge: visual, literary, and performing arts; individuals and societies; and the natural world. To ensure that students wishing to teach elementary school have the breadth of knowledge required for that specialization, they must pass courses in geography, lab science, math, fine arts, literature, history, and child development with a minimum grade of 2.0 out of 4.0.

At baseline, the M.I.T. program admitted about 200 students and graduated about 150 to 170 students per year. Approximately 20 percent of students were non-white.

University of Wisconsin–Milwaukee

UWM is an urban, public university with very close ties to the city of Milwaukee. UWM offers both undergraduate certification majors and post-baccalaureate certification programs.

Students applying to the teacher education programs must have earned a 2.5 cumulative GPA for at least 58 college credits; passed a Pre-Professional Skills Test; and met requirements in English composition, mathematics, and communication proficiency. UWM undergraduates must also complete Education 100, which includes 50 hours of pre-professional field experience. Post-baccalaureate applicants may hold a bachelor's degree in any field from any college or university.

In the academic year 2000–2001, UWM produced 569 teachers, about 175 of whom were in the alternative licensure programs. UWM produces about 500 to 550 teachers a year, accounting for 11 percent of teaching graduates in the entire University of Wisconsin system. Of these, about 10–12 percent are minority students.

We next turn to the changes and activities the institutions have under way as they implement the TNE design principles. The next chapter provides an overview of the grantees' progress in implementing the three major design principles—decisions driven by evidence, engagement of arts and sciences faculty in teacher education, and teaching as an academically taught clinical-practice profession.

CHAPTER FIVE

Implementation Progress and Thoughts About Sustainability of TNE

This chapter provides an overview of our observations and findings on the value that the TNE design principles add to the TNE grantees' teacher education programs and institutional cultures. These findings on the progress of implementation are based on qualitative data from our site visits at the institutions.[1] We also report the institutions' views regarding the sustainability of TNE beyond the life of the grant. A final section presents the TNE funders' thoughts on overall progress, impact, and sustainability of the initiative.

Implementation Progress

Overall, the TNE design principles appeal to and fit well with the teacher education programs at the TNE sites, partly because the sites were chosen for their pre-TNE alignment with these principles and partly because many of these institutions have implemented various versions of these principles in the past as members of other reform networks. At one level, the TNE principles reflect common sense—basing program improvement on evidence, ensuring that teacher candidates get a solid grounding in content knowledge by having arts and sciences faculty deeply involved with the teacher education program, and developing strong relationships with schools and K–12 faculty to ensure that teacher candidates are well-equipped to handle the realities of teaching in a classroom and graduates are provided with support during the early years of teaching. However, as an administrator at one site observed, while seemingly commonsense solutions or ideas are sometimes difficult to implement, these principles nevertheless provide a framework for action.

In this section, we focus on cross-site trends, particularly in the sites' perceptions of the value added by the TNE design principles to the teacher education program and to the broader institutional culture. For each design principle, we first provide some

---

[1] The comments and feedback quoted in this chapter were drawn from on-site interviews conducted from September 2005 to January 2006.

examples of activities undertaken by the sites to demonstrate the range of implementation efforts across the sites, and then we provide a more general discussion of the impact and value added from these efforts. Appendices B through D provide a more detailed picture of how the first and second cohorts of grantees are implementing the major design principles.

We should note that by focusing on the three major design principles, we are not suggesting that the sites are not paying attention to the other TNE principles (listed in Chapter Two under "TNE Design Principles").

Pedagogy is central to all of the sites' teacher education programs, and there have been discussions among administrators and educators at these institutions about what would be the appropriate programs of instruction for elementary school and middle school teachers. In addition, several sites are focusing on issues specific to teachers in lower-income urban areas by incorporating sensitivity of cultural considerations into teaching and recruiting underrepresented groups into teaching programs.

To describe the many activities the sites are undertaking in their reform efforts would be overwhelming; hence, we focus on the activities related to the three major TNE design principles. (Appendix A lists Web sites for further information on each site's TNE program.)

Decisions Driven by Evidence

Examples of the Sites' Activities. The following list of activities provides some examples of what the TNE sites are doing to implement the first TNE design principle—that a teacher education program should be guided by a respect for evidence. Not all sites are conducting these activities.

- Gathering qualitative and quantitative data on small samples of selected teachers (experienced, novice, and/or student teachers) and pupils to understand differences in teaching styles and teaching abilities and their impact on students' work
- Analyzing pupil-learning gains on state assessments (i.e., gains on test scores) in small pilot studies to test the feasibility of doing such analyses on a larger scale
- Analyzing pupil-learning gains on assessments being administered as part of other studies
- Analyzing the performance of teacher candidates on state-mandated tests for licensing
- Developing partnerships with other institutions of higher education to collect and analyze data
- Systematically designing data warehouses for collection and maintenance of longitudinal, comprehensive data on students as they proceed through the program (the data warehouses might include selected pieces of students' work or videos of student teachers in the classroom)

- Developing a conceptual framework and specifying data needed to establish the connections among teacher education, teaching practice, and pupil achievement
- Using mini-grant programs to fund research on TNE design principles
- Conducting small experiments with course curricula and studying their effects through pre- and post-assessments to provide data to inform program improvement
- Establishing a TNE Research Advisory Council and/or establishing TNE Assessment Teams consisting of both arts and sciences and education faculty to oversee and disseminate TNE research
- Mandating the participation of all new teacher candidates in research activities related to teacher education
- Developing and administering surveys (typically online) of faculty, students, and new teacher graduates
- Using evidence to change teacher education courses, create new courses, or change the way student-teaching placements are done
- Creating classroom-observation and data-collection protocols and assessing their validity
- Hiring faculty or staff with expertise in measurement, testing, and value-added modeling
- Hiring a database manager for maintaining and updating the data warehouse.

Overall Impact. All the institutions reported that participating in TNE has led to the development of a "culture of evidence," wherein faculty across the institution as a whole and, most importantly, in teacher education, are paying attention to the need for evidence as a basis for making decisions. The sites credit TNE with three major contributions:

First, TNE has brought a new emphasis on collecting multiple measures of program effectiveness that are valid and reliable, including pupil-learning gains made under the tutelage of program graduates, and using this evidence for program improvement. This new emphasis fits well within the current political and policy context of teacher education, and evidence on effectiveness of their programs will provide sites with ammunition to answer the teacher education critics.

In the same vein, accreditation bodies are increasingly requiring programs and institutions to develop and implement quality-improvement plans and learning objectives and to provide credible evidence of the value added to student learning and subsequent workforce outcomes. For example, the TEAC application asks institutions to identify their "philosophy" of teacher education, on what they base the philosophy, how they measure the effectiveness of their program, and how they use the information to improve the program. While sites might have conducted similar studies for accreditation purposes, they would not have considered extending such studies to include an examination of pupil-learning gains, as required by TNE.

TNE also has brought a greater awareness of and interest in using data to improve teacher education, along with more capacity to collect and analyze data that might be relevant for program improvement. The sites were already moving in the direction of using multiple measures and determining how best to gather data for improvement of their teacher education program or university accreditation processes, but TNE has helped to move them farther and faster in this direction. While there is some doubt as to whether the sites can carry out value-added modeling of the kind envisioned by TNE and use the results for program improvement, some site administrators believe that the effort to think about whether and how such data could be obtained is worth the investment of time. One site administrator noted the following during the site interview:

> One can quibble about the notion that such evidence can be obtained, but the effort to think about whether and how such data can be obtained is worth the investment of time. If it works, this would be a powerful way to drive change in the program and in the curriculum rather than the anecdotal data often used.

Hand in hand with the need for multiple measures is a deeper understanding of the validity and reliability of both the measures and the evidence they collect on the program, teacher candidates, and teacher graduates. Overall, the emphasis on evidence has forced the sites to look at candidate assessment and pupil assessment with a more careful eye. One site has made it mandatory that faculty members provide evidence of effectiveness when seeking changes or additions to the curriculum.

Second, TNE has resulted in a cultural shift across the institutions as a whole—a new emphasis on evidence and assessment is permeating all departments, not just the education program. Teacher education and arts and sciences faculty are now talking about the types of assessments being done, what they actually measure, and the reliability of those assessments. Such discussions are helping faculty to focus their efforts and resources on what they need to know and what measures they need to collect. Administrators at some sites admit that it is difficult to get faculty in general to accept that certain subjects or courses are not being taught well, but they are more likely to be convinced that change is needed when presented with evidence. As one TNE administrator remarked, TNE "has changed the discourse on campus and, in many instances, the practice."

Third, TNE has introduced a realization of the need to develop and implement integrated data systems capable of housing linked data elements, tracking students' progress over time, and being updated and expanded on a regular basis as new data are collected or new data-collection efforts are undertaken. In fact, a number of TNE institutions consider the development of high-quality databases as key to the program-improvement process and are constructing centralized databases (or investigating the possibility of doing so) that will allow them to track the progress of education students over time without having to examine several disparate and often inconsistent data sources. While the sites are beginning to realize the need to collect data for account-ability and accreditation reports, TNE led them to recognize that an infrastructure is needed to handle data and data requests and to move ahead with building this infra-structure. As one TNE administrator reported in this respect, "We are farther ahead than we would have been."

The TNE sites are also aware that using learning gains indicated by standardized test scores to obtain valid evidence of the value added by a program is a complex under-taking. First, due to limitations in state and district data systems and privacy regula-tions, many sites struggle to obtain K–12 student data linked to teachers. Second, even if such linked data were available, it is unclear how those data could and should be used to inform teacher education program improvement. The day that teacher candidates leave the university and enter the teaching profession, they are subject to many other influences—i.e., their district, school, and colleagues. These influences make it diffi-cult to link teacher behaviors and practices to what was learned in teacher preparation programs.

Another site administrator, in discussing the modeling and statistical issues asso-ciated with value-added modeling, said,

> It is necessary to look at the full set of influences on teachers, and it will be diffi-cult to assign attribution. Getting the quantitative data is one thing, but when you think of the qualitative pieces, it is even more complicated. It is an ongoing process forever to find out true value-added dimensions.

Third, the small sample sizes at some sites would not allow the sites to make infer-ences with any degree of confidence. Fourth, test scores offer a narrow view of the real learning that might be taking place. For example, non-cognitive outcomes are com-pletely ignored in such analyses. Fifth, the high rate of student mobility in inner-city schools makes it difficult to get enough data to link teachers to student outcomes over time.

Engagement of Arts and Sciences Faculty in Teacher Education

Although there is not much direct research on the subject, many believe that arts and sciences faculty can help to improve teachers' content knowledge. In evaluating what the sites are doing with respect to implementing this principle, it is important to con-sider the pre-TNE context and the type of teacher education program. For example, Bank Street is a stand-alone graduate institution and, as such, must go outside the institution to collaborate with arts and sciences faculty. Like other institutions that offer graduate teacher education programs, Bank Street has to rely on the quality of undergraduate training at other institutions to ensure that their students have adequate content knowledge. In other institutions, some degree of collaboration already existed between education faculty and arts and sciences faculty, so this principle was not new to these institutions. At some universities, teacher education was already considered to be an all-university responsibility; at other institutions, some collaboration already existed, but it tended to involve only certain departments and/or selected faculty with an interest in teacher education. At other universities, such as Stanford and Michigan State, a number of faculty members have joint appointments in the education department and arts and sciences departments.

We find evidence of arts and sciences department involvement in all aspects of TNE across the institutions. All the TNE institutions, with the exception of Bank Street (a stand-alone college of education), include arts and sciences faculty on the TNE leadership teams and have involvement in TNE from the arts and sciences deans and the provost's office. In many cases, the TNE project manager is from an arts and sciences department.

Examples of the Sites' Activities. The following list of activities provides some examples of what the TNE sites are doing to implement the second TNE design principle—faculty in the arts and sciences must be fully engaged in the education of prospective teachers. Not all sites are conducting these activities.

- Hiring new tenure-track TNE faculty in arts and sciences departments who divide their time among TNE, teaching, and other departmental duties (at some sites, these TNE faculty are required to have extensive experience and interest in preparing teachers and in K–12 education)
- Appointing arts and sciences faculty as TNE fellows to co-teach courses with education faculty members, to serve as liaisons with their home departments, and to work on assessment projects
- Appointing arts and sciences faculty to serve as liaisons at clinical sites, work with K–12 students and teach faculty on-site, recruit arts and sciences mentors, and provide training for mentors
- Forming discussion groups that focus on subject matter and pedagogical content knowledge in several arts and sciences disciplines
- Establishing collaborations between education and arts and sciences departments to
  - develop teacher-knowledge standards
  - examine program coursework to see how well it aligns with knowledge standards
  - redesign programs or courses as needed (for example, statistics, biology, and a course on urban education issues)
  - review general and liberal-education courses taken by teacher candidates and use data on mandated entry examinations to identify gaps in course content or candidates' knowledge
  - develop new courses or lab sections to encourage interest in teaching and/or to model ways to best teach content

- team-teach workshops and courses
- improve advising of teacher candidates.

- Establishing "articulation agreements" (on course content and course goals) with community colleges to improve the rigor of the community colleges' general education courses
- Developing arts and sciences partnerships with outside institutions to provide content-area expertise for teams focusing on the assessment, evidence, and induction pieces of TNE and to develop science content courses for teacher candidates (e.g., an important indicator of the cultural shift at Bank Street is that the Bank Street Curriculum Committee has asked that a representative from arts and sciences sit on the committee)
- Actively involving deans and provosts in TNE leadership activities.

Overall Impact. TNE funds have enabled new and increased arts and sciences participation in teacher education. While arts and sciences participation is strongest in departments with historical ties to teacher education, individuals at the TNE sites report that arts and sciences involvement in teacher education under TNE is broader and stronger than it was before TNE. TNE leaders at most of the sites noted that the initiative is introducing cultural change among both education and arts and sciences faculty. They cited several examples of this change.

First, working together on a common project has led to education and arts and sciences faculty having a greater understanding and respect for each other. Faculty at these sites talked about developing "a common language" and "seeing through new lenses."

Second, education faculty members increasingly are seeking out colleagues to collaborate on and to discuss issues surrounding content knowledge of K–12 teachers. It is also important to mention that, at some sites, teacher education faculty initially were resistant to arts and sciences faculty being involved in the teacher education program. Some faculty members believed that they were already doing a good job preparing teachers, and, in fact, that was one reason why their institution was chosen to be a TNE grantee. Since then, we were told that much of this resistance has been overcome.

Third, the TNE initiative has changed the outlook of many arts and sciences faculty members as well as education faculty members. Arts and sciences faculty now are more aware of how they can contribute to the preparation of teachers. At some sites, arts and sciences faculty are now involved in teacher education program planning and evaluation, joint development of teaching and knowledge standards, improved joint advising, team-teaching courses, on-site activities at K–12 schools, and developing courses or sections aimed at future teachers, among other work. This is not to suggest that many of these activities were not occurring pre-TNE, but the sites report that this sort of involvement in teacher education is now more systematic, and there is a greater recognition of the need for collaboration. Both arts and sciences and teacher education faculty see these developments as a plus. Further, the arts and sciences participants understand more about teaching itself and are making further efforts to improve their own teaching. This is evidenced by the curricular experiments taking place at some sites whose biology and mathematics faculty have become interested in the impact of various methods of teaching and various curriculum materials on education students' understanding of content.

At some sites, the emphasis on involving arts and sciences faculty has resulted in TNE efforts being concentrated primarily on the curriculum for secondary-school teacher candidates. Arts and sciences faculty often find it easier to think about what teachers need to know about a certain discipline (e.g., biology) to teach secondary school students than what teachers need to know (e.g., about science in general) to teach elementary school students.

At the leadership level, many deans are actively fostering collaborative relationships among their various colleges. At several sites, teacher education is becoming more visible across campus and increasingly is being given administrative priority, with greater emphasis on interdisciplinary hires and joint appointments with other departments, cross-college programs within universities, and facilitation of grant applications that involve both education and arts and sciences faculty.

Some sites have hired new arts and sciences faculty with ties to teacher education. These faculty are placed in departments in their discipline but, by contract, are required to spend some amount of time working on teacher education issues and/or acting as a liaison between their departments and the teacher education programs. Some of these faculty members are on joint appointments. These positions, often funded wholly or partially through TNE, are intended to be permanent. One TNE leader observed that as senior faculty are replaced by newer faculty with a different mind-set, these collaborative activities will become the norm. However, we heard concerns voiced at some sites that these new faculty members are not fully accepted by their peers within arts and sciences.

A concern expressed by junior faculty working on TNE is that, given the responsibilities of TNE, they may not have sufficient time to meet their requirements for scholarship and publishing and, as such, may be disadvantaged when it comes time for promotion and tenure decisions. Some deans also expressed these concerns. When these issues are raised, the TNE leadership teams have had several responses. One is to provide ample assurance that research and publications on education issues will count toward promotion and tenure—assurances that do not completely assuage junior faculty members' concerns. The sites' TNE leadership teams also point to new and exciting possibilities for joint research that exist in K–12 schools that might have a good chance of being funded (the National Science Foundation, for example, requires its grantees to show evidence of how their results are disseminated and how they are used to improve K–12 teaching and learning). Some arts and sciences faculty members have been creative about making their own research opportunities by adding research to the TNE activities. Finally, the TNE leadership teams sometimes simply acknowledges that junior arts and sciences faculty need to be less involved in TNE, due to the amount of time that TNE consumes, and they will have those individuals work for only short periods on TNE activities or have senior faculty involved in the TNE work instead.

Teaching as an Academically Taught Clinical-Practice Profession

This principle encompasses both increased involvement of K–12 faculty (e.g., by appointing K–12 faculty as teachers in residence (TIRs), having K–12 faculty work on teams addressing TNE issues, developing clinical sites) and development and implementation of a "residency" program for all new teacher graduates involving both education and arts and sciences faculty, which would track teacher graduates and provide a variety of supports during the first two years of teaching.

Examples of the Sites' Activities. The following list of activities provides some examples of what the TNE sites are doing to implement the third TNE design principle—teaching should be recognized as an academically taught clinical-practice profession. Not all sites are conducting these activities.

Increased K–12 Faculty Involvement

- Hiring teachers in residence in both education and arts and sciences departments whose duties include teaching or team-teaching, coordinating induction activities, supervising student teachers, and interacting with faculty
- Inviting K–12 faculty to participate in TNE teams
- Analyzing data on placements and mentors to improve students' clinical experiences
- Establishing criteria for formal partnerships with clinical sites to ensure that both parties benefit from the arrangement; critically examining current partnerships with schools
- Establishing clinical sites in partnership with districts that meet the criteria for professional development schools and where learning environments can be created that encompass students, teachers, parents, and university faculty
- Hiring a person to serve as a liaison between the university and K–12 schools
- Partnering with local urban districts to recruit minority students to teacher education and to provide more-varied clinical settings for teacher candidates.

Induction

- Collecting data from graduates to better understand what they need in the first few years of teaching
- Developing Web sites for resource materials, helpful tips, and distance-learning opportunities for mentors, those who are being mentored, and new teachers

- Appointing a full-time director of induction (sometimes jointly with the district) to coordinate and oversee the induction program
- Developing curricula for mentor-training programs
- Developing summer institutes focusing on various topics of interest to new educators (e.g., multicultural issues, survival skills, community engagement)
- Developing an alumni-matching program that matches graduates to alumni
- Developing new fifth-year programs in conjunction with school districts and the teachers' union to meet state induction requirements
- Developing pilot induction programs and collecting data on the impact of various levels of support, various formats (online, on-site, summer programs), and various providers (mentors with differing levels of training, arts and sciences faculty, education faculty)
- Offering induction support to all new teachers in participating schools and districts and ensuring that new teachers receive credit for their participation in the support activities.

Overall Impact—Increased K–12 Faculty Involvement. While all the TNE institutions recognize the importance of strong relationships with K–12 schools, and some are developing professional development schools at clinical sites, the institutions have not been uniformly successful in implementing this principle to the degree that TNE envisaged. Most of the TNE sites have some K–12 representation on their work teams, but the degree to which those K–12 representatives are involved in TNE varies considerably by site and across teams.

At some of the institutions, prior to TNE, there was a close and trusting relationship between university faculty and K–12 faculty. The TNE funding and activities have deepened those existing partnerships and have created additional common goals. At other sites, K–12 faculty members were not clear on why they were involved in TNE and were not always in attendance at meetings of the TNE teams. Issues with logistics and incentives were cited as reasons for lack of attendance; some questioned what the payoff was for either K–12 participants or for teacher education programs. However, what the actual impact is of the involvement of K–12 faculty on the redesign of teacher education curricula or coursework at the TNE institutions is uncertain.

In hiring TIRs, some sites have been successful, while others have not, for a variety of reasons. A structural problem that some universities encountered is that many experienced teachers are paid considerably more than assistant professors; as a result, attempting to get those teachers on the university payroll became a difficult task fraught with questions of pay inequity. Teachers were unwilling to join a site's faculty in some instances unless they were given assurances that they could return to their school district with no loss to their retirement contributions or seniority for the time spent on a TNE site's faculty. Further, some districts were reluctant to lose their best and most experienced teachers from the classroom. In some cases of TIRs being hired, the hires were not entirely successful, because neither side was clear on what the role of the TIR should be, how best to use his or her skills and abilities, and how to ensure that the institution's faculty regarded the TIR as a peer, which resulted in unmet expectations on both sides.

Site administrators reported that the clinical-site piece of TNE is difficult to implement because it requires time and resources, and it is hard to judge its eventual overall usefulness to the program. As the experience of the Holmes Group has shown (Fullan et al., 1998), it is difficult to establish and maintain productive and mutually beneficial relationships between universities and K–12 schools, and, after the relationship is established, it requires careful tending. The TNE institutions that have tried to establish clinical sites agree that the clinical site element of TNE is useful in that it provides a model laboratory to distill best practices and it enhances conversations among TNE partners. But these institutions also believe that the usefulness of clinical sites is limited, because finding the money to support a wider number of sites and scale up the program is especially challenging. With respect to the usefulness of the clinical site component of TNE, one site administrator remarked, "The jury is still out" on it.

Nevertheless, the TNE initiative has forced the sites to think more broadly about student teaching and about their relationship with K–12 schools, teacher mentors, and student teachers. Further, many institutions are considering or have made changes to student placements for clinical experiences and the training provided to the K–12 teachers who supervise the student teachers.

Overall Impact—Induction. The induction element of TNE—hailed as one of the most innovative components of the initiative—has proven to be the most difficult to implement in practice. Originally, TNE envisaged the induction component as a two-year program that would provide support to every new teacher graduate and would involve both teacher education faculty and arts and sciences faculty.

The induction concept was new to the sites, and they struggled with it at first in attempting to define their specific role in the endeavor and to find activities that they could actually implement and sustain. Some sites have moved ahead with developing Web sites for new teachers and mentors, which provide a variety of online help; setting up small model induction programs in cooperating districts; and institutionalizing the initiative by creating master's degree programs linked to induction.

Individuals interviewed at some sites believe that induction will become a permanent component of their TNE programs and that it is a natural extension of their current teacher education program. Some of the institutions credit the induction component of TNE with, as one site administrator said, "extending our focus and making us realize the full extent of our responsibilities." Individuals at other sites said that their institutions are not staffed to provide such support and continue to grapple with this element of the TNE design. Almost all interviewees at the sites agreed that involving arts and sciences faculty in direct induction activities—or in supervision of student teaching—is a real challenge. Some sites have addressed this challenge by having arts and sciences faculty provide summer courses—something that many of them were doing as part of their professional development activities for regular teachers.

The sites have faced other significant challenges in implementing this part of the TNE design. First, all of the TNE grantees' states and some of their local school districts have mandated induction programs, and some states and districts provide funding for such programs. As a result, the sites have tried to define a role for themselves in induction that would provide value over and above what states and districts are providing and that would be useful to graduates or new teachers. The issue of demand for such support and whether new teachers would be willing to pay for it if the state or district does not fund it is a matter of serious concern for the sites and has a direct impact on their ability to sustain the induction program. Often, state or district induction programs are provided for free, offered on-site, and required for permanent licensure. Induction programs and assistance offered by universities are often in addition to state or district programs, are offered over a longer period of time, are conducted at the universities, and tend to be relatively expensive. As such, graduates may view such university-based support as an unattractive option.

Second, in some instances, induction programs or courses designed by the sites have not been endorsed by the state and, therefore, do not count toward credit for continuing education or for permanent licensure, making the induction component of TNE a hard sell.

Third, the first two years of a teacher's career may not be the best time to offer additional content learning opportunities. New teachers are already overwhelmed coping with the realities of managing a classroom and the demands of teaching and may have little spare time to take on additional activities, even if those activities are interesting and helpful. Thus, getting new graduates to participate in induction is a challenge. This raises the question of whether it makes sense to target programs to new teachers in the first two years of teaching or target them to teachers when they are more likely to participate in them.

Fourth, scaling up is very expensive, particularly for sites producing large numbers of teacher graduates and/or that have graduates who are spread across a number of districts or states, many of whom fail to provide contact information or to keep in touch with their alma maters. One way of tracking such graduates is through longitudinal teacher files maintained by the state, but this requires that the state is willing and able to share and provide data on a timely basis. This idea, of course, does not get around the problem of students being scattered across a number of states.

Those institutions whose induction programs are offered successfully have worked closely with their local school districts to cater to the districts' needs and to provide support for all new teachers in a district, not just the institutions' graduates.

Sustainability: The TNE Sites' Perspective

The preceding section pointed to a number of changes in both the structure of teacher education programs and institutional cultures that have occurred at or are being contemplated by the TNE sites. In this section, we present the TNE leadership teams' feedback on the sustainability of TNE principles and TNE activities beyond the life of the grant.

In many ways, the TNE principles embody doctrines already practiced to a greater or lesser degree by the sites and that are reinforced by the current political and social climate surrounding teacher education. Some institutions have leveraged their status as a TNE grantee to raise matching funds for activities designed to complement or reinforce TNE. As such, interviewees reported that many of the programmatic and cultural changes (such as those discussed previously) that are being driven by the three major TNE design principles are likely to become institutionalized over time.

First, accreditation requirements and the recent push from policymakers, parents, and students for accountability are forcing all institutions to build databases on students, collect evidence of students' learning, and track students to gather outcome data farther "downstream" from a student's graduation to prove the effectiveness of teacher education. Individuals at two of the TNE sites noted that one of the most valuable contributions of TNE was the development of a database that could be used to track student and course performance. The interviewees were less clear on whether the value-added modeling of the kind envisaged by TNE will continue to be carried out beyond the life of the grant and whether it will be successful in validating the effectiveness of the teacher preparation programs at the TNE sites. Small sample sizes and lack of access to longitudinally linked data are likely to continue to be problems for many sites. Further, sites are unclear on whether such analyses could be used to inform program change. Nevertheless, the discipline of gathering and using evidence to inform program change will persist, said a number of TNE participants.

Second, the current emphasis on accountability and evidence-based programs will require arts and sciences faculty to become more involved in ensuring that students get a good undergraduate liberal education. Thus, the discussions and partnerships between education and arts and sciences faculty—particularly faculty in departments that historically have had a connection to teacher education—are likely to continue and to deepen. The mind-set that results from individuals working together on TNE may well prove to be lasting and pervade the entire institution. In those institutions where large numbers of teachers are produced, arts and sciences faculty have become more aware that the majority of their students are future teachers. Some activities introduced with TNE (e.g., small groups studying pedagogical content knowledge, lab sections aimed at potential teachers, new survey courses, TNE teams) may or may not continue at some of the TNE sites, but most TNE leaders felt that the reform had achieved a momentum that would be difficult to reverse. TNE leaders at some institutions said that they will continue to hire interdisciplinary faculty, and some faculty will continue to apply for joint research grants, while others will continue to pursue their interest in assessment and pedagogy. Where new TNE faculty have been hired, and as they become more numerous and more accepted over time, they will help to sustain a culture in which arts and sciences faculty are involved to some extent in teacher education.

Third, if the TNE induction programs can work with the states and school districts to provide or to extend the induction offerings in ways that the state is willing to endorse and that the states and districts can financially support, induction programs and support systems for graduates being designed now are likely to endure. For example, most sites are developing Web sites that will continue to be sources of support for both their own graduates and for teachers from other institutions. The TNE prospectus (Carnegie Corporation of New York, n.d.) recognizes state policy as an important factor affecting all teacher education institutions, and Carnegie has made explicit attempts through CPRE to inform and influence state policy with respect to access to data on student test scores and teacher education program and certification requirements.

The sites are being cautious in their TNE designs—testing the waters to see what new teachers need, building relationships with school districts, and seeing where they can be a good fit with state- or district-mandated programs that are offered for free. They are very aware of needing to make these programs self-sustaining.

However, whether the two-year residency programs as envisaged in the TNE prospectus—offering support and coursework for all new teacher graduates and involving both education and arts and sciences faculty—will come to fruition remains to be seen.

Progress and Sustainability: The Funders' Perspective

We also interviewed two representatives of the TNE funders in May 2006. This section summarizes their views on the progress of the TNE initiative and its sustainability.

When asked about the overall progress of TNE implementation, the funder representatives reported being encouraged by the depth of commitment to and interest in TNE at each of the institutions and noted some promising indicators across the sites. They acknowledged that the challenges presented by the TNE initiative are profound and that the outcomes of many of the changes now being implemented at the TNE sites may not become apparent for another decade or two.

The funders noted that what makes this reform initiative so difficult to implement is that TNE calls for radical change, and the way the initiative was structured makes change possible but extremely difficult. The teacher education programs selected for TNE were already good ones, and having to change in prescribed ways was difficult for those in the programs. As the funder representatives explained, the TNE grant is not a reward for good practice but rather a challenge to teacher education programs to see how they can improve and lead the nation to a new understanding of teacher education.

The funder representatives noted that the decision to place the TNE grant in the provost's office at each site rather than in the school of education was a good one—it engaged the institutions' leaders in teacher education in new ways and forced the heads of the institutions to look closely at how they were monitoring and assessing their teacher education programs. The funded institutions have created new offices for leading and overseeing TNE, and these offices and positions are likely to continue. According to one funder representative, the sites seem to find the TNE framework "powerful and appealing," and they are implementing it in ways that are appropriate to the culture and mission of their institutions. The general strategy of limiting excuses for failure to implement the reform initiatives by supplying generous grants has worked well, and requiring institutions to raise endowment funds as part of the matching funds requirement should help with sustainability (some of the $5 million TNE funding to be matched by the sites must go into endowments).

Promising Indicators

- The funder representatives observed that all the sites are paying much more attention to evidence as a basis for change, but they reported that it was disconcerting to see how little the institutions were doing in the way of collecting and analyzing data on students and graduates and using those data for program improvement prior to TNE. Now the sites are building databases to track students' progress and carrying out pilot projects to measure student learning under various scenarios. The funders further observed that institutions are struggling with the value-added aspect of the first TNE design principle—that a teacher education program should be guided by evidence of the program's effectiveness—but have accepted responsibility for collecting and analyzing data on their teacher graduates on an ongoing basis.
- The effect of TNE on the arts and sciences faculty has been extraordinarily strong, even in institutions where there had been little collaboration between the college of arts and sciences and college of education and where expectations for success were low. In some of these institutions, new forms of collaboration and curriculum design developed because of the strong backing of new leadership for whom TNE was part of a larger agenda of reform for the institution. A significant number of arts and sciences faculty members at the TNE sites are willing and eager to be involved in TNE, either due to an interest in improving K–12 schools or from a desire to improve the quality of college entrants. Because of

TNE, funders observed, arts and sciences faculty have a greater understanding of pedagogy, and teacher education faculty have a greater understanding of the importance of rigorous content knowledge for teachers.

- The funders reported that the focus on induction and other components of TNE associated with clinical practice was generating a great deal of enthusiasm and energy. How to measure and document effective clinical practice remains a puzzling challenge, leading many sites to undertake valuable research on the validity of the instruments they were currently using to assess student teaching. The funders cited work being done by TEAC that showed zero correlation between teacher-performance ratings based on observations of practice and any given measure of academic performance or preservice course performance. TNE research could help to clarify contradictory findings such as these.

- The TNE institutions' work with induction programs has made them focus on the clinical practice component of their programs and the professional growth of their teacher candidates. Some institutions have discovered that they cannot offer an academically based induction program exclusively for their own graduates but need to provide for other new teachers in a school or district when requested to do so by the school or district.

Sustainability

The funders cited several challenges to sustainability of TNE. First, institutions need to revisit promotion and tenure criteria if they want junior arts and sciences faculty to remain involved in teacher education. Second, changes in institutional leadership may become a threat to an institution's capacity to remain focused on teacher education. Some university or college heads may not be willing to expend the "political capital" they have with faculty or boards of trustees to keep TNE a high priority for the institution. This potential problem has not emerged thus far. In fact, TNE has remained a high priority for the grantee sites despite several changes in the institutions' leadership. Third, the sites need to acquire financial support to continue the TNE activities. Fourth, going to scale with induction programs will prove to be especially challenging for institutions with large numbers of students or widely dispersed graduates.

Despite these concerns, the funders are of the belief that TNE is likely to endure and that TNE has raised the level of awareness of teacher education at each of these institutions. They recognize that institutional inertia is difficult to overcome but are nevertheless seeing positive signs of institutional change. In fact, the funders are considering a second phase of the initiative. If an additional phase of TNE is conducted, it would likely be more modest in scale than the current effort and would focus on increasing the knowledge base for teacher education and strengthening the capacity of teacher education faculty to conduct research on the three TNE design principles.

The funders recognize the vital role of state policy in disseminating the lessons learned through TNE. In 2004, the funders contracted with CPRE to host informational sessions for policymakers, which have been well attended. The expectation is that regulatory policy will change to be more supportive to teacher education reform if the TNE initiative can demonstrate that particular interventions ave beneficial consequences. Thus, evidence is seen as the lever for making policy changes. Evidence will also convince other institutions to follow the example set by the TNE sites in reforming teacher education.

To spread the word on TNE, the TNE funders have been a visible presence at the major professional education conferences, extolling the virtues of TNE, and have established the TNE Learning Network (discussed in Chapter Three) encompassing 30 institutions that will receive small grants to conduct TNE-like projects and to meet occasionally to share ideas. The funders noted that some ucation programs that are part of large university systems have been successful in interesting sister campuses in TNE. The TNE institutions vary with respect to the selectivity and capabilities of students and faculty, so the lessons learned from TNE should generalize to a wide variety of institutions.

CHAPTER SIX

Conclusions

In 2001, Carnegie Corporation of New York launched an ambitious education initiative, Teachers for a New Era, to radically reform teacher education in a handful of selected institutions. Eleven colleges and universities were selected to participate in the initiative. They represent a wide variety of institutions—ranging from large, research universities to a private, stand-alone graduate school of education—that produce the nation's school teachers. The institutions also differ considerably in the number of teacher graduates they produce each year (from 50 to more than 1,500), and they are located across the United States.

The TNE prospectus (Carnegie Corporation of New York, n.d) stated that exemplary teacher education programs are characterized by three major design principles:

- Decisions driven by evidence
- Engagement of arts and sciences faculty in the teacher education program
- Teaching as an academically taught clinical-practice profession requiring increased involvement of K–12 faculty and a two-year residency period in which all new teacher graduates would be provided support and mentoring.

The TNE grantees were provided with a substantial amount of money ($5 million over five years and a requirement for matching funds from the institutions themselves) and external technical assistance in order to align their teacher education programs with the TNE design principles. The TNE grantees were also asked to address other important issues, such as the quality of the general and liberal education that teacher candidates receive, recruitment of underrepresented groups into teacher education, and cultural considerations.

As of September 2005, four institutions had been implementing TNE for three years, and six institutions had been implementing TNE for two years. One institution (FAMU), due to leadership changes, received full approval for the program in spring 2005. In this monograph, we reported on the progress made by these sites in implementing the three major design principles and TNE participants' impressions about the contributions of TNE to the institutions in general and to their teacher education programs in particular. Our findings are based primarily on self-reports from various individuals at the sites during annual two-day site visits.

The Likely Legacy of TNE

Almost a decade ago, Fullan et al. (1998, p. 68) wrote, "Never before has teacher education experienced such a massive outpouring of political and fiscal action." The authors outlined what it would take to reform teacher education:

1. A stronger knowledge base for teaching and teacher education
2. Attracting able, diverse, and committed students to the career of teaching
3. Redesigning teacher preparation programs so that the linkages to arts and sciences, and to the field of practice, are both strengthened
4. Reform in the working conditions of schools
5. The development and monitoring of external standards for programs as well as for teacher candidates and teachers on the job
6. A rigorous and dynamic research enterprise focusing on teaching, teacher education, and on the assessment and monitoring of strategies (Fullan et al., 1998, p. 58).

Over the past decade, an "alphabet soup" of organizations and reformers and reform networks has attempted to promote the same agenda and to radically reform teacher education. TNE is the latest of these reform efforts—albeit perhaps the most ambitious and best funded—that subscribes to the requirements articulated by Fullan et al. We found that the structure and principles of TNE borrow heavily from previous or current reform efforts, all of which have emphasized a culture of evidence-based decisionmaking, engagement of arts and sciences faculty in teacher education, and greater involvement of K–12 faculty (through clinical sites, mentoring, and other work) in teacher education programs.

Of the requirements listed by Fullan et al. (1998), TNE strongly emphasizes the links between teacher education programs and arts and sciences and K–12 faculty, encourages the development of teaching standards and program standards, emphasizes assessment as a basis for continuous improvement, and makes teacher education a priority at the TNE sites. With respect to the second requirement, many of these institutions already attract able students, and some are attempting to attract students from more-diverse backgrounds. The underlying hope is that transformation of the teacher education programs at these sites will attract more-able and more-diverse students. There is little evidence that the research base on teacher education and teaching effectiveness is considerably stronger as a result of research undertaken by the TNE sites; in any event, building a richer research base may take some time. As part of the TNE initiative, the institutions are to develop clinical sites that could act as laboratories for research on teaching and learning, but going to scale is difficult and expensive. Thus, the simultaneous "renewal" of schools and universities is not likely to occur in other than a handful of cases.

We turned to an earlier RAND framework (from Kirby et al., 2004) to sketch out the actual and likely potential outcomes of TNE. In Chapter Three, we noted that there are several different categories of outcomes and impacts—in-program outcomes, intermediate outcomes, and final outcomes—that might result from TNE. None of the intermediate or final outcomes can be measured in the early years of the reform effort, but we can offer some thoughts on the likelihood of these outcomes being achieved by TNE.

In-Program Outcomes

In-program outcomes are those affecting various stakeholders during and because of their direct participation in the TNE program. As outlined in Chapter Three, we saw a number of these in-program outcomes across the sites. We group these outcomes under the three major TNE program design principles.

Decisions Driven by Evidence. Institutions report that participating in TNE has led to their developing a culture of evidence-based decisionmaking across the institution as a whole and, more specifically, in teacher education. Faculty members are developing measures of student learning and the sort of data needed for program improvement. There is a new understanding of the reliability and validity of assessments and the need for multiple measures. One of the most important contributions of TNE is the impetus it has provided for the sites to build integrated, comprehensive databases that will allow them to examine the progress of their teacher candidates (and presumably also other students) over time. Many institutions have launched a number of small research projects aimed at collecting evidence on student learning in college courses.

The one area in which institutions face a real challenge is in collecting pupil-assessment data to assess the value added by their teacher graduates, as required by TNE. The challenge stems from privacy concerns and a lack of longitudinally linked teacher-pupil data. Even when such data are available, many of the sites are not optimistic about being able to use the pupil-assessment data to measure teacher effectiveness and/or to inform program improvement.

Engagement of Arts and Sciences Faculty in Teacher Education. While participation of arts and sciences faculty is strongest in departments with historical ties to teacher education, the sites report an overall deepening of these relationships and new participation from other arts and sciences departments. Faculty noted that working together on a common project has led education and arts and sciences faculty to have a greater understanding of each other's motivations and goals and greater respect for one another, and recognition by arts and sciences faculty that many of their students are future teachers. Across the TNE sites, arts and sciences faculty are involved in teacher education program planning and evaluation; joint development of teaching and knowledge standards; greater coordination in advising of students by faculty of both departments; team-teaching courses, at times on site at K-12 schools; and developing arts and sciences courses or sections aimed at future teachers. In some cases, arts and sciences faculty have become particularly interested in pedagogy and are conducting curricular experiments using various teaching methods, holding study groups to understand effective pedagogical methods, participating in seminars on assessment, and/or undertaking peer coaching. Efforts such as these may improve the quality of teaching across a university.

Some sites are hiring new TNE faculty who are placed within disciplinary departments but who are also, by contract, required to work on teacher education issues. Others have joint appointments in arts and sciences and education. Such faculty members are inculcated in the habits of collaboration and will help to forge further relationships between the departments. However, these faculty members also need to be supported through more-liberal promotion and tenure rules that would allow credit for what might be seen as non-traditional research and service.

Teaching as an Academically Taught Clinical-Practice Profession. Many institutions are considering changes to or have changed student teaching placements and clinical (i.e., student teaching) supervision based on data they have collected. This should help to improve the quality of the student teaching experience and of the student teachers themselves.

Institutions with historically strong K–12 involvement have been successful in making the K–12 community an active and full partner in TNE. Some K–12 faculty members are on TNE leadership teams; others are involved with TNE teams working on design issues. The extent of the involvement is more limited in some sites than in others.

Two elements of this TNE design principle were stressed in the prospectus. One was the appointment of master teachers as university faculty (TIRs), and the other was the establishment of a two-year residency induction program for new teacher graduates. However, most of the sites have not been entirely successful in implementing these TNE components.

Some institutions have been able to hire TIRs, but others have not been as successful because of problems in hiring away experienced teachers from secure and relatively well-paid positions or in getting school districts to "loan" them to the university for one or two years. The districts are understandably concerned about losing their experienced teachers from the classroom. And some sites remain uncertain about the value added by TIRs. State and district policies have a direct impact on the sites' ability to implement the two-year induction programs envisaged by TNE. If such programs are offered for free by the state or district, there is less incentive for graduates to participate in the institutions' offerings. In addition, some institutions' "residency" program activities have not been recognized by the state as fulfilling mandated requirements for continuing education and training. Furthermore, new teachers report being overwhelmed by the various demands of the job; thus, the desire on the part of new teachers for additional induction activities—particularly related to content areas—is likely to be low. Those sites that have been successful in offering or piloting induction programs have collaborated with and sought to fulfill the needs of local districts.

Overall, while the sites have made progress in implementing the TNE design principles and report a distinct and palpable cultural change at their institutions, actual changes to their teacher education programs have been small and marginal. Some courses—both in arts and sciences and in education—are or may be changed, added, deleted, or transformed, and some sites have changed or are considering changes to the structure and timing of student teaching.

Intermediate Outcomes

Intermediate outcomes can be thought of as benefits that accrue later in the process and are valuable in and of themselves but are not seen as final outcomes—e.g., "better" teacher graduates with a strong knowledge of content and pedagogy, building up the teacher education research base and collecting evidence on what works, new and varied ways of assessing students to collect evidence on student learning, and using that evidence for program improvement.

One question that remains to be answered is that of the quality of education students. If the students' academic quality is inferior, it is unlikely that they will do well in more-rigorous and more-demanding subject-area courses. Research has shown that quality of teachers matters in pupils' learning. Thus, the institutions need to pay greater attention to student selection, to ensuring the rigor of general education courses, and to providing support to assist promising but less-well-trained students. However, many high-aptitude students are not attracted to teaching; therefore, teacher compensation systems may need to be overhauled if the quality of teachers is to improve.

If the institutions are able to lend support to graduates through the crucible years of teaching, that support may help to keep more of them in the classroom. But whether these incremental changes will produce highly qualified, competent teachers who will be markedly "better" than the graduates before them is still uncertain. In any case, it will be a long time before credible evidence of these outcomes can be gathered.

The sites have made some attempts to define teacher-knowledge standards and to better understand what "good" teaching is; however, it is not clear how this understanding can or will be used to add to the evidence base for how best to prepare teachers in and for a variety of contexts different from their own unique environment. It should be remembered that several state-specific teacher-knowledge standards already existed prior to TNE.

Assessment is an issue that is front and center at the TNE sites, given TNE's heavy emphasis on the "culture of evidence" and its equally strong emphasis on assessment by accreditation bodies and policymakers. The sites are building databases and collecting evidence in various ways and are examining the validity of the assessment tools they have been using. It is important to note that collecting data, analyzing data, and using data to drive decisionmaking are all distinct and different steps. We saw evidence of the first two steps but much less evidence of the third, largely because it takes time to collect and analyze the data before it can be used. A wide chasm exists between collecting and analyzing data and actually using these data for organizational improvement. Organizations often emphasize the collection of data to convey "an illusory sense of rationality," in which the purportedly rational and deliberate activity to collect data masks the fact that they fail to actually use these data to make decisions (Feldman and March, 1981; Wise, 1979).

It will be interesting to see to what extent TNE sites succeed in transforming themselves into what Senge (1990a) calls long-term "learning organizations," which continually seek to increase their capacity to create results that matter to them. Such a transformation is likely to be heavily dependent on an institution's leadership and organizational culture and whether certain structures and processes are put in place to facilitate that transformation. Whether this activity will result in new or more-rigorous ways of evaluating what students are learning and whether these new assessment methods can be disseminated and used in other academic departments or across institutions—thus adding to the knowledge base for teaching and learning—remain to be seen.

Final Outcomes

Final outcomes are the end result of the change process. The ultimate goal of the TNE initiative is, of course, to improve K–12 student outcomes, and the ultimate outcome measures defined by TNE are pupil-learning gains. Thus, in the long term, TNE will be judged by its impact on the quality of teaching and learning in U.S. schools and its impact on the field of teacher education. If we assume that TNE will result in markedly better teacher graduates—a large assumption, given the preceding discussion—we need to ask (1) how the higher quality of teacher graduates will translate into improvements in pupils' learning and (2) how new methods of teacher preparation will be disseminated and scaled up across the nation.

Likely Impact on Students' Learning and Teacher Retention. To show the effects of teacher graduates on pupil-learning gains, TNE is asking the sites to consider value-added modeling to isolate those effects. However, as the sites are discovering, this method requires a tremendous amount of data, and great care must be taken in including the proper controls and in making inferences from the analyses (McCaffrey et al., 2004; Kupermintz, 2003). To link pupils' achievements back to a teacher preparation institution and to components of a teacher education program, one must control for student, school, and district characteristics and the abilities of individuals when they enter the teacher education program. Numerous studies have shown that improving student outcomes depends on more than just teacher quality—it also depends on federal, state, and district policies; school leadership; school environments and culture;

student characteristics; and community support. The list of factors that could have an impact on student learning is overwhelming, and the best-prepared teachers could well be stymied by unsupportive school and home environments, poor or unstable school leadership, and policies that could result in little learning being accomplished in their classrooms.

For TNE to be considered a success, it is not enough to show that the institutions are producing high-quality graduates. These teachers need to stay in the classroom, particularly in low-performing schools. But if a school is overwhelmed by social and economic problems, is focused solely on test scores, and stifles innovative teaching practices and teachers' enthusiasm, high-quality teachers may well lose heart and leave the school.

Likely Impact of TNE on Peer Institutions. To address the issue of TNE's impact on peer institutions, we need to examine the process by which TNE is presumed to affect other institutions. Under the TNE design, the grantees would become exemplars for other institutions that would learn from the grantees and seek to emulate their TNE program in part or in whole and, thus, extend the reach and impact of TNE in the field of teacher education. TNE asks its grantees to identify and to work with partner institutions and to provide them with small incentives to participate in the reform effort. TNE also invited 30 institutions to be part of its Learning Network.

Several questions arise regarding the incentives for and the ability of peer institutions to change and whether any actual changes can be directly attributed to TNE.

First, will peer institutions follow the example of the TNE sites, even if provided evidence of effectiveness? TNE envisioned that peer institutions will want to adopt successful TNE strategies based on evidence generated by TNE, but earlier reform efforts have shown that institutions are slow to emulate others. The evidence regarding the effect of adopted or proposed changes on the quality of teacher graduates will accumulate over only a long period of time and collecting and analyzing data will require substantial effort. Without such evidence, peer institutions have little incentive to rush to adopt or to adapt TNE principles. However, even provided with evidence, peers may fail to follow suit with TNE institutions. New Institutional Theory, which combines perspectives from several different social sciences to better understand how organizations behave, offers some insights into the process of institutional change. It highlights the fact that rationality is always less than perfect, given individuals' beliefs and organizational cultures, and that procedural ideas and ideologies matter in the process of institutional change. Levin used this theory to explain why it has been so difficult to transform American schools:

> Such institutions operate inexorably to modify and neuter attempts to impose change and innovation, as the school has more power to alter the reform than the reform has to change the school. Finally, this institutionalist umbrella tends to explain why schools serve largely as conserving forces rather than change forces (Levin, 2006 p. 28).

Levin's observation applies equally to universities, and ignoring these aspects of organizational behavior—that organizations do not act simply on evidence—will undermine the ability of even the most innovative reforms to transform institutions.

Second, given the considerable variation within and between traditional and alternative certification programs (and many of the TNE institutions offer several different pathways to teaching), is there likely to be sufficient credible and convincing evidence that there is only a handful of best ways to produce teachers, with guidance specific enough to be followed by peer institutions?

Third, one of the underlying premises on which TNE is based is that it takes substantial amounts of money and external assistance to reform a teacher education program. Indeed, the sites credit a great deal of their progress in implementation to the TNE funding, which has enabled them—among other things—to get buy-in from arts and sciences faculty, develop databases, and hire faculty and data managers.[1] Given this need for substantial resources, how are partner institutions expected to successfully transform themselves, absent this level of funding? And what would be their incentive to do so?

Fourth, the question of attribution is a tricky one. Even if one observed non-TNE institutions adopting principles that seem to resemble those of TNE, how can such a change be attributed to TNE? After all, as we discussed earlier, several reform efforts as well as accreditation bodies share these same principles, particularly the emphasis on the "culture of evidence." From the point of view of correctly identifying the legacy of TNE, this question remains the thorniest.

Likely Impact on Basic Research and Knowledge. Among the six reform requirements listed by Fullan et al. (1998), the one to which TNE and the education field generally has paid the least attention is the development of a codified knowledge base against which to judge the skills and performance of teachers. An earlier report on improving organizational accountability (Stecher and Kirby, 2004) argues that movements to create more-explicit standards of practice or clinical practice guidelines, such as those that exist in the medical and legal fields, could form the basis for more-detailed standards for the teaching profession. Teachers could then be more aggressive about monitoring their own professional competence, and the public could hold teacher-preparation programs accountable for the quality of the teachers they produce.

In an editorial in the *Stanford Educator*, Lee Shulman, president of the Carnegie Foundation for the Advancement of Teaching, delivered a wake-up call, bluntly calling for an end to the current approach of "letting a thousand flowers bloom" that characterizes the field of teacher education:

---

[1] In terms of external technical assistance, the sites recognize the key role that AED played in providing them with the necessary tools to help them organize their work teams and get them jump-started on reform, but, now that they have gained momentum, they see less need for the kind of organizational and technical assistance that AED offered. Thus, in terms of the theory of change, funding has been a key catalyst for change, while external technical assistance appears to be less important than funding for scaling up.

Like our sibling professions, we must rapidly converge on a small set of "signature pedagogies" that characterize all teacher education. These approaches must combine very deep preparation in the content areas teachers are responsible to teach (and tough assessments to ensure that deep knowledge of content has been achieved), systematic preparation in the practice of teaching using powerful technological tools and a growing body of multimedia cases of teaching and learning, seriously supervised clinical practice that does not depend on the vagaries of student teaching assignments, and far more emphasis on rigorous assessments of teaching that will lead to almost universal attainment of board certification by career teachers. The teacher education profession must come to this consensus; only then can accreditation enforce it. Commitment to social justice is insufficient; love is not enough. If we do not converge on a common approach to educating teachers, the professional preparation of teachers will soon become like the professional education of actors. There are superb MFA programs in universities, but few believe they are necessary for a successful acting career (Shulman, 2005, p. 7).

If Shulman's views are correct, greater attention needs to be paid to developing specific standards and signature pedagogies for the preparation of teachers, either under TNE or under other reforms. Indeed, as we have stated, the TNE funders also recognize the need to pay more attention to the research base and to building more-explicit clinical practice guidelines. Perhaps, then, teacher education schools can claim to be closer in spirit and practice to the professional schools with which they frequently compare themselves and to whose status they aspire.

Overall Assessment

Like every reform effort, TNE has several goals. Given that among its goals are changing institutional culture, bringing new awareness of the role that all faculty play in preparing teachers, and helping to make teacher education a priority for institutions of higher learning, the TNE initiative is likely to be a success at least on some levels. The goal of improving teaching more generally across a college or university and improving the quality of general and liberal education that undergraduates receive may also be met, provided the sites collect rigorous evidence and use it for program improvement across their institutions. But attributing these improvements solely to TNE would be a mistake, given the confluence of political, economic, and social forces also driving change.

With respect to whether TNE's other goals—bringing about radical changes in the way teachers are prepared, providing evidence that these changes bring about marked improvements in pupils' learning, providing clear guidance for peer institutions to adopt and to adapt the TNE program design principles, and preparing students to be high-quality teachers who will stay in the classroom and who will improve teaching and learning in our nation's schools—will be met, the answers are less clear, and given the less-than-stellar history and cyclical nature of past teacher education reform efforts, perhaps less optimistic.

Teachers for a New Era Web Sites

Teachers for a New Era Home Page

http://www.teachersforanewera.org

TNE Prospectus

http://www.teachersforanewera.org/index.cfm?fuseaction=home.prospectus

Grantees' TNE Sites

Bank Street College of Education: http://www.bankstreet.edu/TNE/index.html
Boston College: http://tne.bc.edu/
California State University, Northridge: http://tne.csun.edu
Florida A&M University: http://www.famutne.org/
Michigan State University: http://www.tne.msu.edu
Stanford University: http://ed.stanford.edu/tne/
University of Connecticut: http://www.tne.uconn.edu/
University of Texas at El Paso: http://academics.utep.edu/Default.aspx?tabid=31474
University of Virginia: http://www.virginia.edu/provost/tneuva/
University of Washington: http://depts.washington.edu/wactl/tne/about/index.html
University of Wisconsin–Milwaukee: http://www.uwm.edu/Org/TNE/

Implementation Progress: First Cohort of Grantees

In this appendix and in Appendices C and D, we examine the progress made by the first and second cohort of grantees in implementing the three major TNE design principles (Florida A&M is examined separately in Appendix E). The findings presented here are organized according to the three principles: decisions driven by evidence, engagement of arts and sciences faculty in teacher education, and teaching as an academically taught clinical-practice profession.

Several of the TNE activities fall into more than one design-principle category; for example, a curricular experiment in a science course designed to measure student learning would fit under both the evidence principle and the involvement of arts and sciences faculty principle. To avoid repetition, we assign each activity to one of the three categories and describe them under that heading. However, there is considerable overlap across the three categories of activities.

Before we describe what the sites are doing to implement the three major TNE design principles, we need to mention some important caveats: First, the descriptions provided here are not meant to be comprehensive. We elected to highlight major and/ or innovative changes under way in these institutions, rather than provide a laundry list of implementation activities. Second, activities that are directed at implementing one of the other principles, beside the three major ones, listed in the TNE prospectus (Carnegie Corporation of New York, n.d.) are not discussed here, unless they are directly related to the three major principles. The Web sites listed in Appendix A can provide more detailed information on the sites' implementation. In addition, a previous RAND study (Kirby et al., 2004) is a good reference source for readers interested in early implementation of TNE at the first four sites.

Bank Street College of Education

Decisions Driven by Evidence
Bank Street is gathering several different types of evidence to inform its teacher education program, including Action-Oriented Inquiry (AOI) teams, the Bank Street Continuum of Teaching Project, a survey of graduates, curriculum-embedded assess-

ment, and a study of pupil-learning gains as measured by the New York State assessment. A TNE leader at Bank Street said that having overlapping strands of evidence, "like ivy on a trestle," will make the case for program change stronger for faculty and will more likely lead to renewal of the teacher education program. In year four of TNE, Bank Street is to convene a faculty study group to begin systematically analyzing all the data collected from the research activities.

Action Oriented Inquiry Teams. The goal of the AOI component of the TNE initiative is to inform program renewal and to ensure that it is evidence-based. Bank Street plans to use the findings from the AOI project to inform admissions, the induction program, and their teacher education programs. Participants told us that the AOI team process and findings provided faculty with new ways to think about their work.

In years one through three of TNE, teams of Bank Street faculty and arts and sciences partners worked to define the Bank Street approach to teaching based on empirical evidence gathered through observations, interviews, and work samples of pupils from classrooms of teacher education candidates and graduates.

AOI team members observed experienced teachers, recent graduates, and teacher candidates in a specified content area to gather evidence regarding teaching practice across a continuum of teacher experience. For each of the teachers in the study, the researchers conducted an interview with the teacher before each observation, observed three classes (each with a brief pre- and post-discussion), collected the work of three students (representing a range of ability levels), and conducted a post-interview. AOI team members then coded the interviews, observations, and student work. This coded information was entered into a database to allow the group to further analyze the data.

The AOI teams included arts and science faculty from TERC, Sarah Lawrence College, and the Museum of Natural History and faculty from the Bank Street School for Children (SFC) and Bank Street College of Education. TNE participants told us that the dean of the SFC is very supportive of the TNE work and sees it as a chance to help advance progressive education and has facilitated the inclusion of SFC faculty members on the AOI teams. Each year, there has been some turnover among AOI team members. Some members left due to the nature of the work and frustrations with the process, while other members left due to competing commitments. However, at the beginning of year three, six of the original 18 members remained and 12 of the 18 had continued from year two.

Continuum of Teaching Project. The goal of the continuum work is to create an instrument that can be used in ongoing follow-up studies of Bank Street graduates. In addition, the continuum will be one of many tools to help Bank Street evaluate teacher candidates and to support the professional education of candidates. As a teaching tool, the continuum will help candidates identify their own strengths and areas for improvement as teachers. The findings from the follow-up study will also inform courses and coursework.

During the first year of TNE, Bank Street developed a definition of good teaching involving several domains, drawn in part from the California Standards for the Teaching Profession, which could serve as a guide for program improvement and data collection. The framework defines six domains of teaching and establishes explicit constructs for what Bank Street considers to be quality teaching. In year two, Bank Street modified the domains and elaborated them by themes. These themes were further refined in year three.

In year three, in collaboration with arts and sciences partners, Bank Street developed a draft version of the Bank Street Continuum of Teaching Project. *Continuum of Teaching* is a rubric that measures teachers' instructional practices against Bank Street's definition of good teaching. The rubric—which is differentiated by four levels of sophistication of the teaching—allows observers to locate aspects of a teachers' instruction on a continuum. In year four, this instrument is to be used by faculty members and nursery school through grade eight (N–8) teachers in a follow-up study of a sample of graduates. Bank Street plans to use the continuum instrument to assess the knowledge, skills, and dispositions of its graduates.

Leadership team members strategically chose partners to participate in the development of the continuum, including representatives from California who worked to create the California continuum (based on the California Standards for the Teaching Profession), senior Bank Street faculty, and arts and science partners. This group, which met for the first time in October 2004, drafted the continuum for the domains. Bank Street then asked eight Bank Street faculty members to use the continuum with their advisees. Faculty members received a stipend for their participation in the pilot program. Both the advisee and the faculty member placed the advisee at some point on the continuum, and together they discussed their impressions of where the student stands on the continuum. Information from the pilots was used to revise the continuum drafts. Additional changes to the instrument were to be made in year four.

SOLO (Structure of the Observed Learning Outcome) Project. In year three, Bank Street developed and piloted a "curriculum embedded" assessment approach that involves looking at the tasks that teachers assign and pupils' responses to those tasks. Using the SOLO taxonomy (Biggs and Collis, 1982), assigned tasks are analyzed in terms of the demands they place on children. Pupils' responses are analyzed for complexity, sophistication, and completeness. In year four, Bank Street will use this tool to assess the work of its graduates and their pupils. Bank Street hopes to use the results, along with the other inquiry projects, for programmatic renewal of all Bank Street's teacher education programs.

Surveys. In year three, Bank Street conducted an online survey of alumni who had graduated between 1995 and 2004. The survey explored multiple aspects of candidates' preparation for teaching and their current practices and experiences. Bank Street plans to survey incoming candidates as well. The surveys are part of Bank Street's long-range plan for collecting and using information for program renewal. Bank Street will use data from the survey of graduates to also inform its induction offerings.

Analysis of Achievement Test Score Data. Bank Street has contracted with Metis Associates, a research firm, to collect and analyze pupil-achievement data of Bank Street graduates. Metis is analyzing pupil-learning gains of students in grades three through six. For purposes of calculating gains, pupils' previous-year scores on the assessment serve as the "pre" measure of achievement, while their scores on the assessment in the current year serve as the "post" measure. This pilot will compare the performance on a standardized test of a group of pupils taught by Bank Street graduates with the performance of a group of pupils taught by an appropriate comparison group of teachers (e.g., teachers with similar educational backgrounds, teaching tenure). Bank Street would like to analyze these data by pathway—i.e., Teaching Fellows versus traditional graduates of the Bank Street program—and would also like to track candidates in the Teaching Fellows program to see how they progress through their preparation. In addition, Bank Street hopes to compare its graduates pre- and post-TNE. Sample sizes and logistical constraints continue to plague this effort.

Engagement with Arts and Sciences

Because Bank Street is a stand-alone college of education, it does not have arts and sciences faculty in-house. Instead, TNE participants have had to go outside of Bank Street to develop arts and science partnerships. Bank Street has contracted with individuals from TERC, the American Museum of Natural History, and Sarah Lawrence College to provide content-area expertise in its assessment and induction work. The role of each of these outside institutions is discussed below.

TNE leadership said that the involvement of arts and sciences experts in the work has led to a shift in attitude and culture among the Bank Street AOI team faculty members. Some AOI team members on the Bank Street faculty initially resisted the participation of non–Bank Street members or did not believe that a content expert could contribute knowledge and understanding of quality teaching. However, in the process of the AOI work, Bank Street faculty have become more open to drawing upon outside expertise and have expanded their view of quality teaching to include a firm understanding and ability to communicate content knowledge. One indicator of this cultural shift is that members of Bank Street's Curriculum Committee asked to have permanent representation from the arts and sciences on the committee.

TERC. TERC has been involved in the AOI work since the first year of AOI's implementation. In year three, a TERC employee worked to provide support and feedback to AOI teams studying mathematics instruction. TERC served as a resource for teams focused on numeracy, providing feedback on observations across teams and focusing on issues of mathematics content.

Sarah Lawrence College. During year two, Bank Street established a partnership with Sarah Lawrence College. TNE participants told us that the dean of Sarah Lawrence has been very supportive of the partnership and has identified key faculty with a strong interest in K–12 education to work with Bank Street. In year three, two Sarah Lawrence faculty members worked with the AOI teams as content experts (one in social studies and one in science), and one faculty member served as an AOI team member.

In addition, a physicist on faculty at Sarah Lawrence worked with a representative from the Museum of Natural History to develop a science content course for teacher candidates. (The State of New York requires that all middle-school teacher candidates take a college science course to receive a teaching certificate.) Prior to the development of the science content course, incoming Bank Street teacher education candidates needing to fulfill this requirement took any science course. This new science course is specifically designed to provide candidates with the science knowledge they will need to teach in a middle school. The course is conducted at Sarah Lawrence College and/or at the American Museum of Natural History during the summer, and all incoming students needing to fulfill the science requirement are encouraged to take the course.

The science faculty member also worked on the continuum partnership, especially on issues of science content knowledge, to develop and refine the continuum.

American Museum of Natural History. The American Museum of Natural History has a strong focus on access to education for both teachers and students. The museum has more than 100 staff members in its education program departments and has a history of working with teachers. It currently publishes a catalog of resources and offers approved professional development courses for teachers. The museum also has a history of working with Bank Street. In the past, it has provided enrichment activities for Bank Street faculty and students, and it has accepted interns from Bank Street's museum education program. The TNE initiative pushed Bank Street to explore additional ways to collaborate with the museum.

Under TNE, the museum has provided a representative, a biologist, to serve as an AOI team member. In year three, this museum representative helped to develop two courses for Bank Street—the first was the science content course for middle-school teachers developed with the physicist from Sarah Lawrence. The second was a professional development course for graduates, which counts toward full certification in science. Interviewees said that the course for graduates is offered by the American Museum of Natural History and is the least-expensive course counting towards full certification in science available to new graduates in New York City. It is easily accessible online and provides teachers with much-needed help in the sciences. However, even though it was advertised, in the first year of the course offering only one person signed up for it.

Teaching as an Academically Taught Clinical-Practice Profession

K–12 Involvement. All of Bank Street's faculty members are previous K–12 teachers, and faculty from Bank Street's School for Children regularly teach graduate classes. Consequently, additional involvement of K–12 faculty in the teaching of teachers has not been a primary focus of their work. They have, however, increased involvement of PreK-8 (pre-kindergarten through grade 8) teachers in roles in which they have not previously been engaged at Bank Street. With the support of the School for Children administration, their faculty have been actively engaged in all inquiry efforts, and public school PreK-6 teachers and/or administrators have been actively engaged in the SOLO study and the piloting of the Bank Street Continuum of Teaching Project.

Induction. In fall 2004, Bank Street kicked off its induction program, called "Transitions for New Educators," with an event at the Lincoln Center Institute. This event, open to all alumni, provided an opportunity for graduates to reconnect with one another, with their advisors, and with experienced graduates. The event focused on using the arts in education within the current "test-preparation" culture in the schools. Bank Street arranged for the activity to count as continuing professional development credit from the state. However, attendance by new graduates was lower than expected—fewer than 25 new graduates attended. More experienced graduates attended than recent graduates. Consequently, the induction coordinator began developing different types of in-person induction activities. In year four, Bank Street had planned instead to host small study groups of ten to 15 graduates led by a Bank Street faculty member. However, in fall 2005, there were early indications that these groups would not draw the planned number of participants.

At the beginning of year three, Bank Street launched its induction Web site, which has three sections: announcements, yellow pages, and helpful tips for new educators. The yellow pages section contains links to sites and resources that Bank Street faculty and alumni find useful. Bank Street received contributions from several teachers for the helpful tips section of the web site. This section has seasonal themes that change throughout the year (e.g., "How to set up your classroom" at the beginning of the year).

The Web site also contains a link for graduates to express interest in the Alumni Matching Program, which matches graduates to alumni. The Alumni Matching program is not a mentoring system; rather, it is a "buddy" system to provide recent graduates with an additional resource during their first years of teaching. In year three, a number of Bank Street graduates signed up to be a buddy to a new graduate. In year four, Bank Street was to match these veteran teachers with new teachers based on geographic proximity, grade level, and/or specific interest.

In addition, the Web site contains information on the New Perspectives program in the Continuing Education division at Bank Street, which offers professional development opportunities for graduates.

The Induction Group has worked closely with the Alumni Relations Group, and in year three they co-sponsored an event in the spring (a week before graduation), the "Tar Beach Cocktail Party," which drew 20 to 25 soon-to-be graduates. The event also featured an information booth for both the alumni partnership program and the induction program. The Alumni Association also offers workshops and visits to other settings (e.g., science trips), and the Induction Group and Alumni Group are linking to one another's Web sites to cross-list events.

TNE participants told us that Bank Street does not consider induction a "TNE activity." Instead, Bank Street intends that its induction work be sustained regardless of TNE funding. Support for the induction program comes from Bank Street's president and trustees. Furthermore, input for the induction program comes from all divisions at Bank Street, thereby demonstrating an institution-wide commitment to the effort.

California State University, Northridge

Decisions Driven by Evidence

TNE leadership told us that CSUN is attempting to infuse evidence-based decision-making throughout the campus, and not just in teacher education. The TNE effort has merged with the unit assessment required by NCATE accreditation, which requires the university to collect data on the knowledge, skills, and dispositions of its teacher candidates in a manner that can be aggregated across students and to show how these data are used for program changes on an annual basis.

The TNE evidence team developed a conceptual framework and specified the data needed to establish the connections between teacher education, teacher practice, and pupil achievement. This work involved examining pathways to credentialing and winnowing down a broad range of about 40 indicators to a smaller set of key indicators. The team held an evidence symposium for its own faculty, K–12 faculty, and community college faculty and sought outside expertise, including meeting with experts in value-added modeling. The team is recruiting a data manager (a half-time position) and possibly two research associates, one paid for by an Eisner Foundation grant and the other by TNE. The team is contracting with the Center for Research on Evaluation Standards and Student Testing (CRESST) to develop an appropriate hierarchical linear model for the melded CSUN/Los Angeles Unified School District (LAUSD) data. CSUN intends to pilot this approach as a first step in widening the collection and analysis of teacher-effect evidence in the California State University (CSU) system.

Relationships with Partners. Recognizing the need for close collaboration with LAUSD and with other CSU campuses, CSUN has spent considerable time and effort in developing partnerships with the Performance Evaluation Branch of LAUSD. The Chancellor's Office (as part of a larger study) has established a Memorandum of

Understanding with LAUSD, which has greatly facilitated CSUN's negotiations for access to K–12 pupil data. CSUN wants to establish a true partnership with LAUSD and hopes to establish such partnerships with other school districts as well.

CSUN has developed a consortium partnership with several sister CSU campuses that are also interested in pupil achievement data. These campuses have agreed to work together to develop common indicators and data that will allow them to look more broadly across graduates of various programs. They have also agreed to submit a single data request to LAUSD to reduce the burden on the district. California State University, Los Angeles will be conducting a workshop on the use of evidence to facilitate this development work.

CSUN developed a partnership with several community colleges and is examining the courses that math majors and prospective single-subject teachers take at community colleges. CSUN conducted a large survey of community college students and CSUN single-subject teacher candidates. The survey found that students who intended to be math teachers had taken remedial math courses, and a substantial number of students who wanted to be teachers had not asked for or received any advisement. CSUN's content courses for prospective K-6 teachers now include practices to improve what CSUN calls teacher candidates' Mathematical Knowledge for Teaching (MKT), a more narrowly defined version of PCK that focuses on teaching tasks that explicitly demand mathematical knowledge. The results of these approaches are being assessed using an instrument developed by Professors Deborah Ball of the University of Michigan School of Education and Heather Hill, assistant research scientist at the University of Michigan. Scores on this instrument have been correlated with increased pupil performance on national achievement tests. Other measures to increase teacher candidates' knowledge—e.g., adding course time to build MKT skills, such as explanation, procedural fluency, and problem solving—will be considered and pursued in years four and five based on the results of the surveys and the assessments in year three.

Pilot Studies. In year three, CSUN conducted a pilot study that gathered quantitative and qualitative evidence of the impact of teacher preparation on teachers and student achievement that could be built upon for larger-scale studies. The quantitative piece focused on comparing three pathways to licensure—the ACT program, which is small and tightly structured; the traditional fifth-year program, which is the largest at CSUN; and the multiple-subjects intern program targeted at teachers currently in the classroom. CSUN selected a sample of teachers who had been teaching for two years and asked LAUSD to match the teachers in the sample with classrooms and to link student-achievement data with the teacher data. The merged database was used to examine the feasibility of a larger, longitudinal study and to identify problems regarding matching, missing data, inconsistent data, and other issues with data. A preliminary analysis was done in summer 2005 to test hypotheses about links between teacher preparation and pupil performance. During this analysis, several questions surfaced concerning reliability, validity, and comparability of test scores in various forms (e.g., normal-curve equivalents, proficiency levels, raw scores). CSUN is working with LAUSD, CRESST, and the CSU system Chancellor's Office to develop value-added and/or nested models.

The qualitative pilot study focused on a small sample of teachers in each of the three pathways offered by CSUN who are teaching in the third or fourth grades. The purpose was to determine whether teachers prepared through different programs act differently in the classroom, and to understand whether teachers attribute their instructional practice to specific aspects of their teacher preparation. TNE helps support five research assistants, who were trained at LAUSD on how to conduct and script observations. Researchers observed each teacher for three days teaching reading comprehension and literacy related to a content area. Pre-post interviews were conducted with the teachers, and some videotaping was done of lessons and pre-post assessments of the students.

Mini-Grant Program. CSUN started a mini-grant program under TNE, which was in addition to the CSUN Beck Teaching Grants aimed at improving instruction. The purpose of the program was to fund research projects that incorporate one or more of the TNE design principles; that focus on teaching processes and pupils' learning at the elementary, middle or high school levels; and/or that involve a combination of researchers from across the university, community colleges, and local school districts. Funded proposals included, among others, a study of the supply, retention, and performance of graduates from the ACT program and a study examining the breadth and depth of science requirements in California elementary education programs. Another grant was for reciprocal peer coaching in which an arts and sciences faculty member teamed with an education faculty member to improve their teaching through observations and coaching.

Data Warehouse. CSUN is committed to building a comprehensive data warehouse (the Preparation of Education Professionals warehouse) to serve as a secure repository for data on teacher candidates and graduates and to provide data that are consistent, useful, and easily accessible. While CSUN has a broad range of data on students, there are many problems and issues with the current data. Some records, such as some credential information, are available only on hard copy. Data are often inaccurate and not in useful formats. Currently, several departments in the college of education maintain their own "shadow" (duplicate) data systems. While there may be reasons for a shadow system, it is important that the system match the official student database, because separate department files create problems in tracking students. The former CSUN Director of Institutional Research (IR) played an important role in persuading the departments of the need for a unified database across the university. CSUN ensured buy-in from the faculty, administrators, and analysts who would use the database by including them in the development phase.

The focus in this area currently is on cleansing and merging the historic and current student databases and the post-credential database, and on understanding what data TNE will require and how best to store and use the data that will be collected. The new IR director, assisted by recently hired staff in Admissions and Records and one support person hired through TNE funds, has made considerable progress in cleansing the data and making the data fields consistent.

The data warehouse could eventually contain all student teaching evaluations, portfolios, and course grades. The data warehouse will also include data from LAUSD, including teacher characteristics, school characteristics, pupil characteristics and pupil test scores on a variety of tests—e.g., the California Achievement Test, the Stanford-9, curriculum-based tests.

The CSU Chancellor's Office received a Ford Foundation grant to assess pupil learning of CSU-credentialed graduates in several regions, including Los Angeles, Long Beach, and San Diego. The database for that project links to the state employment database as well as the credentialing database. This database could offer one of the best ways to track CSUN graduates who go into the classroom in other districts.

In years four and five of TNE, CSUN will continue to build and expand on the data warehouse and the types of data collected on students and develop a sustainable model for evaluating its teacher preparation programs.

Engagement with Arts and Sciences

In year two, CSUN set as a goal to move from "involvement" of arts and sciences faculty with TNE to "engagement" of arts and sciences faculty with TNE. TNE leadership has conducted workshops to introduce arts and sciences faculty to TNE; for example, within the College of Humanities, faculty from the Departments of Chicano/a Studies, English, Liberal Studies, and Linguistics all participated in these workshops. TNE has also encouraged outreach by other arts and sciences colleges and departments. For instance, the College of Social and Behavioral Sciences has assigned a faculty member to be the College Coordinator for Teacher Education, a formal liaison between teacher education and the College of Behavioral and Social Sciences.

A brief description of four activities engaging arts and sciences faculty at CSUN follows.

Hiring TNE Faculty. CSUN hired new TNE faculty in arts and sciences departments (one each in English, Sociology, Geography, Geological Sciences, and two in History) at the assistant professor level to work on the initiative. These are tenure-track positions funded through reallocation of the university-based budget. TNE leadership noted that there was initial resistance to the idea of TNE faculty serving in some departments, but this resistance is being overcome or dispelled. On average, TNE faculty members spend half of their time on TNE and the other half on teaching and other faculty responsibilities, such as research and service. As required for these positions, TNE faculty members have considerable experience and interest in preparing teachers and in K–12 education. They are involved with a variety of TNE committees and activities (e.g., curriculum redesign, partnerships with schools, assessment, PCK study groups) and play an important role as a bridge between their departments and TNE, teacher education, and the K–12 schools. They are expected to meet the same requirements for promotion and tenure as other arts and sciences faculty, especially in terms of contributions to their field of study. There is agreement that some consideration will be given for TNE involvement and for different types of scholarship; indeed, the university's tenure rules allow this, and the faculty members' appointment letters are clear that such work is expected. Nonetheless, TNE faculty reported that they feel the need to publish in order to be tenured, and they were uncertain about how TNE activities will be treated when they are reviewed for tenure.

Inquiry Groups. CSUN has formed discussion groups focusing on subject matter and pedagogical content knowledge in mathematics, social sciences, English, science, kinesiology, and arts. These inquiry groups studied high-school-level pedagogy and content. Interviewees noted that arts and sciences faculty members are less clear about how to get involved with PCK issues at the elementary school level.

The mathematics study group was the first inquiry group and serves as a model for study groups for the other disciplines. The faculty members themselves formed the group due to their interest in the topic—it was not a directive from TNE leadership. The mathematics group has conducted several workshops, and workshop participants have included mathematics and education faculty, teachers and coaches from local schools, and students. For instance, Deborah Ball of the University of Michigan presented a workshop, and her honorarium was paid out of TNE funds. Two members of the study group (one from the mathematics department and one from the College of Education) traveled to MSU for a workshop titled "Preparing Teachers to Teach Mathematics" in June 2004.

Review of Courses and Programs. As discussed earlier under the "Decisions Driven by Evidence" design principle, arts and sciences faculty in the TNE work group are examining PCK throughout the educational pathways of teacher candidates—at CSUN and community colleges and in both the ITEP and Four-Year Integrated (FYI) Teacher Credential programs.

Another initiative that will have an impact on teacher education and will have implications for the activities of education and arts and sciences faculty is that, independent of TNE, a university task force is reviewing CSUN's general education (GE) courses. Part of the motivation for forming this task force is to make the transition from community colleges to four-year institutions more seamless so as to improve retention and graduation rates. Thirty-nine units of GE are required at the community-college level to earn an associate's degree. CSU as a system wants to formulate an agreement with community colleges on a package of coursework that can be transferred. This sort of agreement is important to teacher education, because GE forms the basis of teacher candidates' knowledge of content. A review of the GE portion of teacher candidates' education showed that most of CSUN's teacher candidates take their GE courses at community colleges.

Involvement with Clinical Sites. Arts and sciences faculty also play a role in the three schools that have been selected as clinical sites and at Northridge Academy High School on the CSUN campus, as is discussed further in the next subsection. There are three arts and sciences site liaisons, one each from kinesiology, arts, and music, who work with K–12 students and faculty on-site. All the arts and sciences liaisons are former teachers.

Teaching as an Academically Taught Clinical-Practice Profession

K–12 Involvement—Teachers in Residence. In Year 2, CSUN hired six TIRs for the College of Education. The roles and duties of TIRs have become further defined over time. Currently, TIR activities include teaching or team teaching (typically six units per semester), coordinating induction activities, serving on the steering committee, supervising student teachers, interacting with faculty, and providing the perspective of a practicing teacher. LAUSD pays the TIRs' salaries so that they may retain their pensions and seniority, and LAUSD then bills CSUN for that cost. TIRs get an extra $1,000 per school year over their regular pay. Because CSU contracts technically do not allow for the hiring of TIRs, CSUN hires TIRs under a "lecturer" contract and provides a letter specifying their duties as a TIR.

In 2004–2005, with support from the Keck Foundation, CSUN hired three new TIRs in English, geography, and mathematics. These were for one-year or two-year positions, and the TIRs were the first ever placed in a department outside of the College of Education. These positions were advertised widely on the CSUN website, at LAUSD schools, and on the National Board for Professional Teaching Standards Web site.

Clinical Sites. CSUN established three clinical sites (Monroe High School, Sepulveda Middle School, and Langdon Elementary School) in addition to Northridge Academy High School and the CHIME Charter School, schools that CSUN faculty helped to develop. By focusing attention on a small number of clinical sites, CSUN believes it will be able to collect evidence of pupil learning and to develop sites that meet the NCATE criteria for professional development schools.

To help in the selection of the sites and development of relationships with those sites, CSUN solicited recommendations from the superintendents of two local districts and made presentations to teachers in potential clinical-site schools that emphasized the goal of creating a joint university/K–12 teacher education reform agenda. The purpose of the joint agenda is to build a real partnership between the university and the schools by creating a learning environment that will help all stakeholders—students, teachers, university faculty, and parents. CSUN refers to these schools as Professional Partnership Schools. Lessons learned from these clinical sites will be disseminated to other LAUSD schools.

In year three, a TNE cohort teacher education model was launched at Sepulveda Middle School. A cohort of 14 teacher candidates was placed at the school full time, and all teacher education courses were taught on-site. In future years, cohorts will be placed at all clinical sites.

CSUN is exploring ways to gather evidence on the success of the cohort model implementation, such as reflective logs kept by student teachers, "learning walks" (organized visits of a school's halls and classrooms in which information is gathered about the instruction and classroom practice) by faculty and teachers, and tracking of retention rates.

Induction. CSUN received a setback in its initial induction plans when the state assigned responsibility for induction to the districts. Originally, the State of California offered beginning teachers the choice of going through a fifth year of university study or a district's induction program to get a professional clear credential. CSUN had developed a fifth year of study that was "induction-like." Subsequently, there was a change in state policy. The new legislation mandated that a beginning teacher had to go through an induction program to earn the professional clear credential. CSUN withdrew the fifth-year program, because there would be little demand for the program from anyone other than charter school or private-school teachers.

CSUN went back to the drawing board to think about how best to design and fund a university-based induction program. Faculty met with LAUSD personnel responsible for induction, who were clearly worried about being able to find the huge cadre of support providers that were needed under the new legislation. If the university rolled out a separate induction program, it would be competing for the same group of veteran teachers. The district had already developed a joint program with California State University, Los Angeles, so it was open to the idea of a joint program with CSUN. The one stipulation was that the courses developed by the university for the induction program had to count toward a master's degree, which was agreeable to CSUN.

The induction team developed a new master's program that is focused on teaching and learning and that will be accepted by the district for new teachers' induction credit. The team worked out a memorandum of understanding with the district about the coursework and program schedule. The team carefully developed the core courses, basing them on California Induction Standards 16-20. CSUN may use some of the United Teachers Los Angeles (UTLA) faculty as part-time instructors for the lesson design study course offered in the master's program.

Literature on beginning teachers and focus-group findings suggest that it will take students three years to finish a master's degree, so CSUN developed its program as a three-year program in which students can take fewer credits each semester and sequenced the courses specifically so as not to overload the new teachers. The CSUN program will require students to conduct a major piece of research over the final three semesters. Three CSUN colleges and five departments also partnered to develop a new course on diversity, which builds upon the current preservice course on diversity.

CSUN was to seek approval for the joint induction-master's program from the graduate studies curriculum committee in fall 2005. If it is approved, the program will be implemented in fall 2006. The current agreement regarding induction credit for the program is with LAUSD, and the next step will be to develop similar partnerships with other districts in which CSUN's graduates teach.

CSUN believes that the program will be self-sustaining if it gets cohorts of about 25 students. However, teachers will have to pay for this program, since it is a master's degree program, whereas the district courses are free.

Michigan State University

Decisions Driven by Evidence

MSU's teacher education assessment work encompasses many different projects, some of which were in place prior to TNE and some of which originated as a result of TNE. TNE leadership told us that the assessment discussions complement MSU's institution-wide focus on regional re-accreditation from the Higher Learning Commission and also will support the College of Education's application for TEAC accreditation.

Teacher Education Program Evaluation. To serve the needs of both the TNE initiative and to satisfy TEAC accreditation requirements, one member of the teacher education faculty has drawn up plans for a comprehensive and ongoing teacher education program evaluation embedded in teacher education courses and experiences. The evaluation's goals are to become part of the normal operation of the teacher education program and to provide data in a timely fashion that are useful to instructors. Digital assessment files (DAFs) will be created for each teacher candidate. These files will incorporate selected pieces of student work and corresponding rubrics, which will be used to assess teacher education courses. Thus, work would accumulate in DAFs as candidates and interns progress through the program. In the aggregate, the DAFs would allow the Teacher Education Department's leadership to understand the impact of a set of required courses. The broad structure of the DAFs allows each discipline to determine those courses from which to collect student assignments and to develop appropriate rubrics for those assignments. In addition, assessment in academic areas outside of teacher education will be used to track teacher education candidates' progress in the disciplines.

In year two, rubrics and other instruments were developed for data collection, primarily for collecting data on students' intern year. MSU piloted a survey of exiting interns in spring 2005 (a survey of exiting interns was to be repeated in 2006) and surveyed all interns in fall 2005. MSU also will field a survey to the interns' university supervisors.

In addition, the Michigan Department of Education has developed an exit survey for those who have completed any education program in the state. Central Michigan

University, Wayne State University, the University of Michigan, and MSU participated in the pilot survey process at the request of the state. The Department of Education will analyze the data and identify potential strengths and weaknesses of the teacher education programs.

The MSU teacher education faculty is using the Teacher Knowledge Standards (TKS) jointly developed by teacher education and arts and sciences faculty (discussed further below) as a guide in a major departmental restructuring of the MSU School of Education. The use of the TKS has led to two structural changes in teacher education. First, MSU has moved from dividing its elementary education students into three cohort teams to dividing them into two teams: one team includes students in local student-teaching placements, the other includes students who are in more geographically distant student teaching placements. In addition, each team now includes subject-area specialists.

Another change to student teaching placements includes more members of the elementary education team being placed in urban settings. MSU adopted a new course in special education and multicultural issues to ensure that all students have some common preparation for addressing these areas, wherever they may teach.

Review of Content Courses and Curricular Experiments. MSU is conducting a number of curricular experiments, which will help to provide a basis for program improvement. For instance, curricular changes were made to an introductory biology course, "Cells and Molecules," to better align the course with the science TKS. Faculty and students documented the effect of the revised instruction in this course (which is team-taught by teacher education and arts and sciences faculty) through multiple assessments of student learning. The instructor of the "Linear Algebra" course is collecting pre- and post-assessment data to track the impact of the changes she has made to that course. New instructional materials aligned with the TKS have been selected for another mathematics course. A more holistic review of the elementary mathematics sequence by a team comprising mathematicians and mathematics education faculty was expected to be produced by June 2006. The review is being informed by classroom assessments of students in these courses and through pre- and post-assessment data.

Analyses of Existing Data on MSU Teacher-Preparation Students. MSU conducted a study of a cohort of 300 to 350 students admitted to MSU's teacher preparation program in spring 2000 to compare the performance of teacher education candidates with that of non-teacher education candidates in their general education classes. The results indicated that teacher education students outperformed non-teacher education students. MSU analyzed certain student characteristics, including students' entering test scores (on the ACT), their high school GPA, and MSU GPA. Data on MSU students' performance on Michigan teacher certification tests and data on course-enrollment patterns of teacher preparation students also have been analyzed.

Pupil Achievement. MSU received a $35 million Math Science Partnership grant from the National Science Foundation. Data that are being collected under this grant include the following:

- An assessment based on the Trends in International Mathematics and Science Study (TIMSS) assessment administered to 250,000 students in grades 3–12 in 750 schools in Michigan and Ohio
- A survey of 15,000 teachers that includes items on teachers' content knowledge and teacher preparation.

The teacher surveys gathered information on where teachers completed their teacher preparation and teachers' knowledge for teaching mathematics and science. Preliminary analyses that compare MSU graduates with other teachers and that examine outcomes, including the learning of their pupils, have been completed. MSU is using this pilot study to help design a system for using data on pupils' learning to inform teacher preparation program decisions.

Engagement with Arts and Sciences

Arts and sciences faculty are involved in many aspects of the TNE initiative at MSU. TNE leadership said that MSU has not hired new faculty members specifically for work on TNE largely because the administration believes that the goal of sustainability of TNE is not well-served by relying on special hires in fixed-term appointments. Nevertheless, according to the dean of the College of Education, TNE participation is an expectation for MSU's recent regular faculty hires. For instance, the recently hired endowed chair in mathematics education is committed to participating in TNE as part of her formal hiring agreement. Another example is a recent hire selected because of prior experience with induction and portfolio assessments. In addition, MSU is working to encourage and facilitate joint appointments and co-teaching across colleges.

TNE participants told us that, as education and arts and sciences faculty have worked together on TNE, initial reluctance on the part of some teacher education faculty to engage with the arts and sciences faculty on this subject has given way to an increasing recognition of the commitment of arts and sciences colleagues to the preparation of quality teachers.

Teacher Knowledge Standards. One of the most important collaborative efforts has been to develop the MSU Teacher Knowledge Standards. These standards outline the disciplinary knowledge required in each subject area. In year two, the disciplinary groups, comprising both teacher education and arts and sciences faculty, completed working drafts of the TKS. During fall 2004, the standards were submitted for input to relevant groups on campus, including the Teacher Education Council, which includes representatives from colleges across MSU that participate in teacher education, and there have been ongoing discussions about TKS among department chairs in teacher education, English, math, and history.

The goal of the work on TKS is to identify curricular gaps within the teacher education program and develop curricular changes that better align the program and courses with the standards. For example, a TNE cross-team group is reviewing the planned curricular program for teacher candidates in elementary education, and the group will use the TKS as a touchstone for recommending revisions to the Teacher Education Department. Several interviewees noted that, although the production of the TKS has taken much time, the process of writing the standards has helped to build buy-in for TNE from a larger group of faculty members, especially those outside of teacher education.

Course and Program Changes. Arts and sciences faculty have played key roles in the design or reconfiguration of courses generated by ongoing TNE work. For example, a TNE cross-team group is reviewing the planned program and the integrated teaching majors. The planned program is a set of courses required of all elementary education candidates and is taken in addition to coursework in the candidate's major or minor. The planned program courses include mathematics, literacy and language arts, science, U.S. history, geography, and the arts. Three integrated teaching majors (language arts, social studies [with concentrations in history and geography] and integrated science) are available for prospective elementary school teachers. These majors, which are housed in the College of Education, provide prospective elementary teachers with the opportunity to focus their academic studies on a set of closely allied subject areas that are central to the core curriculum in elementary and middle schools. The TNE cross-team group plans to use the TKS as a touchstone for recommending revisions of the integrated teaching majors to the Teacher Education Department. Following are several examples of MSU's collaborative work aimed at restructuring courses:

- The Literacy Group identified courses taken by large numbers of teacher education candidates. Group members collected syllabi from the courses, which are both in and outside of the Teacher Education Department, and mapped the content taught in these courses to the literacy TKS. This process highlighted gaps in course content, and the group is planning to use this information to suggest possible changes to the material taught in some of these courses. In addition, a task force is redesigning the three-course elementary teacher education literacy sequence to feature a stronger introduction to *emergent literacy* (the reading and writing behaviors young children demonstrate between birth and the time when they read and write conventionally) and more in-depth work in literacy during the senior year of college and internship year. A pilot revision of "Children's Literature," a teacher education course focusing on multicultural literature, was being offered in 2005–2006. The group also met with both K–12 faculty and former interns to discuss ways to better support teacher candidates during their field experiences; the group is now resequencing candidates' field experiences and ensuring that there are greater opportunities for candidates to engage in more structured and specialized activities.

- The Mathematics Group collected data on elementary school teacher candidates concentrating in mathematics. The group discovered that these students do not receive any instruction in statistics from the courses they must take to complete the teacher education program. As such, the group designed a statistics course for these teacher candidates, which was scheduled to be piloted in 2005–2006.
- The Social Studies Group recommended changes in curricula and graduation requirements for teacher education social studies majors and for all elementary education candidates to provide more interdisciplinary course options.
- The Science Group is working toward improving science teaching for all undergduates. They are experimenting with a popular teaching model used in some biology courses and in other science courses.
- The Urban Education Group in the Teacher Education Department developed a course that combines special education and urban education issues to ensure that every teacher education candidate is exposed to both of these areas.

Dow Corning Internship. A newly funded Dow Corning New Era Internship program was introduced for MSU's teacher education graduates. MSU-prepared teachers on the internship will work with industrial scientists and MSU science faculty mentors on laboratory research.

Teaching as an Academically Taught Clinical-Practice Profession

Induction. The Induction Team assembled information about induction practices and beginning teachers' needs in order to develop a framework for an induction curriculum. The group realized that MSU could be successful with its own induction plans only if the university worked to build induction capacity at the state level. To help fund this work, one of the induction coordinators received a grant from the State Board of Education for a program called Advocating Strong Standards-Based Induction Support for Teachers (ASSIST), which is developing support materials consistent with statewide induction standards. This grant is considered to count as TNE matching funds.

Through its work for the Michigan Department of Education, MSU designed three levels of induction:

1. Basic: New teachers can obtain support materials from the ASSIST Web site (http://assist.educ.msu.edu/ASSIST/index.php).
2. Collaborative: New teachers can receive support from a district mentor and from the ASSIST Web site, which also includes support materials for mentors.

3. Comprehensive: New teachers can receive support from university-trained mentors, and support includes attendance at multiple workshops, trained mentors matched by subject area to beginning teachers, and study groups for new teachers and their mentors.

Under this grant, MSU developed the Web-based resources for the ASSIST Web site. The Web site includes materials for mentors and beginning teachers and is divided into three sections: "In the School" focuses on creating learning communities in a school, preparing the school administration to work with new teachers, and preparing mentors; it also includes advice for beginning teachers and veteran teachers on new assignments (based on materials from the Santa Cruz New Teacher Project). "In the Classroom" features resources for new teachers related to such issues as lesson planning, assessment, and classroom management. "In Further Study" includes curriculum modules for new teachers and mentors to work on together throughout the novice's first year of teaching. MSU's induction program will utilize this resource.

In addition, MSU designed a pilot induction program for beginning teachers in the Lansing school district, which recently hired more than 100 new teachers due to a buyout of the contracts of veteran teachers. In this program, MSU is conducting an experimental study of the impact of two levels of mentoring—collaborative and comprehensive. The experimental group consists of 15 novice teachers matched with veteran classroom teachers in mathematics, science, English, special education, and elementary education who were trained as Lansing Intensive Mentors. TNE is paying the Lansing school district $20,000 for five mentors to be released one day a week to work with three new teachers each, matched by subject area. These 15 novice teachers will be observed and compared with another 15 who were being mentored by district-assigned mentors trained through ASSIST.

MSU will scale up its induction support for the Lansing school district and will offer support to all new hires (up to 40 in a year) and 30 teachers in their second year of teaching. Information generated by these programs will be provided to the state to help inform state induction policies.

K–12 Involvement—TNE Teams. The Induction, Literacy, and Mathematics teams and the Urban Education Group partnered with groups of K–12 teachers, including MSU graduates, and administrators. K–12 practitioners met periodically with the teams to discuss drafts of the TKS, to help in shaping the content and structure of the Induction Program, and to give general advice on the work of the teams. The Literacy Team developed a plan for structured field experiences, which was piloted in 2005-2006, with a set of K–12 teachers. In fall 2005, the Social Studies Team initiated conversations with K–12 teachers regarding a plan similar to the Literacy Team's plan.

K–12 Involvement—Partnership with Detroit Public Schools. MSU received a grant from the Broad Foundation to partner with the Detroit Public Schools (DPS) to create a "pipeline" of teachers for the school system. The grant includes three components: creating scholarships for MSU students who commit to teaching in DPS upon graduation; developing a three-week summer-school program at MSU, focused on teaching, for DPS juniors and seniors; and establishing a DPS summer program for rising MSU seniors in the teacher preparation program to provide them with experience teaching in an urban setting. The Broad Foundation grant has caused MSU education faculty to focus more closely on urban issues and recruitment for high-needs areas, and it led MSU to reexamine admission processes for the teacher education program. Currently, teacher education candidates apply in their sophomore year of college to be admitted to the program in their junior year, and the decision to admit a candidate is based on written essays and his or her GPA. MSU has begun shifting to a more holistic process for evaluating candidates and now looks at additional evidence including experience, background, and desire to teach in high-need areas. MSU also plans to recruit a cadre of freshmen from urban high schools for early offers of contingent admission to teacher education following high school, if the students express interest in working in high-needs areas. Up to one-third of a teacher education class might be admitted to MSU's teacher education program in this way. MSU will couple the early admission with more attention being paid to mentoring in the first and second years of college. MSU's goal is to prepare students to teach in all contexts and to attract more students who are willing to teach in urban schools.

University of Virginia

Decisions Driven by Evidence

By year three of the TNE initiative, UVa established an overarching vision for its assessment work, which moved the UVa TNE program from a "mini-grant" structure toward a comprehensive research effort. This effort focuses on tracking teacher candidates' progress through the teaching lifecycle (preservice and beyond throughout a teaching career) using a variety of data sources, including new observation instruments and pupil learning measures.

Research Advisory Council. The UVa provost selected several faculty members from arts and sciences and education, who were among attendees at his monthly seminar on evidence and education, to serve as his TNE Research Advisory Council (RAC) and to provide centralized management and strategic guidance. The RAC is serving as an advisory board to the new Center for Advanced Study of Teaching and Learning, which, with three years of start-up funds from the provost, will inherit, expand, and disseminate TNE research.

Research Participant Pool. With the TNE initiative, the Curry School of Education at UVa now mandates five hours of participation in research activities by all incoming teacher candidates. All teacher candidates must participate in interactive activities and surveys and allow Curry to have access to their transcripts and PRAXIS scores. Research activities in which Curry candidates are asked to participate include:

- **In-Take Survey.** This online survey will be used to characterize the students entering UVa's teacher education programs. Survey questions are used to gather data on students' attitudes and abilities in regard to education. The study is worth 0.5 hours toward the required five hours of research activities.
- **Q-Sort Exercise.** This activity measures the qualities, attributes, and beliefs of preservice teachers. Students are asked to sort a set of cards, each of which displays a single statement about education, into five categories ranging from "least characteristic of my approach/beliefs" to "most characteristic of my approach/ beliefs." This study is worth one hour toward the required five hours of research activities.
- **Life Experiences Inventory.** The life experiences questionnaires ask students about certain aspects of their lives that may play a role in their future job as a teacher. This study is worth one hour toward the required five hours of research activities.
- **Interactive Teaching Instrument.** This multimedia instrument attempts to simulate real-time interactive teaching in a middle-school classroom. Students are asked to watch videos of middle-school classrooms and respond to a series of questions related to what was viewed. This study is worth 0.5 hours toward the required five hours of research activities.

These activities are designed to generate data for a variety of ongoing research projects that will inform TNE and to make teacher candidates aware of research as part of the life of a teaching professional.

Mini-Grant Program. In years one and two, UVa funded faculty mini-grants to support research related to teacher education and the TNE principles. In year one, 14 research and six development proposals were produced. Sixteen proposals were submitted, and 12 were selected for year-two funding. One of these grants was used for the pupil-learning gains pilot. This study assessed the effectiveness of public school teachers who received their teacher education training at UVa compared with the effectiveness of teachers who were not trained at UVa. Effectiveness was measured by pupils' academic achievement on the eighth-grade Standard of Learning (Virginia's state assessment) Algebra I assessment. The sample included 259 pupils taught by UVa graduates and 115 pupils taught by non-UVa graduates. Small sample sizes appeared to prevent detection of significant achievement results in the first round.

UVa also conducted a study that examined dual-placement and single-placement student-teaching experiences. This study relied on student teachers' self-assessments and survey responses about their student teaching experience. Both sets of student teachers responded that their experience was positive. However, the findings suggested that the student teachers who conducted their student teaching in one classroom saw themselves as being engaged in teaching to a greater degree as "doers," while the student teachers who split their student teaching between two classrooms saw themselves more as "observers" in the classroom. The data from the dual-placement/single-placement study showed that the single placement led to outcomes that were more highly desired by the teacher education faculty. As a result, in year three, all student teachers will be placed in a single classroom for their entire student teaching semester.

Observation Tools. UVa created a formalized preservice program of classroom observation and data collection, which includes a higher-inference observation protocol and a lower-inference protocol. Beginning in year three, the teacher education department within the Curry School of Education will mandate that at least three of the six observations of student teaching will use the higher-inference protocol. Both observational systems will be used to periodically describe the practices of third- and fourth-year students in the teacher education program.

Curry Teacher Education Database. UVa is developing a database that contains information on teacher education candidates, including data from the research activities that teacher education candidates in the Curry Participant Pool complete. UVa expects that the database will enable teacher education faculty and TNE researchers to chart the development of groups of students and study the effects of modifications to the teacher education program.

Pilot Study on Induction. A small pilot study with a group of 21 novice teachers was conducted to learn more about what new teachers need. A second round of the study is under way. The findings will be used to inform the design of UVa's induction program. UVa will survey novice teachers and their advisors to measure their self-efficacy and perceptions of their teaching practice. UVa will also look to measure the value of the mentor program and the quality of the relationship between the mentors and the new teachers they are mentoring.

Engagement with Arts and Sciences

TNE leadership noted that active participation in TNE by the provost, deans, associate deans, and senior research faculty has been key in signaling the importance of TNE to UVa faculty and to students, especially faculty and students in arts and sciences departments. In our interviews, the dean of arts and sciences was credited with raising awareness regarding teacher education among the faculty and students. In fact, in year three, he sent a letter to all arts and sciences students telling them about teacher education options. Another important strategy for encouraging involvement by arts and sciences faculty is the research focus of TNE at UVa. Involvement in TNE and K–12 schools is presented as an opportunity to enhance research opportunities, to obtain access to new types of data, and to collaborate in seeking funding. TNE leadership noted that a clear difference in the relationship between arts and sciences and teacher education faculty members is already apparent. The simple fact that more faculty know one another is considered a benefit.

Assessment Seminars. One key way that UVa engages arts and sciences faculty in teacher education is through monthly lunchtime assessment seminars hosted by the provost. The purpose of this seminar series is to raise awareness of assessment techniques, develop a culture of research and practice, and foster further interaction between teacher education and arts and sciences faculty. Faculty participants include Curry School of Education faculty (ten to 12 members) and arts and sciences faculty (eight to ten members); the provost also participates. School district personnel began attending the seminars in year two. Many of the assessment seminars focus on methods of measuring pupils' learning and the effect of teacher education. These seminars are considered to be quite successful.

New Courses. Under TNE, UVa has developed two new series of courses— Common Courses and Counterpoint Seminars. Common Courses are large survey courses in the arts and sciences with an interdisciplinary focus. The Common Courses take the multidisciplinary knowledge required of elementary school teachers as the model for all liberal arts training. In year two, the first TNE Common Course, Designing Matter, was taught, and UVa solicited proposals from faculty members interested in developing a new course, which resulted in three funded proposals for courses that were offered in year three.

A teacher education faculty member noted that the Common Courses raise some longer-term questions for teacher education that need to be answered once the Common Courses have a track record. For instance, should UVa require Common Courses for all teacher candidates? If so, how many should be required, and what should be their focus?

Counterpoint Seminars, taken by B.A./M.T. students, are linked to an arts and sciences survey course that B.A./M.T. students have taken and focus on how a course's content can best be taught in a middle school or high school setting. B.A./M.T. students can use these courses to synthesize the two degree programs, similar to what is done with "capstone" courses (courses generally targeting students nearing completion of their studies; the courses are designed to build on knowledge and skills acquired in earlier studies). In year two, UVa offered the first two Counterpoint Seminars, for English and for history. The dean of arts and sciences, a renowned historian, was a guest speaker for the history Counterpoint Seminar.

Advising Teams. As discussed earlier, UVa has a five-year B.A./M.T. program. As part of this program, teacher education candidates have two advisors: an arts and sciences advisor to inform them about their major and a teacher education advisor. While the goal always has been to have coordination among advisors, TNE participants told us that, before TNE, this system was not working as well as it was envisioned. UVa formed seven advising teams to create improved advising for teacher education students in seven arts and sciences subject areas—English, foreign languages, history, liberal arts/elementary education, mathematics, psychology, and sciences. The dean of arts and sciences personally sent out invitations to arts and sciences faculty members asking them to participate in these advising teams and charged an appropriate associate dean or department chair from arts and sciences with heading each of these groups. The new advising structures developed by the teams were up and running in year three, and TNE participants said that it has resulted in increased coordination among advisors.

Teaching as an Academically Taught Clinical-Practice Profession

K–12 Involvement. In year two, teacher education faculty began re-envisioning their relationships with schools by creating school partnerships. Curry School leadership hosted a faculty retreat to discuss school partnerships, and during the retreat decided to move forward by creating school partnerships in two pilot schools, an elementary school and a high school in Albemarle County, in year three. After the pilot year, UVa hopes to expand the program to the Charlottesville schools.

If the partnership model is a success, UVa will face the question of how to select additional partner schools and how to expand the program to other schools to meet the demand, given the relatively small size of the teacher education program.

Induction. The Induction Steering Committee is responsible for induction work in the schools within the two districts with which UVa has induction partnerships. The committee is chaired by a full-time TNE induction coordinator. Other participants include two representatives from each of the two school districts, the director of TNE, the director of the teacher education program, and a teacher education faculty member who is responsible for student teaching placements.

UVa plans to have a two-tiered induction system—one tier focused on its graduates and the other focused on all new teachers in the local area. Current plans for providing induction support to graduates are to offer services online, possibly using Tapped In, an online dialogue platform. However, as of year three, UVa had concentrated its efforts on developing the district induction program.

In year one, UVa focused on engaging the local school districts and determining the districts' needs for support. In year two, the district induction work gained focus. Interviewees told us that the turning point for the induction work was the TNE conference in fall 2004. UVa included a district representative in the UVa team attending the conference. At the conference, a representative from the Santa Cruz New Teacher Center (NTC) spoke about the NTC induction model, which is one of the induction models that the state of Virginia considered to be acceptable under its new mentoring regulations. The district representative became very enthusiastic about the NTC induction model, and in winter 2004, UVa sent district representatives to Santa Cruz, California, to learn more about the program. They came back energized about the program's possibilities and eager to work on the program with UVa.

A UVa induction coordinator was hired in April 2004. The hiring decision was made jointly by the districts and the university. In fact, principals from the school districts conducted the final round of interviews for the position. The coordinator of induction helped the districts to adapt the NTC model to meet local needs and got the induction program up and running in fall 2004. In year three, the program was operational in all Charlottesville schools and in all Albemarle secondary schools and some elementary schools (another 12 schools will be added in future years).

The UVa-supported district induction program is divided into three tiers. In tier one, three full-time mentors cover about 16 novice teachers across several schools. Tier-two mentors are part time, work only with novices in the same school, and receive a stipend for mentoring in addition to their regular duties. Tier three is the mentoring system that the districts previously had in place. Tier three varies a great deal from school to school. The districts provided some training and manuals for mentors, but there was very little structure to the system and no requirements for regular meetings, evaluation, or reflection. Often, the mentoring took place only in the first few weeks of the school year to go over the nuts and bolts of the local school system.

The mentors applied for the positions and were selected by a hiring committee comprising school division and UVa faculty. Mentors in the new program went through three days of summer training at UVa and receive five hours of ongoing training each month on such topics such as formative assessments.

Novice teachers are required to participate in the UVa induction program if their schools are participating. First-year novices get help mainly with pedagogy, classroom management, and administrative issues. Help with content issues will be of greater focus in the second year of induction.

Mentors are required to have weekly meetings with each novice and keep logs to monitor the novice's progress. Mentors are also expected to help the novices locate any additional, outside assistance they may need.

Novice teachers were invited to attend four 2.5-hour-long workshops throughout the year: Knowledge of Classroom and Students—Classroom Routines and Management; Developing Professional Networks—Communication and Collaboration; Planning, Instruction, and Assessment; and Lifelong Learning and Reflection—Goal-Setting. Interviewees told us that the local induction program has reduced attrition among new teachers participating in the program.

TNE leadership noted that the relationship between UVa and the local school districts has improved as a result of TNE, particularly due to the induction work. There is a better understanding on both sides that a partnership is beneficial for UVa, the districts, and, most important, the pupils in the schools. A key shift in attitude is that UVa is first listening to the schools and districts on what their needs are and then offering appropriate assistance.

Another positive sign is that the local districts have sped up their hiring process and are hiring greater numbers of UVa's teacher education graduates. There were 40

UVa graduates (first-and second-year teachers) in the local school districts in 2005–2006, a dramatic increase from when only a handful of teacher education graduates would end up in local district schools.

Second Cohort of Grantees: Sites Included in the National Evaluation

This appendix and Appendix D examine the progress made by the second cohort of grantees in implementing TNE. This appendix discusses three of the four sites in that cohort—BC, UConn, UTEP—that were part of the funded national evaluation, which allowed for site visits.[1] Appendix D covers the three sites—Stanford, UW, and UWM—that were not part of the funded evaluation (as stated earlier, we were able to obtain information on these three sites through other means in order to include them in this analysis). The reason for dividing the institutions in this manner is twofold: First, the sites are at different points in their implementation, and we found it useful to group sites by the number of years that they have been implementing TNE principles. Second, we have differing amounts of information on the individual sites (depending on whether we were able to conduct a site visit).

Boston College

Decisions Driven by Evidence

Assessment Team. BC formed an Assessment Team that is responsible for conducting surveys, collecting qualitative data, and leading a value-added assessment study. However, gathering evidence on what is happening in BC's teacher education program is seen as the joint responsibility of all the teams working on TNE. For example, a faculty member who has been working on a new initiative to help teachers develop competencies to work with English-language learner (ELL) students has asked for help in developing an evaluation of her work. BC has asked its external evaluator

---

[1] Florida A&M University—the fourth site in the second cohort with a funded evaluation—is not included here. Because of changes in leadership at FAMU and delays in its grant-approval process, Florida A&M did not receive final approval of its design proposal until May 2005. While FAMU received preliminary funding of $110,000 in April 2004, the first regular reimbursement of university costs for grant activities was in September 2005. Consequently, we provide a brief overview of Florida A&M University's TNE activities separately in Appendix E.

to help faculty members develop assessment tools and research questions to evaluate course offerings and new initiatives.

As a result of the TNE work, BC revamped its required Inquiry Project for teacher candidates so that it has a greater focus on student learning. BC developed a new scoring rubric for Inquiry Projects, focusing on teaching practice, pupil learning, social justice, and teachers as researchers, which will be used in year three of TNE.

The Assessment Team noted that, in BC's next accreditation cycle, it is applying for TEAC rather than NCATE accreditation, so there will be a greater focus on presenting claims and evidence to support the accreditation application. The Assessment Team developed a portfolio approach (including case studies, survey work, observations, interviews, document review, and multiple assessments) to gather evidence, which comprises a collection of instruments and assessments encompassing a mix of process and outcome goals.

Surveys. In year two, the Assessment Team developed and fielded the following survey instruments to track students and graduates:

- An entry survey, which surveys incoming students on their expectations and characteristics
- An exit survey, which surveys students' beliefs and attitudes about children and teaching and students' future plans
- A one-year-out survey, which asks graduates about their perceptions of how well their teacher education program prepared them for teaching.

TNE participants noted that all three surveys have considerable overlap and common items that will allow longitudinal and cohort analyses and follow-up over time. The surveys include a 12-question "social justice scale," which evaluates how well the teacher education program fosters awareness of social justice issues. Response rates on these three surveys were approximately 90 percent, 91 percent, and 60 percent, respectively. BC piloted the exit survey with its 2004 graduates and modified it based on those results for the 2005 cohort. Faculty members were also given opportunities to participate in the survey modification, which, we were informed, helped to increase faculty buy-in.

Pupil Learning-Gains Study. In year two, BC began planning a study to compare pupil-learning gains for BC's graduates with pupil-learning gains for another group of teachers using a state assessment as a measure of pupil learning. Faculty members have been discussing what the appropriate comparison group should be. In preparation for the study, BC completed several simulations. BC will continue working on additional simulations in year three and will continue working with the Boston Public Schools (BPS) to obtain actual student-level data. However, it is uncertain whether there will be a large enough number of cases to conduct the value-added analyses being considered. Approximately 50 BC graduates are hired by BPS each year; however, the value-added models require three years of consecutive data per teacher, and, at this point, BC does not know how many of its graduates remain in BPS for three years. Further, some graduates may be teaching non-tested grades. The Massachusetts Department of Education has expressed some interest in the VAM work, so BC believes its work may create greater access to state-level data.

Qualitative Studies. BC has gathered qualitative evidence through interviews, observations, documents, reviews of lesson plans, and pupils' work. BC created a new observation protocol that focuses on student learning and social justice as well as on teaching. Developing this protocol led to important discussions about what BC wants its teachers to "look like" when they exit the program and how BC can develop its programs to meet those goals.

In year two, BC planned 24 case studies of its teacher candidates in the master's degree program. In year three, BC will begin following candidates through their entire pre-service training and into their first year of teaching, conducting interviews and observations of the candidates. BC plans to conduct cross-case analyses to try to understand, among other things, how their teacher candidates are assessing student learning.

Social Justice. As noted above, the surveys developed for teacher candidates and teacher graduates include a 12-item social justice scale. In addition, BC created interview and observation protocols related to social justice and is developing a series of vignettes about social justice in the classroom. The idea is to create a battery of assessments to evaluate the ways in which BC's teacher education program fosters awareness and teaching of social justice issues.

Evaluation and Dissemination. BC hired a database manager who is responsible for maintaining a database that includes all information on teacher candidates and graduates. Having collected much information, Boston College is focusing at this point on strategic planning and thinking about how to use the evidence to guide its curricular decisions. In Year 2, the Assessment Team used several forums to present the results from its work, including teacher education faculty meetings.

Engagement with Arts and Sciences

Members of BC's TNE leadership team noted that, through various TNE initiatives, the college has cultivated greater involvement of arts and sciences faculty in the teacher education program. The hope is that this increased involvement will help arts and sciences faculty members to better understand how to translate subject-area content for various audiences so that it can feed into improving the preparation of teacher education candidates. TNE leadership noted that there had been some backlash initially among education faculty to the notion that arts and sciences involvement was needed in teacher education, but this feeling has dissipated over time. Also, we were told that involvement in TNE has been enlightening for arts and sciences professors and has changed the way they view the teacher education students in their classes.

Below, we highlight two categories of activities in which BC has engaged arts and sciences faculty in teacher education—TNE courses and mentoring and advising.

TNE Courses. In year two, BC defined the characteristics of a "TNE course." A TNE course is mindful of the Massachusetts curriculum frameworks for public school children and what K–12 students need to learn in general. BC faculty developed or modified 16 courses in 2004-2005 to meet TNE objectives. The courses were taught in the teacher education department and in several arts and sciences departments, including biology, geology, history, English, and fine arts. Some are pedagogical lab courses, e.g., a course on Shakespeare with an optional one-credit lab on how to teach Shakespeare. Others are core arts and sciences or required teacher education courses— e.g., a geology course on how to integrate mathematics into a science class. BC circulated this list of TNE courses to academic advisors so that the advisors can provide useful information to education and arts and science students about course options.

Mentoring and Advising. In 2004–2005, BC began utilizing arts and sciences faculty to provide one-on-one content mentoring to secondary teacher education candidates. Three times a semester, the content mentor helps a student teacher develop a lesson, observes the student teacher implementing the lesson, and debriefs the student teacher after the lesson. Eleven faculty members from English and history attended three training sessions prior to serving as mentors for the 2004–2005 school year. BC recruited 15 English faculty members for 2005–2006.

BC believes that having Ph.D. researchers with expertise in various subjects mentoring pre-service teachers will help the teacher candidates understand what it means to think like a scientist or think like an historian. However, BC realizes that it does not have the capacity to provide mentoring to all candidates through this sort of one-on-one relationship. As a result, faculty members will work to create alternative opportunities (e.g. one-on-two mentorships) that can involve more students.

All secondary-education student teachers were invited to participate in two content workshops. These workshops were run by arts and sciences faculty from various departments, teacher education faculty, and cooperating teachers. The workshops focused on teaching methods and pedagogy within particular content areas. Secondary-education students in English and history were assigned arts and sciences advisors in their respective content areas.

Finally, BC funded advising seminars for freshmen in BC's Lynch School of Education that introduce teacher education students to arts and sciences faculty and disciplines.

Teaching as an Academically Taught Clinical-Practice Profession

K–12 Involvement. Throughout the course of BC's TNE program, BPS teachers and principals have been serving on the TNE leadership team and other teams and committees, co-teaching teacher education courses, and assisting with content-knowledge mentoring. In year two, BC expanded its leadership team to include more school-based practitioners. There are now as many K–12 representatives as there are arts and sciences, teacher education, and administrative participants put together, which the TNE leadership believes provides a "comfort zone" for K–12 practitioners and creates deeper engagement in TNE and increased interaction among participants.

BC already had a number of K–12 teachers in adjunct faculty positions and was interested in getting more BPS teachers on full-time faculty appointments in teacher education, but it found that it cannot match the teachers' salaries at BPS. In addition, the district is reluctant to let its good teachers go, even temporarily, and there may be associated legal issues with the teachers' union.

Partnership Schools. The leadership team noted that BC has taken on a systems approach to thinking about relationships with schools—e.g., by considering what types of schools should be involved in teacher education, what a K–12 partnership ought to mean, and what the schools (and BC) need and want. BC is working to build true partnerships and to be responsive to the schools' feedback and needs. The goal is to develop formal parameters on what a good partnership constitutes—one in which both sides benefit and achieve shared goals.

BC began this endeavor by drawing up a short list of Partner Schools in which to pilot its partnership program in the hope of growing the program from there. Faculty members noted that BC was fortunate in that it already had a number of partnerships in place. Through TNE, BC has begun to centralize information about its relationship with each of 11 partner schools and all the various BC programs at a given school. This task has allowed TNE staff to serve as "air traffic control" to integrate initiatives, to prevent program overload at the schools, and to avoid redundancy and manage demand. BC is working to keep its TNE initiatives, research, and inquiry projects focused in these schools. TNE faculty at BC believe that deep involvement in these schools will teach the cooperating teachers and their student teachers about communities of practice and collaboration. Many of the partner schools are in BPS, but BC is beginning to expand into other local communities, such as Waltham and Newton. Representatives from all 11 partner schools serve on the TNE Leadership Team, and BC hired a liaison to work with the university and the schools.

Improving Clinical Experiences for Teacher Education Candidates. BC offers a number of programs to help prepare cooperating teachers at the school districts for their role in TNE. For instance, BC offers Supervision in Action, a course that helps teachers to learn mentoring skills. The leadership team noted that TNE-sponsored activities have made a considerable impact on the in-service cooperating teachers who host their student teachers. Faculty noted that they are confident that the cooperating teachers actually model BC's vision of good teaching for their student teachers.

Induction. BC started offering induction activities in year two of TNE. Its Project SUCCESS provides a number of induction opportunities for teachers in the field. First-year teachers from BPS schools may participate in the three-day Summer Start Institute, which features discussion of practical issues related to teachers setting up their first classroom. Follow-up includes six support seminars throughout the school year and ongoing support from a mentor for the first 60 days. Second-year teachers attend a three-day Maintaining Your Balance Institute during the summer and, beginning in 2005–2006, had the opportunity to participate in monthly follow-up seminars. Third-year teachers participate in a one-day institute during which they investigate a classroom-based research question related to pupil achievement and prepare papers and presentations on what they learned in the investigation. All BC graduates with teaching positions, along with school-based professionals from local area schools, are invited to attend these institutes. BC also is having an impact on teacher education more broadly by inviting neighboring universities to the Summer Start program. Representatives from Bridgewater State University observed the program in summer 2005.

The summer institutes for the first- and second-year teachers are scheduled concurrently so that the second-year teachers can work with the first-year teachers for a portion of the time. So far, BC has received very good reviews from the new teachers who participate in the program, and we were told that the participation was good at the monthly follow-up meetings. BC is negotiating with BPS so that its graduates who teach in the district may have the opportunity to receive professional development credit for their participation in the Project SUCCESS programs.

Currently, arts and sciences faculty are not involved in the Summer Start Institute; instead, the program focuses on survival skills to help new teachers to set up their classrooms and to start the school year. In summer 2005, BC invited representatives from the Santa Cruz New Teacher Project to speak at the Summer Start Program about content-knowledge issues. While the second-year teachers greatly enjoyed hearing about content-knowledge issues, the first-year teachers were less receptive.

In addition to its on-site induction activities, in year two, BC began developing a set of online resources and distance-learning opportunities that will be available to graduates through an induction Web site.

At the request of BPS, the team leader for BC's TNE induction program developed and published a yearlong month-by-month curriculum for use by student/mentor training programs. This curriculum helped to fill a void in the district's mentoring program. The district purchased a copy of the curriculum for every new teacher and mentor.

University of Connecticut

Decisions Driven by Evidence

Over the first two years of TNE, UConn developed and fielded a number of surveys to inform its TNE work, conducted focus groups, developed a comprehensive database of teacher education students, started a syllabus study, worked on developing a pupil-learning pilot program, and funded a program for small research grants.

Student Surveys. UConn administered an entry survey to all students entering its teacher education program in 2005. UConn will use the student survey data to compare the experiences of students in its teacher education programs. The survey asks about expectations, perceptions of the program, and students' goals. An end-of-year survey was administered to students in the teacher education program in spring 2005. Survey topics included self-efficacy, level of preparation to use assessment methods, integration of technology into the classroom, teaching methods, and domain-specific knowledge. Response rates on the student surveys have been high—around 90 percent. The chance to win an iPod was used as an incentive for participating in the surveys, which proved to be successful.

Alumni Survey. A survey was administered to teacher education alumni six months after graduation to gather information for planning an induction program and for improving the teacher education program. Graduates were asked about their perceptions of the program, their experiences with it, their level of preparation, and suggestions for program improvement.

Survey of Practicing Teachers. To understand what defines excellent teaching, UConn conducted a survey of 569 practicing teachers in the United States (using a convenience sample) that asked respondents about their perception of what makes an excellent teacher. UConn is fielding the same questions to a sample of college and high school students.

Faculty Survey. A survey developed in spring 2005 was administered to faculty members to explore their familiarity with the requirements of the state's induction program, Beginning Educator Support and Training (BEST).

Focus Groups. UConn conducted focus groups in spring 2005. Participants included 27 arts and sciences faculty members, seven faculty members in education, and 46 students in the Integrated Bachelor's/Master's program. Major themes addressed by the groups included content knowledge, diversity, technology, assessment, characteristics of teacher education students, and relationships between teacher education programs and PDSs and arts and sciences departments.

Analysis of the BEST Program Survey. The Connecticut Department of Education administered a Web-based survey to 15,000 individuals—including beginning teachers (those in the first through fifth years of teaching), district facilitators, and mentors—to solicit information about the BEST program. Approximately 2,300 teachers responded to the survey. UConn began analyzing the survey data for the state Department of Education in year two and will analyze the BEST experiences of UConn graduates. UConn will use these data to better understand what role UConn might play in induction.

Database. UConn hired a database manager to organize existing and incoming data on students and graduates. Before TNE, multiple data sets were kept by many programs and departments. The database manager has merged all these data sets and is developing a coherent system, which will allow faculty members to use the data to form research questions and make decisions. TNE leaders told us that the database is one of the most significant contributions of the TNE work, because without a comprehensive and current database, it would be impossible to make decisions based on evidence.

Syllabus Project. In year two, UConn introduced its syllabus project. Using the new comprehensive database, faculty members identified the most-popular courses (and sections of those courses) taken by teacher education students. In year three, UConn will collect and analyze the syllabi from these courses to determine how well course content matches the state's teacher standards.

Pupil-Learning Pilot. In year two, UConn worked with an elementary school that was implementing a system that allows teachers to enter results of student assessments into a computer program and upload the program to the Web for access and data entry. The system then makes suggestions based on student-assessment results to help teachers individualize instruction based on the data. However, TNE participants told us that participation by teachers was sporadic. UConn plans to analyze the pupil-learning data provided by the system, which would give UConn additional experience in analyzing data of this type. However, due to teachers' limited participation in the pilot, the analyses will not provide solid information on the system's impact.

TNE Research Program. To push forward the TNE agenda for reform and develop enthusiasm for TNE overall, UConn instituted a program of small research grants for faculty, graduate students, and undergraduate students. To administer this program, UConn formed a six-member research committee including a principal from a local school. In fall 2004, the research committee hosted a conference to assist those planning to submit a research proposal. UConn spent $50,000 on the grants in year two.

Engagement with Arts and Sciences

UConn has established four committees to focus on aspects of the TNE work—assessment, curriculum design, induction, and research; the committees are co-chaired by school of education and arts and sciences faculty. A history professor on the Curriculum Design Team is working on a history course within arts and sciences that all teacher education students would be required to take. The plan is to add a lab for one section of this course that would be targeted toward education majors. The lab will focus on how to teach K–12 students to think about history.

In addition, UConn developed two mechanisms to help institutionalize the involvement of arts and sciences faculty in TNE—a TNE Fellows Program and TNE graduate assistants.

TNE Fellows. Faculty in the TNE Fellows Program dedicate a minimum of 25 percent of their academic time to TNE and play a significant role in the TNE project. TNE Fellow positions are one-year, renewable positions that are appointed by the provost. UConn appointed six TNE fellows in year one and seven in year two. Three of the TNE fellows were tenure-track faculty from the arts and sciences, and two were in new tenure-track positions in the arts and sciences that were specifically created for new hires working on TNE. An interest in pedagogy was explicitly included in the job opening announcements.

TNE fellows help to lead the TNE committees, co-teach courses with education faculty members, serve as liaisons with their home departments, and work on assessment projects. For instance, one TNE fellow, a modern and classical languages assistant professor, co-teaches a methods course in foreign-language instruction with a teacher education professor.

TNE Graduate Assistants. UConn created TNE graduate assistant positions for both education and arts and sciences graduate students. All graduate assistants share a common office space in UConn's TNE office suite. By bringing together the graduate assistants, UConn believes it has improved communication among its TNE teams and is developing a cadre of young professionals who may be more inclined toward such collaboration in the future.

Teaching as an Academically Taught Clinical-Practice Profession

K–12 Involvement. UConn has K–12 education representation on all of its TNE teams. We were told that some representatives from the K–12 schools have been very actively involved in TNE, while others have been involved to only a limited degree.

Induction. UConn formed a committee to lead the induction work that includes one arts and sciences faculty member, one State Department of Education representative, and two school principals, in addition to education faculty members.

TNE participants told us that UConn's teacher education program and the state context both strengthen and challenge its induction efforts. Because the program provides graduates with both a master's degree and teaching certification, UConn finds it difficult to motivate those graduates with post-baccalaureate credit (e.g., a master's, degree) to participate in an induction program. In addition, there is a statewide induction system, called BEST, which is a mandatory, two-year program that requires teachers to submit a portfolio of their teaching work at the end of year two of the program. However, UConn has access to BEST program data, and faculty have experience with the program, which would enable UConn to identify gaps in BEST that the university could fill for its graduates.

In year two of TNE, UConn developed five induction pilots for implementation in the following year. Each pilot is led by a faculty member and includes five or six participating graduates. The pilots vary in at least one of four ways: by provider (inductees' prior instructors or faculty members unknown to the inductees), by format (online or in person), by focus (geographic, i.e., where graduates teach, or subject-matter), and by "artifacts" and practice around which the pilots are centered. UConn will use the pilots to understand what can be learned from various induction formats and to develop its formal induction offerings.

University of Texas at El Paso

Decisions Driven by Evidence

UTEP's assessment work under TNE has involved research-unit representatives from the local school districts as well as education and arts and sciences faculty from the university. Key efforts in this area include a number of mini-grants to support TNE research, pupil-learning-growth pilot studies, and research on and review of courses and teacher education program elements.

Pilot Studies. TNE participants told us that the TNE requirement for gathering evidence on teacher effectiveness at first seemed "amorphous," particularly when attempting to build a chain of attribution between teacher education and pupil learning. UTEP decided to begin with a pilot study on a specific intervention in middle-school mathematics instead of tackling a much broader set of questions on the worth of teacher education. Picking a specific intervention and linking it to pupil achievement was seen as a more reasonable approach.

The core pilot study was to take place during the 2005–2006 school year and was to include 15 teachers trained under UTEP's Teacher Quality program and up to 500 of their students. A classroom intervention with pre-tests and post-tests for teachers and pupils and an analysis of selected items from the state achievement test were planned for the pilot.

A pre-pilot study was conducted during a two-month TexPREP program in summer 2005 for middle school and high school students in math and science, although the pilot involved only four teachers in the program who were using methods they learned through the Teacher Quality initiative. These teachers were linked to 100 of their summer students.

Two complementary studies were designed to use overlapping samples. One compared two curricula for teaching the application of logic to mathematics and the other examined the performance of bilingual pupils on cognitive ability and achievement tests.

Mini-Grant Program. UTEP has used TNE resources to fund a mini-grant program similar to small-grant programs at other TNE sites. The program has funded nine studies relating to TNE principles and research activities. Examples of these studies include a study that aims to link special-education teacher effectiveness to pupils' progress and another that involves mathematics-teacher candidates' use of technology in learning content, in clinical applications, and in assessment of pupils' learning. The grant program has drawn participants from across the university and local community. Faculty from fine arts, mathematics, English, psychology, chemistry, teacher education, and educational psychology have become involved in the program, as have representatives from El Paso Community College and three local school districts—El Paso, Socorro, and Ysleta.

Other Research. Several data-collection and research efforts are being conducted by TNE work groups at UTEP. The science work group developed and fielded a high school science teacher survey to learn more about the characteristics of science teachers in local districts. One goal was to learn more about science teachers who received alternative certification (AC). The survey drew 144 responses, 46 percent of which were from AC teachers. The teachers who were being closely mentored and who were provided with support (within a particular school) were doing very well, so this may be a model that UTEP's induction group should study.

TNE participants told us that there are very few secondary science-education majors (students who major in the sciences and train to be secondary-school science teachers) at UTEP. Instead, most students get a science degree and then enroll in an AC program. Some faculty members advise students to go the alternative certification route; therefore, the science work group also wants to examine how students are advised, how those students progress, and whether they go into teaching. UTEP is gathering data on 570 students who had been counseled by a student advisor sometime over the past few years and who showed an interest in science education, and it will try to track the students who are teaching in the local school districts.

Several other data-collection efforts are being considered or are under way, including a study linking college entrance scores, GPAs, and teacher education program experiences to performance on the TExES certification test.

Other TNE work groups at UTEP have been using assessments and other evidence to review and revise core courses and other courses in the arts and sciences disciplines. These efforts are further discussed under "Engagement with Arts and Sciences."

Data Coordination. A full-time TNE research associate was hired in summer 2005 to provide the work groups with technical support in statistical design and analysis and in survey methodology and other efforts to collect evidence, and to help with Institutional Review Board issues.

UTEP's student data reside in several places that are not interconnected. UTEP is working to collect all the available data that reside in various places and is considering designating a work group to guide the coordination efforts. UTEP plans to purchase teacher certification data from the state and has scheduled a training session, to be led by a consultant, on how to use the data. Efforts to obtain pupils' test scores will be facilitated by existing close ties to local districts that are already involved with TNE and through long-term involvement with the El Paso Collaborative for Academic Excellence.

Engagement with Arts and Sciences

TNE is building upon other initiatives at UTEP that have encouraged collaboration between arts and sciences and education faculty. UTEP's Math Science Partnership (MSP) program has resulted in partnerships between the science faculty and K–12 schools. TNE participants told us that TNE and MSP will bring about cultural change and improvements in teaching. UTEP leadership promotes the idea that there is value and importance in performing research on education. Several years ago, a National Science Foundation grant prompted UTEP to fund improvements in teaching and to include teaching evaluations in tenure decisions.

TNE program leadership at UTEP noted that TNE committees have introduced increased collegiality and have brought about greater trust and sharing of ideas among faculty. The TNE leadership hosted a TNE retreat in July 2005, which was attended by more than 50 UTEP faculty members and faculty from El Paso Community College and the local school districts.

TNE and Joint Faculty. TNE has funded and filled two new faculty positions, one in psychology and one in history. A search is under way for another TNE hire in the College of Education. In addition, there are new hires in English, who are focused on teacher preparation, funded by the university. The new hires promote awareness of assessment and TNE overall among the departments. The new faculty members reportedly have been welcomed by their colleagues and are seen as productive additions to the faculty, largely because of the careful selection of faculty with strong content knowledge and education backgrounds.

In addition, a number of arts and sciences faculty members were hired to focus on teacher education and engagement with K–12 schools prior to TNE. UTEP has five MSP faculty members in tenure-track positions. The mathematics department has three faculty members in math education, one of which is a tenured joint appointment in mathematics and teacher education; another joint appointment is in the anthropology department and the College of Education. The physics and history departments also have faculty positions that require a focus on pedagogy and education.

Review of Courses. The mathematics work group surveyed all mathematics faculty regarding the content of their courses. These data, along with an analysis of TExES pre-certification test scores, were used to develop a capstone course in mathematics that reviews the mathematics competencies and domains covered in the TExES test. The test scores will enable the group to identify potential gaps and weaknesses in course content and will help them to better align the course content with the test. UTEP is developing a bank of test items that will allow students to take practice tests and will enable faculty to monitor students' progress toward their learning goals. This information will be used to reconfigure courses to provide instruction in areas where students are weak. A capstone course has also been designed for future social studies teachers.

The fine arts work group is partnering with El Paso Community College to analyze the preparation of fine arts teachers. The work group surveyed fine arts faculty and also examined the performance of their students on the TExES state certification test. The results of this analysis led to the redesign of the Whole Arts course, including separating the lecture from the lab and having the course shared by the music, theater, and arts departments.

The core curriculum work group is examining the required core coursework and how these core courses map to what teachers need to know to effectively teach in the classroom. In summer 2006, UTEP was to offer seminars in which high school, community college, and UTEP faculty members examine common content and syllabi.

Teaching as an Academically Taught Clinical-Practice Profession

Clinical Sites. UTEP already had a set of auxiliary schools, partner schools, and PDSs pre-TNE, although only a few schools meet the criteria for being in the highest level of PDSs. As part of TNE, UTEP plans to expand the development of PDSs to promote "communities of learners."

Teachers in Residence. In year two, UTEP began its search for a TNE teacher in residence. The TIR, who was hired in October 2005, will be responsible for teaching university courses and for participating in various TNE activities, including collecting data on undergraduates who are interested in teaching and tracking their progress through the university and into teaching careers.

Induction. TNE participants told us that while Texas has state-mandated induction, it is not funded at the state level; therefore, all induction programs are run at the district level, and what is offered varies a great deal across districts. This situation creates opportunities for UTEP to assist with induction activities.

As part of TNE, UTEP formed an induction work group. The group's 25 members include many K–12 participants—new teachers, experienced teachers, and representation from several districts. A large part of the work group's efforts in year two focused on developing a conceptual model of simultaneous renewal of K–12 schools and the university. This model has three components—beginning teachers, experienced teachers, and school organization and climate. UTEP plans to build on what the districts are already doing in terms of induction and on what they have learned through their affiliation with the National Network for Educational Reform. UTEP plans to gather data to inform its program choices and develop new surveys of teachers, mentors, and administrators.

In year two, UTEP advertised a position for an induction coordinator, who was hired in year three. This individual, with the help of the work group, will be responsible for designing a two-tier induction program featuring on-site and online support.

Second Cohort of Grantees: Sites Not Included in the National Evaluation

This appendix and the previous appendix examine the progress made by the second cohort of TNE grantees. Appendix C examined TNE activities at the four sites that were part of the funded national evaluation; this appendix examines the three sites that were not part of the funded evaluation.

Stanford University

Decisions Driven by Evidence

Over the first two years of TNE, Stanford funded a number of studies to help inform its TNE work and developed a comprehensive data-management system, which allows Stanford to store and analyze data on its current students and on its graduates. The system will also be used to store data from research studies.

Stanford's TNE Research and Assessment Team provided ongoing advice on the development of the TNE research, including assigning faculty in the development of proposals and reviewing all proposals to ensure sound research design. Stanford funded large and small research studies—some of which focus on teacher education and some of which place greater emphasis on outcomes for teachers and pupils. Each funded study employs doctoral students, because one of Stanford's goals is to develop a cadre of doctoral students who are knowledgeable about teacher preparation. The Stanford-funded studies are briefly described next.

Survey of Graduates. Stanford continues to survey its teacher education program alumni, which it has done since 1998. The 84-question survey asks alumni to answer questions regarding their feelings of preparedness for the teaching profession.

Survey of Elementary Education Preservice Students. In 2003–2004, faculty in Stanford's School of Education developed a survey of its elementary education pre-service students. Students were surveyed on their views of education, background, expectations of the program, and approach to literacy instruction. The survey was administered in 2004–2005. Stanford will re-administer the survey to its students at the completion of the program and use the data from the survey to inform program decisions.

Survey of Student Teachers. Two experts in language acquisition for second-language learners developed a survey instrument to measure student teachers' attitudes toward English-language learners. This instrument was administered to student teachers before and after their placement to determine changes in their attitudes. Faculty members are analyzing the survey results to determine the impact of two courses, Teaching in Heterogeneous Classes and Language Policies and Practices, and the effect of clinical placements on students' attitudes regarding ELL students.

Research Studies. A study on teaching practices is being conducted jointly by Stanford faculty and an external evaluator, SRI International. Stanford designed the study in 2003–2004 and launched it in 2004–2005. This study examines the teaching practices of a set of Stanford teacher education graduates and non-Stanford teacher education graduates in their first years of teaching. This research will provide Stanford with important data on teacher education programs, allow it to develop tools for studying beginning teachers and their pupils, and enable it to develop instruments to link pupils' progress with teacher education programs.

Another study is assessing the Performance Assessment for California Teachers (PACT), which all Stanford student teachers must complete. PACT requires student teachers to analyze their teaching effectiveness by using various assessment strategies to track pupils' learning and to articulate their findings from the assessment. The PACT assignment was implemented in 2003–2004 and was revised for 2004–2005. All results will be shared with other schools of education in the PACT consortium.

A third study follows Stanford teacher education graduates into secondary schools in the San Francisco Bay Area. The study will collect data on all teachers in six high schools, collect comparable data on pupil achievement for all teachers who teach a course in any one of four core academic areas (mathematics, science, history, English language arts), and examine the teaching practices of a selected subsample of teachers who represent high, modal, and low levels of teacher effectiveness, as measured by their pupils' achievement. A survey of teachers will provide information about their academic backgrounds, preparation and induction experiences, teaching experiences, and teaching practices. The goal is to determine how certain aspects of teacher education programs and other experiential and contextual factors influence teaching practices and outcomes, independent of teachers' participation in a particular teacher education program. School participation and survey administration were to start in 2005–2006.

Other studies measure the content knowledge of teacher education candidates, the application of knowledge learned in a teacher education program, and the connection between mathematics instruction and pupils' learning under student teachers.

Stanford asked SRI to conduct a study of its graduates and their teaching practices to better understand the key characteristics of the teacher education program, how the program impacts graduates' teaching practices, and the nature of a beginning teachers' practice. The ultimate purpose of the study is to understand the teacher education program's impact on its participants so that its leaders can chart improvement strategies. SRI will conduct in-depth case studies of eight graduates and in-depth case studies of eight comparable first-year teachers. Case study participants will be observed and interviewed in the spring of the school year. Researchers will also interview individuals who are considered to be influential in a participant's development as a teacher (e.g., principal, mentor).

Engagement with Arts and Sciences

Arts and sciences faculty and graduate students are included in the majority of TNE activities and are active in the Content and Design TNE study groups. In addition, education faculty members are becoming more greatly involved in non-education school courses. For example, the associate dean of the School of Education and a professor from the humanities program developed a section for the Introduction to Humanities course, which focuses on social justice.

Following are selected examples of Stanford's teacher education activities that include arts and science faculty:

- In 2003–2004, two new courses focusing on literacy were developed, and the literacy course for the secondary Stanford Teacher Education Program (STEP) students was redesigned.
- Arts and sciences faculty who are experts in language acquisition for second-language learners developed a survey of student teachers to determine attitudes toward ELL students.
- Arts and sciences faculty have played key roles in developing the elementary pre-service program and new courses for the preservice undergraduate students. For instance, in winter 2004–2005, Stanford offered a new undergraduate course on teaching Shakespeare. The university also developed a new mathematics course for its elementary education program, which will be co-taught by a mathematics faculty member and faculty from the Carnegie Center for the Advancement of Teaching. Faculty from the visual arts department developed and offered an undergraduate course, Elementary Visual Arts, which included a lecture, studio, and field work.
- Stanford's string quartet and its conductor conducted sessions for teacher education students and taught classes in one of Stanford's professional development schools.
- In addition, arts and sciences faculty and graduate students offered a professional development workshop, which focused on Shakespeare and reading of literature,

for STEP English graduates. Participants earned a $350 stipend for participating in the workshop. They also were asked to participate in a case study following the workshop.

Teaching as an Academically Taught Clinical-Practice Profession

K–12 Involvement. Teacher education students at Stanford have participated in a tutoring project for struggling readers in the local schools. Stanford is developing two additional tutoring projects, one of which will include a pre- and post-test of pupils in the tutoring program and will compare tutored pupils with a control group that did not receive tutoring support.

Stanford developed the Council for Partnerships Schools, which brings together administrators, teachers, and teacher education faculty to work on various topics, such as differentiated instruction.

Stanford has taken over the charter for the East Palo Alto High School and will expand the school to serve both secondary and elementary school students. Stanford plans to make the East Palo Alto school a site for clinical placements for student teachers.

Stanford is analyzing the strengths and weaknesses of the clinical placements in the secondary STEP program. In summer 2004, student teachers used guided questions to complete a paper in which they reflected on their first clinical placement. These papers were analyzed, and the findings were reported to the STEP Steering Committee and Cabinet and will be used to guide future teacher education policies and practices.

Induction. Stanford is in the planning stages of induction. It is working to develop induction opportunities for graduates and to enhance the professional development programs at the schools where they teach. Arts and sciences faculty will also provide specific types of professional development that targets graduates who teach locally. For example, quarter-long courses and departmentally designed teacher workshops will be offered to participants at a reduced cost and for credit. Stanford will also host summer institutes that offer seminars in content-specific pedagogy, classroom management, and other topics of interest to new teachers. Recent graduates will be invited to attend these institutes and will receive professional development credit for attendance. Stanford also plans to offer Web-based support and resources for all graduates.

University of Washington

Decisions Driven by Evidence

Database. UW has begun preliminary work on a new database that will track teacher candidates from graduation into the field and link pupils' work with information on teachers and the school's context. The database will include information on entering students' beliefs and knowledge, learning opportunities within the program, post-student-teaching learning, teaching practice and perceptions of graduates, and evidence of the learning gains of graduates' pupils.

Mini-Grant Program. The Executive Committee created an RFP encouraging faculty members and P–12 representatives to develop research projects on teacher development issues. The projects will be funded at $25,000 to $75,000 for one year. Three proposals had been received and one was funded as of the beginning of year two. Recipients of TNE monies will be asked to share their findings with others in the university, in journal articles, and at local, regional, and national conferences.

Research Studies. UW has initiated several studies that will help to inform its teacher education program renewal efforts. One study followed a cohort of graduates from an urban education certification program into its first two years of teaching to learn more about the types of induction supports that were available and most useful in improving retention and teacher learning. Data sources included online surveys, interviews, and document reviews.

The Urban Study Group reviewed data and relevant literature to draft recommendations for specific urban-related initiatives for the renewal of the teacher education program. Another study group has been learning about the practices of other TNE sites and teacher education programs related to ELL education and will be developing a set of recommendations based on its studies.

Another study is examining UW's teacher education program through an ethnographic lens, focusing on the student-teaching experience. Data include interviews and observations of student teachers, cooperating teachers, and university supervisors. Preliminary findings on student teachers' interests related to teaching were presented at a conference in year two of TNE.

UW has also launched a project to examine the experiences of students of color in its teacher education program. Interviews and focus groups will be used to produce a handbook of pedagogical strategies for teacher education faculty, and a survey will be conducted to monitor changes and progress in this area.

A study group has been formed around renewal of the elementary education program. In year two, the group planned for two inquiry projects and several seminar discussions to help members of the teacher education program and other stakeholders to discuss priorities for renewal.

UW has made preliminary progress toward a study of pupil-learning gains tied to teacher education graduates. A pilot study is planned that will link students' test score gains to 20 to 30 teachers in Seattle public schools.

Engagement with the Arts and Sciences

Arts and sciences faculty are incorporated into all TNE workgroups. One TNE recruiting mechanism used by UW was the creation of a database of arts and sciences faculty members' current involvement with P–12 schools, teachers, and/or pupils, which enabled TNE leadership to identify arts and sciences faculty with a natural interest in teacher education.

Following are selected examples of TNE activities that include arts and science faculty:

- The divisional dean of Natural Sciences met with science department chairs to discuss improving science teaching and learning and the possibility of a new undergraduate major in general science.
- In year two, the Puget Sound Science Supervisors group provided feedback on how to better prepare science teachers. Their input will be used by the Developing a General Science Undergraduate Degree Committee, which was to be convened in fall 2005.
- The Study Group on English Language Arts prepared a report and a set of recommendations to be presented to the English department. The recommendations include establishing a new pathway toward a degree in English, creating a new seminar series for students interested in teaching, creating a series of workshops to show English department faculty how to incorporate PCK into their teaching, and jointly appointing a faculty member in the Schools of Education and Arts and Sciences to specialize in English education.
- UW plans to utilize arts and sciences faculty in its Video Traces computer program, which enhances teachers' professional growth through the use of video. UW envisions using asynchronous feedback from a variety of experts to form a virtual professional learning community that can help emerging teachers to learn about ways to improve their practice.

Teaching as an Academically Taught Clinical-Practice Profession

K–12 Involvement. P–12 educators are represented in all three study groups, on the Evidence of Learning Team, and in various committees. In addition, UW has appointed a former P–12 principal as a full-time Distinguished Educator on a three-year appointment and named her as co-director of the new Washington Center for Teaching and Learning. She also co-teaches one of the teacher education courses.

The Bridging Theory and Practice for Novice Teachers Project of the Urban Scholars Program is working to redesign a mathematics methods course to include topics covered over a weeklong period with lecture-based introductions to the topics, field-based activities, and follow-up debriefings on what was learned through the activities. TNE funds allow for a first-year UW graduate to provide "release time" for P–12 mathematics teachers in the school where the project is being implemented so that these teachers can participate in and help to teach the field-based portion of the course.

UW has refined its goals for P–12 partnerships and its process for identifying partner schools. Faculty are working to reduce the number of schools in which teacher candidates are placed to better concentrate their resources for the benefit of both the university and the schools. In year one, schools were invited to nominate themselves to be partner schools, and the Partner School Committee developed a rubric to evaluate the schools' nomination materials and evaluated those materials from the schools. In year two, 19 schools in five districts were invited to join the Ackerley Partnership for Teacher Development Network. Meetings of the network to date have focused on induction and new possibilities for reciprocal collaborative work.

UW created new field-based Reflective Seminars for student teachers, in which cooperating teachers share their experiences and help to facilitate discussion and reflection on teaching experiences.

Induction. The pilot of UW's T-LINC (Teachers Learning in Networked Communities) online induction support system went "live" on the Seattle Public Schools' Web site in year two. The site includes district-specific links to standards, materials, strategies, forms and other documents, and vetted educational Web sites for new teachers. The project will eventually be expanded to serve all UW teacher graduates.

UW is preparing to implement a new Master in Instructional Leadership for Teachers program geared toward cooperating teachers, mentors, and instructional coaches beginning in fall 2006. The program has been approved by the university, and applications are currently being accepted for enrollment in the first class.

UW is making efforts to ensure that its induction offerings fit into the local district's system. As stated above, one UW research study tracked graduates from an urban education certification program to learn more about what types of induction supports are available and most useful in improving retention and teacher learning. Also, a UW TNE representative is participating in a task force to evaluate new Professional Practice Standards for evaluation and professional growth of teachers in Seattle public schools.

University of Wisconsin–Milwaukee

Decisions Driven by Evidence
UWM has assembled two groups that are working specifically on issues of assessment and evidence. The Pupil Learning Gains Coordinating Group is charged with studying student-learning gains accomplished under the tutelage of UWM teacher graduates, while the Program Assessment Coordinating Group is charged with supporting the assessment of UWM pre-service teachers' development. Both groups include faculty members from arts and sciences and education, and the pupil learning-gains group also includes a representative from the Milwaukee Public Schools (MPS). These groups met every two or three months during the 2004–2005 school year and accomplished several objectives.

Work on Pupils' Learning Gains. The Pupil Learning Gains Coordinating Group spent the first portion of 2004–2005 reviewing the literature on VAM and writing a report on the use of VAM within the context of UWM and MPS. One major concern of the group has been finding ways to measure teacher behavior in addition to measuring student achievement and various teacher and student characteristics. As the group's 2004–2005 activity report states, "We have concluded that it is not enough to say that teacher X graduated and was certified by UWM. We need some assurance that what teacher X is doing in the classroom is what UWM prepared, and expected, the teacher to do."

As of spring 2005, the Pupil Learning Gains Coordinating Group had developed a plan for a pilot study of learning gains in the Milwaukee Public Schools and had collected achievement data from MPS for students in grades three, seven, and ten. The group was working on developing an online survey for teachers and on database design and analysis. Additional data collection was anticipated in fall 2005 and spring 2006, at which point the group will have enough data to begin testing various analytical models of value-added teacher effects.

Assessment Work. The Program Assessment Coordinating Group conducted a literature review and examined work at other TNE sites as a starting place for its work. Members of the group felt that there was no common understanding of "content knowledge" and "subject matter knowledge" at UWM; as such, the group worked to develop an operational definition of those terms to help ground the TNE work. Plans for summer 2005 and the 2005–2006 school year included planning and implementing a series of assessment forums for MPS teachers and UWM faculty that would include external experts presenting work on assessments; collecting and archiving existing assessment tools from content courses, general education courses, school of education courses, and student teaching experiences; and developing and planning a number of new assessments geared toward evaluating teachers' development at various points in their teacher preparation and induction period.

Other Work. Some work related to evidence was conducted by other TNE design teams. For example, the Arts and Culture Design Team met at the end of the 2004–2005 school year to review portfolios of current MPS teaching (e.g., lesson plans, pupils' work) in the arts to provide a foundation for the development of new common assessment rubrics and evaluation tools across the various arts disciplines.

Engagement with Arts and Sciences

Arts and sciences faculty members are involved in the work of TNE through their roles on six content-focused teams—the Humanities, Social Sciences, Science, Mathematics, Arts and Culture, and Cultures and Communities Design Teams. A seventh team, focusing on foreign languages, was added for the 2005–2006 academic year. Design teams met approximately once a month during the 2004–2005 school year. They were charged with studying the alignment of the UWM teacher education program with

School of Education courses and typical pre-education courses and with national, state, and local K–12 content standards in each content area, and were charged with developing recommendations for correcting any misalignment. As of spring 2005, most of the design teams had completed their alignment reviews, but a number of curriculum revisions were still in the planning phase. However, the recommendations from the various teams had several similar strategies:

- **Changes to content requirements in major or minor areas of study.** The Humanities, Social Sciences, and Science Design Teams recommended significant changes to the requirements for teacher education students' content-area majors and minors in several teaching fields.

- **New courses.** Several design teams recommended new content-area courses. For example, the Social Science Design Team in its final 2005 report recommended developing a new multidisciplinary course that will "examine one theme with contemporary relevance, e.g., poverty or inequality, from multiple disciplinary perspectives." The Science Design Team initiated a new course, Introductory Biology for Teachers, to complement similar courses in physics and chemistry; the new course was offered for the fall 2005 semester. In addition, the Cultures and Communities Design Team recommended assembling a team of faculty members to develop a new service learning (community service activities) core course on Global Cultures and Communities.

- **Course revisions.** Several design teams recommended revisions to existing courses to improve alignment of teacher education students' preparation with K–12 teaching standards. For example, the Science Design Team is planning a new lab component for the Basic Physics for Teachers course and plans to make revisions to the Basic Chemistry for Teachers course based on students' comments. In its final 2005 report, the Humanities Design Team expressed particular concern regarding "conceptual" alignment and recommended that there be "a congruency between the content taught in a particular course and the theory/practice needs of teachers in training." As a result, UWM assembled a working group over summer 2005 to begin making plans for curricular revisions, using Introduction to English Studies, a required course for all English majors, as a starting place. The group hopes to revise the course goals to pay more attention to critical literacy and has discussed the need to improve coordination among sections in multi-section courses.

- **Prerequisite changes.** The Humanities Design Team recommended a change to the prerequisite policy for upper-level courses in the English Department; 300- and 400-level courses had been limited to students with junior standing or above, but this requirement made it difficult for teacher education students to complete their English major requirements in a timely manner. The English Department reviewed this requirement at the recommendation of the TNE Humanities Design Team and approved a new policy making 300- and 400-level classes open to students with sophomore standing or above.

- **New programs.** The Cultures and Communities Design Team formed an action team that is planning a new master's degree track in the Department of Curriculum and Instruction in partnership with the College of Letters and Science that will focus on "Cultures and Communities"; the goal was to launch the degree program by offering two courses in summer 2006.

Teaching as an Academically Taught Clinical-Practice Profession

K–12 Educators' Involvement in Teacher Education. UWM involves K–12 educators in its teacher education program in a variety of ways. First, TNE funds helped to support two new TIRs on two-year appointments to the university. The TIRs worked with the various design teams, advised student teachers, and worked with students in their methods courses; however, the TIR program was in place prior to TNE, and four additional TIRs have already been funded through the Milwaukee Mathematics Partnership.

K–12 educators are also well-represented on the various Design Teams; most include a principal, a district curriculum specialist, and at least one teacher. Furthermore, several of the design teams have sought input from current MPS teachers to help inform their work. For instance, the Humanities and Social Sciences Design Teams are planning surveys of second- and third-year in-service teachers, while the Science Design Team and the Induction Team conducted focus groups with in-service teachers during the 2004–2005 school year.

Induction. UWM's Induction Team is charged with developing plans for a comprehensive induction program in conjunction with MPS, although several other design teams have also included induction activities in their work. The Induction Team is composed of faculty in education and arts and sciences, MPS central-office staff, MPS teachers, and one MPS parent. This group functioned dually as the TNE Induction Team and as a workgroup for the Milwaukee Partnership Academy. The group met biweekly during the 2004–2005 school year and accomplished several objectives.

First, the team developed a document titled "Characteristics of a High-Performing Urban Classroom," which will help to create a common language regarding the practice of teaching in MPS to structure induction support. The team then trained MPS literacy and mathematics specialists in piloting discussions of this document in 16 MPS schools. The group also conducted a series of focus groups of first-year MPS teachers to learn about their induction experiences and found that these teachers generally do not feel that they receive adequate support during this period. The team worked to catalog the "status quo" for first-year teachers in MPS from the time the teacher candidates apply for a teaching position with the district until they get into a district school. Using these various data, the group developed a comprehensive induction plan for MPS that includes explicit definitions of the role of each stakeholder (MPS, UWM, the teachers' union, new teachers). This plan was presented to the district in June 2005. Using this plan, the group developed a brochure for new MPS teachers, which outlines what new teachers should expect in terms of support and their responsibilities during the induction period; the group is also developing similar guides for district personnel, school principals, the teachers' union, and UWM faculty on their specific roles in induction.

In addition to the comprehensive plan, the Induction Team is also piloting a new "induction cohort" in their master's program, with a particular focus on reflective practice (the process by which teachers actively reflect upon or analyze their teaching practice in hopes of making improvements in it). The group plans to do a research study of this program.

Several other TNE design teams at UWM have also worked on induction and professional development activities for teachers. The Cultures and Communities Design Team, for example, is developing a summer Teacher Institute for 2007 that will showcase available resources and best practices in multicultural studies and community engagement in K–12 education. The Arts and Cultures Design Team is focusing almost entirely on providing induction and professional development opportunities, including graduate courses and summer programs (one idea was a theme-based program for MPS teachers on using storytelling through the arts) to help new teachers become master teachers of the arts.

Florida A&M University

Florida A&M University had undergone a number of leadership changes since the inception of the TNE grant process. Changes had occurred in the offices of the President, Provost and Vice President for Academic Affairs, Vice President for Finance and Administrative Affairs, and Vice President for Research. As a result of these and other personnel changes, there have been delays in the grant approval process. The TNE grant agreement for FAMU was finalized in May 2005. While preliminary funding in the amount of $110,000 was received in April 2004, it was not until September 2005 that FAMU received its first regular reimbursement for grant activities. Therefore, in this appendix, we provide a brief overview of FAMU's TNE activities; however, we did not include the TNE data for FAMU in our examination of cross-site trends.

Project Structure and Staffing

The Provost and Vice President for Academic Affairs serves as principal investigator for the TNE project at FAMU. A full-time TNE Project Manager and a full-time Curriculum and Assessment Coordinator were hired in August 2004. FAMU's TNE Leadership Team includes the Principal Investigator, Project Manager, Associate Vice President for Academic Affairs, Dean of General Studies, Dean of Education, Associate Dean of Arts and Sciences, Assistant Dean of Education, Assistant Dean of Arts and Sciences, the Coordinator of the National Board Resource Center at FAMU, and the Director/Superintendent of the FAMU Developmental Research School.

TNE Design Teams

FAMU formed six TNE design teams. The teams included faculty from the Colleges of Education and Arts and Sciences, teacher education candidates, and in-service teachers from FAMU's Developmental Research School. The first three design teams—Assessment, Elementary Education, and Chemistry—started work in summer 2004 and the remaining three teams—Biology, Mathematics, and English—began work in spring 2005.

The Assessment Design Team compiled an inventory of assessments used at FAMU and identified elements to be included in a TNE database that will be used to track the progress of students and graduates. The Assessment Design Team also began work on a pupil-learning-growth pilot study. This pilot study will track pupil learning gains made by the 2000–2001 cohort of FAMU graduates. FAMU has received data from the Florida K–20 Education Data Warehouse, which enables FAMU to longitudinally link teachers to students.

The Elementary Education Design Team established two work groups—the Upper Division Work Group and the Social Studies Course Work Group. Both groups have been working to revise teacher education courses, program requirements, and field experiences to help better prepare students for the Florida Teacher Certification Examination (FTCE). FAMU has requested more-detailed FTCE data from the state to help in these efforts. The team is also collecting data from several other sources: surveys of field-experience supervisors, focus groups consisting of recently tested students, and evaluations of revised courses. In addition, the Social Studies Course Work Group designed an arts and sciences course to be piloted in fall 2006. The course will prepare students for the FTCE K–6 Subject Area Exam, which includes questions on history, geography, economics, government, and civics. One member of the workgroup is conducting an experiment in her Cultural Geography course sections to better understand the impact of more-interactive pedagogies.

The Mathematics Design Team identified high-stakes, statewide exams for which FAMU is responsible for preparing students, including the College Level Academic Skills Test and three specific pieces of the FTCE. The team created a list of tested skills that it will use to guide curriculum changes. The goal is to create diagnostic tests and computer-generated individualized study plans to increase the pass rates in courses and on the statewide examinations.

The Biology Design Team is engaged in a similar standards realignment based on FTCE standards. The team is considering customizing a biology course section (Biological Science), which is taken by many education majors, to meet the needs of elementary education students. The Chemistry Design Team began work on curriculum mapping and standardization of courses by reviewing Florida Teacher Competencies (state teaching standards), Sunshine State Standards for K–12 students, National Science Standards for science teachers, and the American Chemical Society Guidelines. Subteams were organized to work on general chemistry, organic chemistry, physical chemistry, and biochemistry curricula. Revised courses, exams, and grading criteria are being piloted. For example, one faculty member is experimenting with a section of his General Chemistry course using a personal response system (PRS)[1] to determine if the use of this system results in improved student performance. Another professor piloted a revised Organic Chemistry course during summer 2005 and implemented it department-wide in fall 2005.

The English Design Team has been collecting input from pre-service teachers, K–12 teachers, and FAMU faculty to help produce a program assessment plan.

FAMU also planned a Design Team Colloquium that was conducted in fall 2005, which allowed teams to meet and to share their progress.

Promoting TNE

FAMU introduced a series of professional development seminars to stimulate the faculty's interest in teaching, pedagogy, and assessment. These "Lunch and Learn Seminars" have been well received, drawing participants from across the campus, including faculty from arts and sciences and FAMU's Development Research School. The seminars have such titles as "Using Bloom's Taxonomy to Promote Critical Thinking," "Syllabus Analysis," "Teaching and Assessing to Standards," "Learning Styles," and "Culturally Relevant Pedagogy." The seminars are designed to help FAMU faculty find ways to improve their understanding of pedagogy and their own teaching.

---

[1]   A PRS enables large groups of people to vote on a topic or to answer a question via remote control. Typically, the results are instantly displayed on a projection screen for participants. PRSs are increasingly used in teaching situations.

Bibliography

Adams, T. L., "Prospective Elementary Teachers' Mathematics Subject Matter Knowledge: The Real Number System," *Journal for Research in Mathematics Education*, Vol. 20, No. 2, 1998, pp. 35–48.

Adcock, E. P., and G. W. Phillips, "Accountability Evaluation of Magnet School Programs: A Value-Added Model Approach," paper presented at the Annual Meeting of the American Educational Research Association, New Orleans, La., April 2000.

Agenda for Education in a Democracy, "Twenty Postulates," n.d. (http://depts.washington. edu/cedren/Publications/postulates.htm; accessed February 2006).

Allen, M., *Eight Questions on Teacher Preparation: What the Research Says*, Denver, Colo.: Education Commission of the States, 2003.

Allexsaht-Snider, M., J. G. Deegan, and C. S. White, "Educational Renewal in an Alternative Teacher Education Program: Evolution of a School-University Partnership," *Teaching and Teacher Education*, Vol. 11, September 1995, pp. 519–530.

Ball, D. L., "The Mathematical Understandings that Prospective Teachers Bring to Teacher Education," *Elementary School Journal*, Vol. 90, March 1990a, pp. 449–466.

————, "Prospective Elementary and Secondary Teachers' Understanding of Division," *Journal for Research in Mathematics Education*, Vol. 21, No. 2, 1990b, pp. 132–144.

Barnett, C., "Rethinking Organizational Learning Theories: A Review and Synthesis of the Primary Literature," unpublished manuscript, Whittemore School of Business and Economics, University of New Hampshire, n.d.

Biggs, J., and K. Collis, *Evaluating the Quality of Learning: The SOLO Taxonomy*, New York, N.Y.: Academic Press, 1982.

Blocker, L. S., and C. Mantle-Bromley, "PDS Versus Campus Preparation: Through the Eyes of the Students," *The Teacher Educator*, Vol. 33, Autumn 1997, pp. 70–89.

Boe, E. E., S. A. Bobbitt, L. Cook, S. D. Whitener, and A. L. Weber, "Why Didst Thou Go? Predictors of Retention, Transfer, and Attrition of Special and General Education Teachers from a National Perspective," *The Journal of Special Education*, Vol. 30, Winter 1997, pp. 390–411.

Borko, H., M. Eisenhart, C. A. Brown, R. G. Underhill, D. Jones, and P. C. Agard, "Learning to Teach Hard Mathematics: Do Novice Teachers and Their Instructors Give Up Too Easily?" *Journal for Research in Mathematics Education*, Vol. 23, May 1992, pp. 194–222.

Bryk, A. S., Y. M. Thum, J. Q. Easton, and S. Luppescu, *Academic Productivity of Chicago Public Elementary Schools*, Chicago: Consortium on Chicago School Research, 1998.

Bullough, R. V., Jr., "Planning and the First Year of Teaching," *Journal of Education for Teaching*, Vol. 13, No. 2, 1987, pp. 231–250.

————, *First Year Teacher: A Case Study*, New York, N.Y.: Teachers College Press, 1989.

————, "Supervision, Mentoring and Self-Discovery: A Case Study of a First-Year Teacher," *Journal of Curriculum and Supervision*, Vol. 5, No. 4, 1990, pp. 338–360.

Bullough, R. V., Jr., J. G. Knowles, and N. A. Crow, "Teacher Self-Concept and Student Culture in the First Year of Teaching," *Teachers College Record*, Vol. 91, No. 2, Winter 1989, pp. 209–233.

Bush, R. N., "The Beginning Years of Teaching: A Focus for Collaboration in Teacher Education," paper presented at the World Assembly of the International Council on Education for Teaching, Washington, D.C., 1983.

Button, K., J. Ponticell, and M. J. Johnson, "Enabling School-University Collaborative Research: Lessons Learned in Professional Development Schools," *Journal of Teacher Education,* Vol. 47, January/February 1996, pp. 16–20.

Carnegie Corporation of New York, "Teachers for a New Era Prospectus," *The Corporation's Program,* n.d. (http://www.carnegie.org/sub/program/teachers_prospectus.html; accessed June 2004).

Carter, K., K. Cushing, D. Sabers, P. Stein, and D. Berliner, "Expert-Novice Differences in Perceiving and Processing Visual Classroom Information," *Journal of Teacher Education,* Vol. 39, May/June 1988, pp. 25–31.

Charles A. Dana Center, *Texas Beginning Educator Support System Evaluation Report for Year Three—2001–02*, Austin, Tex.: Charles A. Dana Center, 2002.

Choi, T., and O. Behling, "Top Managers and TQM Success: One More Look After All These Years," *Academy of Management Executive,* Vol. 11, No. 1, 1997, pp. 37–47.

Choo, C. W., *The Knowing Organization: How Organizations Use Information to Construct Meaning, Create Knowledge, and Make Decisions*, New York: Oxford University Press, 1998.

Civil, M., "Prospective Elementary Teachers' Thinking About Teaching Mathematics," *Journal of Mathematical Behavior*, Vol. 12, No. 1, 1993, pp. 79–109.

Cleary, M. J., and S. Groer, "Inflight Decisions of Expert and Novice Health Teachers," *Journal of School Health,* Vol. 64, No. 3, 1994, pp. 110–114.

Cochran-Smith, M. and K. Fries, "The AERA Panel on Research and Teacher Education: Context and Goals," in *Studying Teacher Education: The Report of the AERA Panel on Research and Teacher Education*, Washington, D.C.: American Educational Research Association, 2005a.

————, "Researching Teacher Education in Changing Times: Politics and Paradigms," in *Studying Teacher Education: The Report of the AERA Panel on Research and Teacher Education*, Washington, D.C.: American Educational Research Association, 2005b.

Cochran-Smith, M., and K. M. Zeichner, eds., *Studying Teacher Education: The Report of the AERA Panel on Research and Teacher Education*, Washington, D.C.: American Educational Research Association, 2005.

Conant, J., *The Education of American Teachers*, New York, N.Y.: McGraw-Hill, 1963.

Connor, K. R., and N. Killmer, "Cohorts, Collaboration, and Community: Does Contextual Teacher Education Really Work?" *Action in Teacher Education,* Vol. 23, No. 3, 2001, pp. 46–53.

Cornett, L. M. "A Comparison of Teacher Certification Test Scores and Performance Evaluations for Graduates in Teacher Education and in Arts and Sciences in Three Southern States," unpublished report submitted by the Southern Regional Education Board, Atlanta, to the National Endowment for the Humanities, 1984.

Crosby, P. B., *Quality Is Free*, New York, N.Y.: McGraw-Hill, 1979.

Cuban, L., "School Reform by Remote Control: SB813 in California," *Phi Delta Kappan*, Vol. 66, November 1984, pp. 213–215.

Daft, R. L., *Organization Theory and Design,* 5th ed., St. Paul, Minn.: West Publishing Co., 1995.

———, *Organizational Theory and Design*, 6th ed., Cincinnati, Ohio: South-Western College Publishing, 1998.

Daft, R. L., and N. B. Macintosh, "A Tentative Exploration into the Amount and Equivocality of Information Processing in Organizational Work Units," *Administrative Science Quarterly*, Vol. 26, No. 2, 1981, pp. 207–224.

Dean, J. W., Jr., and M. P. Sharfman, "The Relationship Between Procedural Rationality and Political Behavior in Strategic Decision Making," *Decision Sciences*, Vol. 24, No. 6, 1993, pp. 1069–1083.

deGues, A., "Planning as Learning," *Harvard Business Review*, March/April 1988, pp. 70–74.

Deming, W. E., *Out of Crisis*, Cambridge, Mass.: MIT Center for Advanced Engineering Study, 1986.

Desimone, L., M. S. Garet, and B. F. Birman, "Improving Teachers' In-Service Professional Development in Mathematics and Science: The Role of Post-Secondary Institutions," *Educational Policy*, Vol. 17, No. 5, 2003, pp. 613–649.

Drucker, P., "Knowledge-Worker Productivity: The Biggest Challenge," *California Management Review*, Vol.41, No. 2, 1999, pp. 79–94.

Druva, C. A., and R. D. Anderson, "Science Teachers' Characteristics by Teacher Behavior by Student Outcome," *Journal of Research in Science Teaching*, Vol. 20, No. 5, 1983, pp. 467–479.

Earley, P. E., *Guaranteeing the Quality of Future Educators: A Report of a Survey on Teacher Warranty Programs*, Washington, D.C.: American Association of Colleges for Teacher Education, AACTE Education Policy Clearinghouse, February 2000 (http://www.edpolicy.org/publications/documents/warranty.htm; accessed March 2006).

Ehrenberg, R., and D. Brewer, "Did Teachers' Verbal Ability and Race Matter in the 1960s? Coleman Revisited," *Economics of Education Review*, Vol. 14, No. 1, 1995, pp. 1–21.

Elmore, R. F., *Building a New Structure for School Leadership*, Boston, Mass.: Harvard University, Albert Shanker Institute, 2000.

Ernst and Young, *International Quality Study: The Definitive Study of the Best International Quality Management Practices—Top-Line Findings*, Cleveland, Ohio: Ernst and Young, 1992.

Eskildson, L., "Improving the Odds of TQM's Success," *Quality Progress*, Vol. 27, No. 4, 1994, pp. 61–63.

Falch, T., and B. Strom, *Teacher Turnover and Non-Pecuniary Factors*, Trondheim, Norway: Norwegian University of Science and Technology, 2002.

Feldman, M. S. and J. S. March, "Information in Organizations as Signal and Symbol," *Administrative Science Quarterly*, Vol. 26, No. 2, 1981, pp. 171–186.

Ferguson, R. F., "Paying for Public Education: New Evidence on How and Why Money Matters," *Harvard Journal on Legislation*, Vol. 28, No. 2, 1991, pp. 465–498.

Ferguson, R., and H. Ladd, "How and Why Money Matters: An Analysis of Alabama Schools," in H. Ladd, ed., *Holding Schools Accountable: Performance-Based Reform in Education*, Washington, D.C.: The Brookings Institution, 1996, pp. 265–298.

Fetler, M., "High School Staff Characteristics and Mathematics Test Results," *Education Policy Analysis Archives*, Vol. 7, No. 9, 1999 (http://epaa.asu.edu/epaa/v7n9; accessed June 2006).

Fisher, T. J., "The Impact of Quality Management on Productivity," *Asia Pacific Journal of Quarterly Management*, Vol. 1, No. 1, 1992, pp. 44–52.

Fletcher, S., M. Strong, and A. Villar, A. *An Investigation of the Effects of Variations in Mentor-Based Induction Programs on the Performance of Students in California*, Santa Cruz, Calif.: Santa Cruz New Teacher Project, 2005.

Floden, R., and M. Meniketti, "Research on the Effects of Coursework in the Arts and Sciences and in the Foundations of Education," in *Studying Teacher Education: The Report of the AERA Panel on Research and Teacher Education*, Washington, D.C.: American Educational Research Association, 2005.

Fones, S. W., J. R. Wagner, and E. R. Caldwell, "Promoting Attitude Adjustments in Science for Preservice Elementary Teachers," *Journal of College Science Teaching*, Vol. 28, No. 4, February 1999, pp. 231–236.

Fullan, M. G., *The New Meaning of Educational Change*, New York, N.Y.: Teachers College Press, 1991.

Fullan, M., G. Galluzzo, P. Morris, and N. Watson, *The Rise and Stall of Teacher Education Reform*, Washington, D.C.: American Association of Colleges for Teacher Education, 1998.

Fuller, E., "Beginning Teacher Retention Rates for TxBESS and Non-TxBESS Teachers," unpublished paper, State Board for Educator Certification, Texas, 2003.

Fuller, F. F., "Concerns of Teachers: A Developmental Conceptualization," *American Educational Research Journal*, Vol. 6, No. 2, 1969, pp. 207–226.

Gallagher, J. J., "Teaching and Learning: New Models," *Annual Review of Psychology,* Vol. 45, 1994, pp. 171–195.

Garet, M. S., A. C. Porter, and L. Desimone, "What Makes Teacher Professional Development Effective? Results from a National Sample of Teachers," *American Educational Research Journal*, Vol. 38, No. 4, 2001, pp. 915–945.

Gess-Newsome, J., and N. G. Lederman, "Preservice Biology Teachers' Knowledge Structures as a Function of Professional Teacher Education: A Yearlong Assessment," *Science Education*, Vol. 77, No. 1, 1993, pp. 25–45.

Gilbert, J. D., "TQM Flops: A Chance to Learn from the Mistakes of Others," *National Productivity Review*, Vol. 11, No. 4, 1992, pp. 491–499.

Gill, B. P., and A. Hove, *The Benedum Collaborative Model of Teacher Education: A Preliminary Evaluation*, Santa Monica, Calif.: RAND Corporation, DB-303.0-EDU, 2000.

Gitlin, A., and F. Margonis, "The Political Aspect of Reform: Teacher Resistance as Good Sense, *American Journal of Education,* Vol. 103, No. 4, 1995, pp. 377–405.

Goldhaber, D. D. and D. J. Brewer, "Does Teacher Certification Matter? High School Teacher Certification Status and Student Achievement," *Educational Evaluation and Policy Analysis*, Vol. 22, No. 2, Summer 2000, pp. 129–145.

Goodlad, J. I., *Educational Renewal: Better Teachers, Better Schools,* San Francisco: Jossey-Bass, 1994.

Graeber, A. O., D. Tirosh, and R. Glover, "Preservice Teachers' Misconceptions in Solving Verbal Problems in Multiplication and Division," *Journal for Research in Mathematics Education*, Vol. 20, No. 1, January 1989, pp. 95–102.

Greenwald, R., L. V. Hedges, and R. D. Laine, "The Effect of School Resources on Student Achievement," *Review of Educational Research*, Vol. 66, No. 3, 1996, pp. 361–396.

Grissmer, D. W., and S. N. Kirby, "Teacher Turnover and Teacher Quality," *Teachers College Record, Vol. 99,* No. 1, 1997, pp. 45–56.

Grossman, P. L., and A. E. Richert, "Unacknowledged Knowledge Growth: A Reexamination of the Effects of Teacher Education," *Teaching and Teacher Education,* Vol. 4, No. 1, 1988, pp. 53–62.

Hanushek, E. A., "The Trade-Off Between Child Quantity and Quality," *Journal of Political Economy*, Vol. 100, No. 1, 1992, pp. 84–118.

Hanushek, E .A., J. F. Kain, and S. G. Rivkin, *Teachers, Schools and Academic Achievement*, Cambridge, Mass.: National Bureau of Economic Research, 1998.

———, *Why Public Schools Lose Teachers*, Cambridge, Mass.: National Bureau of Economic Research, 2001.

Hanushek, E. A., and R. R. Pace, "Who Chooses to Teach (and Why)?" *Economics of Education Review*, Vol. 14, No. 2, 1995, pp. 101–117.

Harari, O., "Three Very Difficult Steps to Total Quality," *Management Review*, Vol. 82, No. 4, 1993, pp. 39–42.

Hawkins, E. F., F. B. Stancavages, and J. A. Dossey, *School Policies and Practices Affecting Instruction in Mathematics: Findings from the National Assessment of Educational Progress*, Washington, D.C.: U.S. Department of Education, 1998.

Heckman, J. J., "Investing in Disadvantaged Young Children Is an Economically Efficient Policy," presentation at the Committee for Economic Development/The Pew Charitable Trusts/PNC Financial Services Group Forum on Building the Economic Case for Investments in Preschool, New York, N.Y., January 10, 2006, (http://www.ced.org/docs/report/report_2006heckman.pdf, accessed June 2006).

Henke, R. R., X. Chen, and S. Geis, *Progress Through the Teacher Pipeline: 1992–93 College Graduates and Elementary/Secondary Teaching as of 1997*, Washington, D.C.: National Center for Education Statistics, 2000.

The Holmes Group, *Tomorrow's Teachers*, East Lansing, Mich.: The Holmes Group, 1986.

———, *Tomorrow's Schools*, East Lansing, Mich.: The Holmes Group, 1990.

———, *Tomorrow's Schools of Education*, East Lansing, Mich.: The Holmes Group, 1995.

Holt-Reynolds, D., "Good Readers, Good Teachers? Subject Matter Expertise as a Challenge in Learning to Teach," *Harvard Educational Review*, Vol. 69, No. 1, Spring 1999, pp. 29–50.

Hopkins, W. S., S. Q. Hoffman, S.Q., and V. D. Moss, "Professional Development Schools and Preservice Teacher Stress," *Action in Teacher Education*, Vol.18, No. 4, 1997, pp. 36–46.

Huberman, A. M., and M. B. Miles, *Innovation Up Close: How School Improvement Works*, New York, N.Y.: Plenum Press, 1984.

Hudson-Ross, S., "Intertwining Opportunities: Participants' Perceptions of Professional Growth Within a Multiple-Site Teacher Education Network at the Secondary Level," *Teaching and Teacher Education*, Vol. 17, No. 4, 2001, pp. 433–454.

Humphrey, D., et al., *Insights into Alternative Certification: Initial Findings from a National Study*, Menlo Park, Calif.: SRI International, September 2005.

Imazeki, J., "Teacher Attrition and Mobility in Urban Districts: Evidence from Wisconsin," white paper, San Diego State University, 2002 (http://www-rohan.sdsu.edu/~jimazeki/papers/Milwaukee_0202.pdf, accessed June 2006).

Ingersoll, R. M., "Teacher Turnover and Teacher Shortages: An Organizational Analysis," *American Educational Research Journal, Vol. 38*, No. 3, 2001, pp. 499–534.

Ingersoll, R. M., and J. M. Kralik, *The Impact of Mentoring on Teacher Retention: What the Research Says*, Denver, Colo.: Education Commission of the States, 2004.

Ingersoll, R. M., and T. M. Smith, "Do Teacher Induction and Mentoring Matter?" *NASSP Bulletin*, Vol. 88, No. 638, 2004, pp. 28–40.

Johnson, S. M., et al. *Finders and Keepers: Helping New Teachers Survive and Thrive in Our Schools*, San Francisco, Calif.: Jossey-Bass, 2004.

Juran, J. M., *Juran on Planning for Quality*, New York, N.Y.: Free Press, 1988.

Kagan, D. M., "Professional Growth Among Preservice and Beginning Teachers," *Review of Educational Research*, Vol. 62, No. 2, 1992, pp. 129–179.

Kain, J. F., "The Impact of Individual Teachers and Peers on Individual Student Achievement," paper presented at the Association for Public Policy Analysis and Management, 20th Annual Research Conference, New York, N.Y., November 1998.

Kain, J., and K. Singleton, K., "Equality of Educational Opportunity Revisited," *New England Economic Review*, May/June 1996, pp. 87–111.

Kennedy, M. M., *Learning to Teach Writing: Does Teacher Education Make a Difference?* New York, N.Y.: Teachers College Press, 1998.

Kirby, S. N., M. Berends, and S. Naftel, "Supply and Demand of Minority Teachers in Texas: Problems and Prospects," *Educational Evaluation and Policy Analysis*, Vol. 21, No. 1, 1999, pp. 47–66.

Kirby, S. N., and D. W. Grissmer, "Teacher Attrition: Theory, Evidence, and Suggested Policy Options," paper presented at the World Bank/Harvard Institute for International Development Seminar on Policies Affecting Learning Outcomes Through Impacts on Teachers, Cambridge, Mass., 1983.

Kirby, S. N., J. S. McCombs, S. Naftel, H. Barney, H. Darilek, F. C. Doolittle, and J. J. Cordes, *Reforming Teacher Education: A First Year Progress Report on Teachers for a New Era*, Santa Monica, Calif.: RAND Corporation, TR-149-EDU, 2004.

Kupermintz, H. "Teacher Effects and Teacher Effectiveness: A Validity Investigation of the Tennessee Value-Added Assessment System (TVAAS)," *Educational Evaluation and Policy Analysis*, Vol. 25, No. 3, 2003, pp. 287–298.

Labaree, D. *The Trouble with Ed Schools*, New Haven, Conn.: Yale University Press, 2004.

Lagemann, E., *An Elusive Science: The Troubling History of Education Research*, Chicago, Ill.: University of Chicago Press, 2000.

Lankford, M., S. Loeb, and J. Wyckoff, "Teacher Sorting and the Plight of Urban Schools: A Descriptive Analysis," *Educational Evaluation and Policy Analysis*, Vol. 24, No. 1, 2002, pp. 37–62.

Leinhardt, G. C., "Math Lessons: A Contrast of Novice and Expert Competence," *Journal for Research in Mathematics Education*, Vol. 20, No. 1, January 1989, pp. 52–75.

Levin, H. M., "Why Is Educational Entrepreneurship So Difficult?" in F. Hess, ed., *Educational Entrepreneurship*, Cambridge, Mass.: Harvard Education Press, 2006.

Livingston, C., and H. Borko, "Expert-Novice Differences in Teaching: A Cognitive Analysis and Implications for Teacher Education," *Journal of Teacher Education*, Vol. 40, No. 4, 1989, pp. 36–42.

Lucas, C., *Teacher Education in America: Reform Agendas for the Twenty-First Century*, New York, N.Y.: St. Martin's Press, 1999.

MacDonald, H., "Why Johnny's Teacher Can't Teach," *City Journal,* Spring 1998, (http://www.city-journal.org/html/8_2_a1.html; accessed June 2006).

Malone, D., B. J. Jones, and D. T. Stallings, "Perspective Transformation: Effects of a Service-Learning Tutoring Experience on Prospective Teachers," *Teacher Education Quarterly,* Vol. 29, No. 1, 2002, pp. 61–81.

Markus, M. L., "Power, Politics, and MIS Implementation," *Communications of the ACM,* Vol. 26, No. 6, 1983, pp. 430–444.

Mayer, D., et al., *Identifying Alternative Certification Programs for an Impact Evaluation of Teacher Preparation,* Cambridge, Mass.: Mathematica Policy Research, Inc., 2003.

Mazmanian, D. A., and P. A. Sabatier, *Implementation and Public Policy,* Lanham, Md.: University Press of America, 1989.

McCaffrey, D. F., D. M. Koretz, J. R. Lockwood, and L. S. Hamilton, *Evaluating Value-Added Models for Teacher Accountability,* Santa Monica, Calif.: RAND Corporation, MG-158-EDU, 2004.

McDiarmid, G. W., and S. M. Wilson, "An Exploration of the Subject Matter Knowledge of Alternate Route Teachers: Can We Assume They Know Their Subject?" *Journal of Teacher Education,* Vol. 42, No. 2, 1991, pp. 93–103.

McDonald, F., "The Problems of Beginning Teachers: A Crisis in Training," in *A Study of Induction Programs for Beginning Teachers,* Princeton, N.J.: Educational Testing Service, 1980.

McDonnell, L. M., and W. N. Grubb, *Education and Training for Work: The Policy Instruments and the Institutions,*" Berkeley, Calif.: National Center for Research in Vocational Education, University of California at Berkeley, 1991.

McLaughlin, M. W., "Learning from Experience: Lessons from Policy Implementation," *Educational Evaluation and Policy Analysis,* Vol. 9, No. 2, 1987, pp. 171–178.

———, "The RAND Change Agent Study Revisited: Macro Perspectives and Micro Realities," *Educational Researcher,* Vol. 19, No. 9, 1990, pp. 11–16.

McNeal, B., and M. A. Simon, "Mathematics Culture Clash: Negotiating New Classroom Norms with Prospective Teachers," *Journal of Mathematical Behavior,* Vol. 18, No. 4, 2000, pp. 475–509.

Mendro, R., H. Jordan, E. Gomez, M. Anderson, and K. Bembry, "An Application of Multiple Linear Regression in Determining Longitudinal Teacher Effectiveness," paper presented at the 1998 Annual Meeting of the American Educational Research Association, San Diego, Calif., 1998.

Mikulecky, M., G. Shkodriani, and A. Wilner, "A Growing Trend to Address the Teacher Shortage," *Policy Brief: Alternative Certification,* Education Commission of the States, December 2004, (http://www.ecs.org/clearinghouse/57/12/5712.pdf; accessed May 2, 2006).

Mitchell, K. S., D. Z. Robinson, B. S. Plake, and K. T. Knowles, eds., *Testing Teacher Candidates: The Role of Licensure Tests in Improving Teacher Quality*, Washington, D.C.: National Academy Press, 2001.

Mohrman, S. A., S. G. Cohen, and A. M. Mohrman, Jr., *Designing Team-Based Organizations*, San Francisco, Calif.: Jossey-Bass, 1995.

Monk, D. H., "Subject Area Preparation of Secondary Mathematics and Science Teachers and Student Achievement," *Economics of Education Review*, No. 13, 1994, pp. 125–145.

Monk, D. H., and J. King, "Multilevel Teacher Resource Effects on Pupil Performance in Secondary Mathematics and Science: The Role of Teacher Subject-Matter Preparation," in R. G. Ehrenberg, ed., *Contemporary Policy Issues: Choices and Consequences in Education*, New York, N.Y.: ILR Press, 1994, pp. 29–58.

Mont, D., and D. I. Rees, "The Influence of Classroom Characteristics on High School Teacher Turnover," *Economic Inquiry, Vol. 34*, No. 1, 1996, pp. 152–167.

Murnane, R. J. "Selection and Survival in the Teacher Labor Market," *The Review of Economics and Statistics*, Vol. 66, No. 3, 1984, pp. 513–518.

Murnane, R. J., and R. J. Olsen, "The Effects of Salaries and Opportunity Costs on Duration in Teaching: Evidence from Michigan," *Review of Economics and Statistics, Vol. 71*, No. 2, 1989, pp. 347–352.

———, "The Effect of Salaries and Opportunity Costs on Length of Stay in Teaching: Evidence from North Carolina," *The Journal of Human Resources*, Vol. 25, No. 1, 1990, pp. 106–124.

Murnane, R. J., J. D. Singer, and J. B. Willett, "The Influences of Salaries and 'Opportunity Costs' on Teachers' Career Choices: Evidence from North Carolina," *Harvard Educational Review*, Vol. 59, No. 3, 1989, pp. 325–346.

Murnane, R. J., J. Singer, J. Willett, J. Kempe, and R. Olson, *Who Will Teach: Policies That Matter*, Cambridge, Mass.: Harvard University Press, 1991.

National Council for Accreditation of Teacher Education, "Professional Development Schools," NCATE Web site, 1997–2006, (http://www.ncate.org/public/pdswhat.asp?ch=133; accessed February 2006).

National Council for Accreditation of Teacher Education, *Professional Standards for the Accreditation of Schools, Colleges, and Departments of Education*, Washington, D.C.: NCATE, 2002, (http://www.ncate.org/documents/unit_stnds_2002.pdf; accessed June 2006).

National Research Council, *Testing Teacher Candidates: The Role of Licensure Tests in Improving Teacher Quality*, Washington D.C.: National Academy Press, 2001.

Noell, G. H., *Year One Report: Assessing Teacher Education Program Effectiveness: A Pilot Examination of Value Added Approaches*, Baton Rouge, La.: Louisiana State University, 2004.

———, *Year Two Report: Assessing Teacher Education Program Effectiveness: A Pilot Examination of Value Added Approaches*, Baton Rouge, La.: Louisiana State University, 2005.

Nonaka, I., "The Knowledge-Creating Company," *Harvard Business Review*, Vol. 69, No. 6, 1991, pp. 96–104.

O'Connor, E. A., M. C. Fish, and A. E. Yasik, "The Influence of Teacher Education on the Elementary Classroom System: An Observational Study," *Journal of Classroom Instruction*, Vol. 39, No. 1, 2004, pp. 11–18.

Odell, S. J., and D. P. Ferraro, "Teacher Mentoring and Teacher Retention," *Journal of Teacher Education*, Vol. 43, No. 3, 1992, pp. 200–204.

Ostrom, E., *Governing the Commons: The Evolution of Institutions for Collective Action*, New York, N.Y.: Cambridge University Press, 1990.

Pennsylvania Department of Education, *Pennsylvania Value-Added Assessment System: PVAAS Overview*, n.d., (http://www.pde.state.pa.us/a_and_t/lib/a_and_t/pdepvaasoverview.pdf; accessed March 2006).

Peterson, P. L., and A. M. Comeaux, "Teachers' Schemata for Classroom Events: The Mental Scaffolding of Teachers' Thinking During Classroom Instruction," *Teaching and Teacher Education*, Vol. 3, No. 4, 1987, pp. 319–331.

Pfeffer, J. *Competitive Advantage Through People: Unleashing the Power of the Work Force*, Boston, Mass.: Harvard Business School Press, 1994.

Podgursky, M., "Improving Academic Performance in U.S. Public Schools: Why Teacher Licensing Is (Almost) Irrelevant," in R. Hess, A. Rotterham, and K. Walsh, eds., *A Qualified Teacher in Every Classroom? Appraising Old Answers and New Ideas*, Cambridge, Mass.: Harvard Education Press, 2004.

Powell, T., "Total Quality Management as Competitive Advantage: A Review and Empirical Study," *Strategic Management Journal*, Vol. 16, No. 1, 1995, pp. 15–37.

Pressman, J., and A. Wildavsky, *Implementation*, Berkeley, Calif.: University of California Press, 1973.

Prestine, N. A., "Political System Theory as an Explanatory Paradigm for Teacher Education Reform," *American Educational Research Journal*, Vol. 28, No. 2, 1991, pp. 237–274.

The Renaissance Group, "TRG Governance: Principles," 2005–2006, (http://education.csuf-resno.edu/rengroup/principles.htm; accessed February 2006).

Reynolds, A., S.M. Ross, and J. H. Rakow, "Teacher Retention, Teaching Effectiveness, and Professional Preparation: A Comparison of Professional Development School and Non-Professional Development School Graduates," *Teaching and Teacher Education*, Vol. 18, 2002, pp. 289–303.

Rickman, B. D., and C. D. Parker, "Alternative Wages and Teacher Mobility: A Human Capital Approach," *Economics of Education Review*, Vol. 9, No. 1, 1990, pp. 73–79.

Rivers, J. C., *The Impact of Teacher Effect on Student Math Competency Achievement*, Ann Arbor, Mich.: University Microfilms International, Number 9959317, 2000.

Rivkin, S. G., E. A. Hanushek, and J. F. Kain, *Teachers, Schools, and Academic Achievement*, Cambridge, Mass.: National Bureau of Economic Research, NBER Working Paper W6691, 2000.

Rowan, B., F. S. Chiang, and R. J. Miller, "Using Research on Employees' Performance to Study the Effects of Teachers on Students' Achievement," *Sociology of Education*, Vol. 70, October 1997, pp. 256–284.

Rowan, B., R. Correnti, and R. J. Miller, "What Large-Scale Survey Research Tells Us About Teacher Effects on Student Achievement: Insights from the *Prospects* Study of Elementary Schools," *Teachers College Record*, Vol. 104, No. 8, 2002, pp. 1525–1567.

Sabatier, P., and D. Mazmanian, "The Conditions of Effective Implementation: A Guide to Accomplishing Policy Objectives," *Policy Analysis*, Vol. 5, No. 4, 1979, pp. 481–504.

Sabers, D. S., K. S. Cushing, and D. C. Berliner, "Differences Among Teachers in a Task Characterized by Simultaneity, Multidimensionality, and Immediacy," *American Educational Research Journal*, Vol. 28, No. 1, 1991, pp. 63–88.

Sandholtz, J. H., and K. Wasserman, "Student and Cooperating Teachers: Contrasting Experiences in Teacher Preparation," *Action in Teacher Education*, Vol. 23, No. 3, 2001, pp. 54–65.

Sanders, W., A. Saxton, and B. Horn, "The Tennessee Value-Added Assessment System: A Quantitative Outcomes-Based Approach to Educational Assessment," in J. Millman, ed., *Grading Teachers, Grading Schools: Is Student Achievement a Valid Educational Measure?* Thousand Oaks, Calif.: Corwin Press, Inc., 1997, pp. 137–162.

Sanders, W. L., and J. C. Rivers, *Cumulative and Residual Effects of Teachers on Future Student Academic Achievement*, Knoxville, Tenn.: University of Tennessee Value-Added Research and Assessment Center, 1996.

Schein, E. H., "How Can Organizations Learn Faster?" *Sloan Management Review*, Vol. 34, 1993, pp. 85–92.

Scheirer, M. A., "Designing and Using Process Evaluation," in J. S. Wholey, H. P. Hatry, and K. E. Newcomer, eds., *Handbook of Practical Program Evaluation*, San Francisco, Calif.: Jossey-Bass Publishers, 1994, pp. 40–60.

Schmoker, M., *Results: The Key to Continuous School Improvement*, Alexandria, Va.: Association for Supervision and Curriculum Development, 1996.

Senge, P., *The Fifth Discipline: The Art and Practice of the Learning Organization*, New York, N.Y.: Doubleday, 1990a.

———, "The Leader's New Work," *Sloan Management Review*, Vol. 32, No. 1, 1990b, pp. 7–23.

Shen, J., "Teacher Retention and Attrition in Public Schools: Evidence from SASS91," *Journal of Educational Research, Vol. 91*, No. 2, 1997, pp. 81–88.

Shulman, L. S., "Teacher Education Does Not Exist, *Stanford Educator,* Fall 2005, (http://ed.stanford.edu/suse/educator/fall2005/EducatorFall05.pd; accessed February 2006).

Simon, H. A. "Bounded Rationality and Organizational Learning," *Organization Science*, Vol. 2, No. 1, 1991, pp. 125–134.

Simon, M. A., "Prospective Elementary Teachers' Knowledge of Division," *Journal for Research in Mathematics Education*, Vol. 24, No. 3, 1993, pp. 233–254.

Singer, J. D., and J. B. Willett, "Detecting Involuntary Layoffs in Teacher Survival Data: The Year of Leaving Dangerously," *Educational Evaluation and Policy Analysis,* Vol. 10, No. 3, 1988, pp. 212–224.

Smith, D. C., and C. A. Anderson, "Appropriating Scientific Practices and Discourses with Future Elementary Teachers," *Journal of Research in Science Teaching*, Vol. 36, No. 7, 1999, pp. 755–776.

Stecher, B., and S. N. Kirby, *Organizational Improvement and Accountability: Lessons for Education from Other Sectors,* Santa Monica, Calif.: RAND Corporation, MG-136-WFHF, 2004.

Stinebrickner, T. R., "An Empirical Investigation of Teacher Attrition," *Economics of Education Review,* Vol. 17, No. 2, 1998, pp. 127–136.

————, "Estimation of a Duration Model in the Presence of Missing Data," *Review of Economics and Statistics,* Vol. 81, No. 3, 1999, pp. 529–542.

————, "Compensation Policies and Teacher Decisions," *International Economic Review,* Vol. 42, No. 3, 2001a, pp. 751–779.

————, "A Dynamic Model of Teacher Labor Supply," *Journal of Labor Economics*, Vol. 19, No. 1, 2001b, pp. 196–230.

Stoddart, T., M. Connell, R. Stofflert, and D. Peck, "Reconstructing Elementary Teacher Candidates' Understanding of Mathematics and Science Content," *Teaching and Teacher Education,* Vol. 9, No. 3, 1993, pp. 229–241.

Strong, M. S., *A Comparison of SCNTP Beginning Teachers and Experienced Teachers as Measured by Student Performance*, Santa Cruz, Calif.: Santa Cruz New Teacher Project, 1998.

————, *Induction, Mentoring and Teacher Retention: A Summary of the Research*, Santa Cruz, Calif.: Santa Cruz New Teacher Project, 2005.

Szwergold, J., "Why Most Quality Efforts Fail," *Management Review*, Vol. 81, No. 8, 1992, p. 5.

Tabachnick, R., and K. Zeichner, "The Impact of the Student Teaching Experience on the Development of Teacher Perspectives," *Journal of Teacher Education,* Vol. 35, No. 6, 1984.

Teacher Education Accreditation Council, "Summary Outline of the TEAC Accreditation Process," TEAC Accreditation Process Web site, 2004, (http://www.teac.org/accreditation/summaryoutline.asp; accessed June 2006).

Tirosh, D., and A. O. Graeber, "Preservice Teachers' Explicit Beliefs About Multiplication and Division," *Educational Studies in Mathematics*, Vol. 20, No. 1, 1989, pp. 79–96.

"TNE Widens the Circle: 30 Institutions Selected for the Learning Network," Teachers for a New Era Web site, Carnegie Corporation of New York, n.d., (http://www.teachersforanewera.org/index.cfm?fuseaction=happenings.showHappening&happening_id=19; accessed February 2006).

Turban, E., E. McLean, and J. Wetherbe, *Information Technology for Management*, New York, N.Y.: Wiley, 1998.

U.S. Department of Education, Office of Postsecondary Education, Office of Policy Planning and Innovation, *Meeting the Highly Qualified Teachers Challenge: The Secretary's First Annual Report on Teacher Quality*, Washington, D.C.: U.S. Department of Education, 2002.

————, *Meeting the Highly Qualified Teachers Challenge: The Secretary's Third Annual Report on Teacher Quality*, Washington, D.C.: U.S. Department of Education, 2004.

Valli, L., with A. Agostinelli, "Teaching Before and After Professional Preparation: The Story of a High School Mathematics Teacher," *Journal of Teacher Education*, Vol. 44, No. 2, 1993, pp. 107–118.

Veenman, S., "Perceived Problems of Beginning Teachers," *Review of Educational Research*, Vol. 54, No. 2, 1984, pp. 143–178.

W. K. Kellogg Foundation, *Using Logic Models to Bring Together Planning, Evaluation, and Action: Logic Model Development Guide*, Battle Creek, Michigan: W. K. Kellogg Foundation, 2004.

Walling, B., and M. Lewis, "Development of Professional Identity Among Professional Development School Preservice Teachers: Longitudinal and Comparative Analysis," *Action in Teacher Education*, Vol. 22, No. 2A, 2000, pp. 65–72.

Walsh, K., *Teacher Certification Reconsidered: Stumbling for Quality*, Baltimore, Md.: The Abell Foundation, 2001.

Wayne, A., and P. Youngs, "Teacher Characteristics and Student Achievement Gains: A Review," *Review of Educational Research*, Vol. 73, No. 1, 2003, pp. 89–122.

Weatherly, R., and M. Lipsky, "Street-Level Bureaucrats and Institutional Innovation: Implementing Special Education Reform," *Harvard Education Review*, Vol. 47, No. 2, 1977, pp. 171–197.

Weinert, F. E., F. W. Schrader, and A. Helmke, "Educational Expertise: Closing the Gap Between Educational Research and Classroom Practice," *School Psychology International*, Vol. 11, 1990, pp. 163–180.

Weiss, C. H., *Evaluation Research*, Englewood Cliffs, N.J.: Prentice Hall, Inc, 1972.

————, "Ideology, Interests, and Information," in D. Callahan and B. Jennings, eds., *The Social Sciences and Policy Analysis*, New York, N.Y.: Plenum Press, 1983, pp. 224–250.

Wenglinsky, H., "How Schools Matter: The Link Between Teacher Classroom Practices and Student Academic Performance," *Education Policy Analysis Archives*, Vol. 10, No. 12, 2002.

Westerman, D. A., "Expert and Novice Teacher Decision Making," *Journal of Teacher Education*, Vol. 42, No. 4, 1991, pp. 292–305.

Westphal, J., R. Gulati, and S. Shartell, "An Institutional and Network Perspective on the Content and Consequences of TQM Adoption," *Administrative Science Quarterly*, Vol. 42, No. 2, 1997, pp. 366–394.

Wideen, M., J. Mayer-Smith, and B. Moon, "A Critical Analysis of the Research on Learning to Teach: Making the Case for an Ecological Perspective on Inquiry," *Review of Educational Research*, Vol. 68, No. 2, 1998, pp. 130–178.

Wilson, J. D., "An Evaluation of the Field Experiences of the Innovative Model for the Preparation of Elementary Teachers for Science, Mathematics, and Technology," *Journal of Teacher Education*, Vol. 47, No. 1, 1996, pp. 53–59.

Wilson, M., "One Preservice Secondary Teacher's Understanding of Function: The Impact of a Course Integrating Mathematical Content and Pedagogy," *Journal for Research in Mathematics Education*, Vol. 25, No. 4, 1994, pp. 346–370.

Wilson, S., R. Floden, and J. Ferrini-Mundy, *Teacher Preparation Research: Current Knowledge, Gaps and Recommendations*, Washington, D.C.: Center for the Study of Teaching and Policy, 2001.

Wilson, S. M., and S. S. Wineburg, "Peering at American History Through Different Lenses: The Role of Disciplinary Knowledge in Teaching," *Teachers College Record*, Vol. 89, No. 4, 1988, pp. 529–539.

Wise, A. E., *Legislated Learning; The Bureaucratization of the American Classroom*, Berkeley, Calif.: University of California Press, 1979.

Wiseman, D. L., and P. L. Nason, "The Nature of Interactions in a Field-Based Teacher Education Experience," *Action in Teacher Education*, Vol. 17, No. 3, 1995, pp. 1–12.

Wisniewski, R., *ReCreating Colleges of Teacher Education*, Atlanta, Ga.: BellSouth Foundation, n.d., (http://www.bellsouthfoundation.org/pdfs/recreate01.pdf; accessed February 2006).

W.K. Kellogg Foundation, *Logic Model Development Guide: Using Logic Models to Bring Together Planning Evaluation and Action*, Battle Creek, Mich.: W.K. Kellogg Foundation, January 2004, (http://www.wkkf.org/DesktopModules/WKF_DmaItem/ViewDoc.aspx?LanguageID=0&CID=281&ListID=28&ItemID=2813669&fld=PDFFile; accessed June 2006).

Wright, S. P., S. P. Horn, and W. L. Sanders, "Teacher and Classroom Context Effects on Student Achievement: Implications for Teacher Evaluation," *Journal of Personnel Evaluation in Education*, Vol. 11, No. 1, pp. 57–67.

Wruck, K. H., and M. J. Jensen, "Science, Specific Knowledge, and Total Quality Management," *Journal of Accounting and Economics*, 1994, pp. 247–287.

Yerian, S., and P. L. Grossman, "Preservice Teachers' Perceptions of Their Middle-Level Teacher Education Experience: A Comparison of a Traditional and a PDS Model," *Teacher Education Quarterly*, Vol. 24, No. 4, 1997, pp. 85–101.

Yin, R., *Changing Bureaucracies*, Lexington, Mass.: Lexington Books, 1979.

Zumwalt, K., and E. Craig, "Teachers' Characteristics: Research on the Demographic Profile," in *Studying Teacher Education: The Report of the AERA Panel on Research and Teacher Education*, Washington, D.C.: American Educational Research Association, 2005.